World Anthropologies in Practice

ASA Monographs ISSN 0066-9679

World Anthropologies in Practice
Situated Perspectives, Global Knowledge

Edited by
John Gledhill

Bloomsbury Academic
An imprint of Bloomsbury Publishing Plc

B L O O M S B U R Y
LONDON · OXFORD · NEW YORK · NEW DELHI · SYDNEY

Bloomsbury Academic
An imprint of Bloomsbury Publishing Plc

50 Bedford Square	1385 Broadway
London	New York
WC1B 3DP	NY 10018
UK	USA

www.bloomsbury.com

Bloomsbury is a registered trademark of Bloomsbury Publishing Plc

First published 2016

British Library Cataloguing-in-Publication Data
A catalogue record for this book is available from the British Library.

ISBN: HB: 978-1-47425-260-7
PB: 978-1-47425-261-4
ePDF: 978-1-47425-263-8
ePub: 978-1-47425-262-1

Library of Congress Cataloging-in-Publication Data
A catalog record for this book is available from the Library of Congress.

Typeset by Fakenham Prepress Solutions, Fakenham, Norfolk NR21 8NN
Printed and bound in India

Contents

List of Illustrations

Acknowledgements

This Association of Social Anthropologists (ASA) monograph is based on papers given to the Seventeenth Congress of the International Union of Anthropological and Ethnological Sciences, held in Manchester in August 2013. The ASA did not hold a conference of its own in that year in order to support the International Union of Anthropological and Ethnological Sciences (IUAES) event, and past and current ASA officers contributed in an important way to its organization and delivery. The congress organizing committee was chaired by the editor of this volume, John Gledhill, at that time Max Gluckman Professor of Social Anthropology at the host institution, the University of Manchester. I would like to take this opportunity to thank ASA for its truly generous support and all my colleagues on the committee for their sound advice and creative suggestions.

The organizing committee members were Simone Abram (Durham University and Leeds Beckett University), Filippo Aureli (Liverpool John Moores University), Laura Bishop (Liverpool John Moores University), James Fairhead (University of Sussex), Katherine Homewood (University College London), Tim Ingold (University of Aberdeen), Nayanika Mookherjee (Durham University,), Giuliana Prato (University of Kent), Sara Randall (University College London), and Trevor Stack (University of Aberdeen). The late Steven Rubenstein, of the University of Liverpool, also made an important contribution to planning the congress before his untimely death in March 2012.

On behalf of IUAES, I gratefully acknowledge the support given to the congress by the Wenner-Gren Foundation for Anthropological Research, which provided funding to support the participation of delegates from lower-income countries; Manchester City Council, whose support enabled us to hold the congress opening ceremony and reception in the city's Bridgewater Hall; the ASA, which provided funds to support the participation of postgraduate students and its Firth distinguished lecture, given by Lourdes Arizpe; the Royal Anthropological Institute, which contributed its Huxley distinguished lecture, given by Howard Morphy; and the World Council of Anthropological Associations, which sponsored several large panels, including a final plenary roundtable on world anthropologies. Much appreciated local subsidies in support of some aspects of the congress programme and participation by delegates from low-income countries were also received from University of Manchester sources: the Hallsworth Conference Fund, the Faculty of Humanities, the School of Social Sciences and the Department of Social Anthropology.

Notes on Contributors

Cristina Amescua Chávez is a Researcher at the Regional Centre for Multidisciplinary Research of the National Autonomous University of Mexico, Mexico. She has published several edited books in Spanish, and most recently, in English, *Anthropological Perspectives on Intangible Cultural Heritage*, co-edited with Lourdes Arizpe.

Paul Chambers is Lecturer in International Relations at the Institute of South Asian Affairs of Chiang Mai University, Thailand. His most recent books are *Democratization and Civilian Control in Asia*, co-authored with Aurel Croissant, David Kuehn and Philip Lorenz, and the edited volume *Knights of the Realm: Thailand's Military and Police, Then and Now*.

John Gledhill is Emeritus Professor of Social Anthropology at the University of Manchester, UK, and was Chair of the ASA from 2005 to 2009. His most recent books are *The New War Against the Poor: The Production of Insecurity in Latin America*, and *New Approaches to Resistance in Brazil and Mexico*, co-edited with Patience Schell.

Srisompob Jitpiromsri is Director of the Centre for Conflict Studies and Cultural Diversity at Prince of Songkla University, Thailand. He is one of the founders of *Deep South Watch*, which aims to use academic knowledge to correct biased media portrayals and government misinformation and challenge popular misconceptions about the Muslim community.

Maria Kastrinou is Lecturer in Anthropology at Brunel University, UK. Her published articles include 'Sect and House in Syria: History, Architecture, and Bayt Amongst the Druze in Jaramana', *History and Anthropology* 25 (3) and 'A Different Struggle for Syria: Becoming Young in the Middle East', *Mediterranean Politics* 17 (1).

Robert Layton is Emeritus Professor of Anthropology at Durham University, UK. His wide-ranging interests and expertise are reflected in books such as *The Anthropology of Art; Uluru: An Aboriginal History of Ayers Rock; Anthropology and History in Franche-Comté: A Critique of Social Theory*; and *Order and Anarchy: Civil Society, Social Disorder and War*.

Winnie Lem is Professor in International Development Studies and Women's Studies at Trent University, Canada. Her most recent books are *Migration in the*

21st Century: Political Economy and Ethnography, co-edited with Pauline Gardiner Barber, and *Culture, Economy, Power: Anthropology as Critique, Anthropology as Praxis*, co-edited with Belinda Leach.

Shalina Mehta is Professor of Social and Cultural Anthropology at Panjab University, India. Her most recent books are the edited volume *Anthropology Today: Contemporary Trends in Social and Cultural Anthropology* and *Globalized Environmentalism and Environmental Organizations in India*, co-authored with Priscilla Weeks.

Susana Narotzky is Professor of Social Anthropology at the University of Barcelona, Spain. Her most recent books are *Industry and Work in Contemporary Capitalism: Global Models, Local Lives?*, co-edited with Victoria Goddard, and *Immediate Struggles: People, Power and Place in Rural Spain*, co-authored with Gavin Smith.

Peter Redfield is Professor of Anthropology at the University of North Carolina at Chapel Hill, USA. His most recent books are *Life in Crisis: The Ethical Journey of Doctors Without Borders* and *Forces of Compassion: Humanitarianism Between Ethics and Politics*, co-edited with Erica Bornstein.

Carmen Rial is Professor of Anthropology at the Federal University of Santa Catarina, Brazil and Director of its Centre for Audiovisual Anthropology and Studies of the Image. She was President of the Brazilian Anthropological Association from 2013 to 2015. Her most recent book is *Migration of Rich Immigrants: Gender, Ethnicity and Class*, co-edited with Alex Vailati.

Steven Robins is Professor of Social Anthropology at the University of Stellenbosch, South Africa. His books include the monograph *From Revolution to Rights in South Africa: Social Movements, NGOs and Popular Politics*, and the edited volume *Limits to Liberation: Citizenship, Governance and Culture After Apartheid*.

Mallika Shakya is Assistant Professor of Sociology at the South Asian University, New Delhi, and was a Postdoctoral Fellow in the Human Economy Programme of the University of Pretoria, South Africa. Her publications include 'Marwari Traders Animating the Industrial Clusters of India–Nepal Border', in K. Hart and J. Sharp (eds), *The Human Economy*, and 'Nepali Economic History through the Ethnic Lens: Changing State Relationships with Entrepreneurial Elites', in M. Lawoti and S. Hangen (eds), *The Changing Face of Ethnic Movements in Nepal*.

Pan Shouyong is Professor of Anthropology and Museology at Minzu University, China. His recent articles in English include 'The Social Benefits of Heritage and Chinese Ethnic Minorities' and 'Museums and the Protection of Intangible Cultural Heritage', both published in the journal *Museum International*. Vol. 62, Issue 1–2 (2011); Vol. 60, Issue 1–2 (2008).

Hiroki Takakura is Professor of Social Anthropology and Siberian Ethnography at the Centre for Northeast Asian Studies, Tohoku University, Japan. His recent publications include *Good to Eat, Good to Live With: Nomads and Animals in Northern Eurasia and Africa*, co-edited with Florian Stammler, and 'The Shift from Herding to Hunting among the Siberian Evenki: Indigenous Knowledge and Subsistence Change in Northwestern Yakutia,' *Asian Ethnology* 71 (1).

Napisa Waitoolkiat is Lecturer in Political Science at the Institute of South Asian Affairs of Chiang Mai University, Thailand. Her publications include the book chapter 'Khaki Veto Power: The Organization of Thailand's Armed Forces', co-authored with Paul Chambers, and 'Effect of District Magnitude on Electoral Corruption Under a Block Vote System: The case of Thailand', *Asia-Pacific Social Science Review* 10 (2).

ASA Foreword

Practising Scales in Anthropology

The ASA's annual conference comprises its primary forum for the exchange of anthropological knowledge. This extends beyond the UK: many of its members continue to valorize longstanding Commonwealth ties, and to welcome opportunities for joint international conferences. The Association's decision to subsume its annual conference into the IUAES's international congress in Manchester reflected its members' enthusiasm for inclusivity and a commitment to encouraging a flow of diverse knowledges through our discipline. In taking up a formal responsibility as Chair of the ASA at the congress, I felt that this openness to alternate perspectives, both ethnographically and professionally, suggests a discipline with sound intellectual and ethical foundations.

As the chapters in this volume illustrate, flows of knowledge are deeply affected by the social and political contexts from which they are generated and through which they travel, and by related distributions of intellectual and economic resources. The collection fulfils the intention of the congress in providing a culturally diverse array of anthropological perspectives. While the topics may seem equally diverse – ranging from sanitation to reincarnation – they share a cross-cutting concern with power and the multiple ways in which it is manifested and contested. Thus, in a political arena dominated by neoliberal ideologies, we hear how labour movements, counter-movements and social critics struggle to make their voices heard in debates about ownership, democracy and governance. There are striking ethnographic examples of efforts to promote the interests and identities of subaltern groups, through protests against unequal access to sanitation; through careful navigations of religiously embedded gender inequalities; and through valorizations of intangible and material cultural heritage.

A recurrent theme is the difficulty of resolving tensions between widely differing discursive scales. Shalina Mehta explores the incommensurability between UN efforts to reconcile ideas about universal human rights with specifically cultural perspectives. Pan Shouyong considers efforts to construct localized identities in relation to the state through museum developments in China. Winnie Lem reflects directly on issues of scale through an analysis of the forces that frame and 'condition' anthropology in the different epistemes created locally, nationally and internationally. And ongoing questions about the potential for ethnographic comparison through shared theoretical frameworks are highlighted in Maria

Kastrinou and Robert Layton's chapter on beliefs about reincarnation in Syria and Australia.

These examples lead John Gledhill to consider whether we should be promoting world anthropology in the singular, or world anthropologies in the plural. As he observes, navigating the complexities of knowledge exchange has been a core concern for anthropology since our discipline's earliest reflexive critiques. Working in a number of postcolonial contexts (in particular Australia and New Zealand) I have seen this debate progress, for the most part, from pejorative caricatures of anthropology as a colonial handmaiden (often met with indignation by anthropologists familiar with long-term disciplinary commitments to social justice), to more productive dialogues exploring the complexities of historical and contemporary engagements between ethnographers and host communities, and the *realpolitiks* affecting distributions of power and resources at every level.

The question about pluralities is framed, to some extent, as an alternative between either being complicit in upholding a singular and hegemonic 'integrated knowledge system' based on 'dominant metropolitan paradigms', or advancing a vision of anthropology as being composed of multiple decentred and diverse knowledges. While favouring the latter, Gledhill notes Dipesh Chakrabarty's defence of universalizing Enlightened reason, and Eric Wolf's view that comparison and analytic generalization is only possible with some common conceptual ground. He also acknowledges João de Pina-Cabral's related argument: that all anthropologists now share a 'meta-tradition' based on global exchanges and influenced by multiple sub-traditions, and so establishing 'pluralities' risks merely reinforcing boundaries and impeding intellectual exchange.

Gledhill charts the progress of these debates from attempts by forward thinkers such as Sol Tax, to facilitate scholarly exchanges across national boundaries, to more recent deeply reflexive efforts, by many anthropologists, to eschew their socio-political 'conditioning' and engage on an equal basis not just with 'others' in the academy, but with the worldviews – or as Pina-Cabral puts it, the 'local intellectual universes' – of the communities with whom they conduct research.

This latter point interests me particularly, as I have long thought (and argued in *Current Anthropology* a decade ago) that assumptions about anthropologists exerting vast power as lone scholars in ethnographic contexts may be rather illusory. Perhaps some of us are less inclined to feel powerful! But my experience of working with indigenous communities suggests that reciprocal and egalitarian relationships are not so hard to achieve. More to the point, I would suggest that the exchanges of knowledge that occur in the course of ethnographic research have been highly influential in the composition of anthropological theories over time. It is this flow of diversity into our intellectual developments that sets anthropology apart from the other social sciences.

Gledhill is, of course, absolutely right to say that we need to keep a sharp eye on the conditions that create and maintain inequalities, but I would argue that a rendition of these relationships that assumes an exploitative one-way street also risks denying the agency of others and erasing the historical and contemporary co-authorship of our discipline. If ethnographic engagement brings diverse cultural and sub-cultural ideas into core theoretical debates, it is surely possible – and necessary – to recognize the distinctive voices and their contributions at each level of our discipline, while simultaneously valorizing the collectively constituted meta-discursive theories that enable us to talk across cultural and geographic boundaries. Unity and plurality are not mutually exclusive.

It may be beyond anthropologists' capacities (though that doesn't mean we should stop trying) to resolve the many inequities that continue to distort global intellectual exchanges. But we can at least subvert these by including those with less access to resources for mobility and self-expression; by sharing resources as best we can; and by openly co-producing – and acknowledging the co-authorship of – our theories and methodological approaches. Clearly there is a role here for international anthropological associations such as the IUAES and WCAA, and at a national level, for organizations such as the ASA. But perhaps the most important achievement of the Manchester Congress has been to encourage collaborative efforts that link their activities at different scales.

Veronica Strang
Chair, Association of Social Anthropologists of the UK and the Commonwealth

IUAES Foreword

Like any professional association or scholarly community, the International Union of Anthropological and Ethnological Sciences (IUAES) depends on the cooperative endeavours and collaborative initiatives developed among its members. These often emerge in the context of the scientific commissions, the nearly thirty constituent units that are the intellectual heart of the IUAES. Also integral to the IUAES's intellectual vitality and organizational efficacy are the joint efforts undertaken with allied associations, such as the World Council of Anthropological Associations (WCAA) and, of immediate relevance to this monograph, the Association of Social Anthropologists of the UK and Commonwealth (ASA). A productive partnership with the ASA made the IUAES' Seventeenth World Congress possible. The successes of the 2013 Manchester Congress owe a tremendous amount to John Gledhill's leadership and the well-coordinated work of those who formed and fulfilled the objectives of the organizing committee. Those collective efforts are deeply appreciated by all who participated in what was a genuinely memorable congress. In some important respects, that congress, as Gledhill suggests in the Introduction, increased the visibility and affirmed the legitimacy of the IUAES in the North Atlantic, where the organization was not as well-known as in other parts of the world. However, the earliest impetus for promoting the internationalization of anthropology emanated from Europe and the United States. As the epicentre of interest in the IUAES shifted from North to South, and West to East, the criteria for disciplinary internationalization also changed. With this shift, the IUAES is learning to navigate the complex terrain of 'world anthropologies'.

The seventeenth World Congress offered a global space and thematic focus ('Evolving Humanity, Emerging Worlds') for stimulating a multiplicity of conversations that encouraged anthropologists to move across the boundaries that mark differences along lines of culture, gender, race, nation, and hemisphere. The potentially cross-fertilizing outcomes of democratized forms of intercultural communication – whether straight-forward exchanges of information and perspectives or more contentious debates – may help create some of the conditions for asking new questions, creating new syntheses and co-producing new knowledge. It is our hope that world congresses that frame and facilitate effective 'intercommunications' among world anthropologists will play a meaningful role in creating alternatives to trends that sustain the knowledge divides that characterize the contemporary social sciences worldwide. The overlapping activities of the IUAES, the WCAA and the ASA demonstrate that we believe that different kinds of relations of global knowledge production are possible. To achieve them requires concerted, decolonizing work. Some of that work is underway and reflected in what Gledhill calls the 'snapshot' from the Manchester Congress that this book presents.

The IUAES welcomes this new addition to the ASA Monographs Series. *World Anthropologies in Practice: Situated Perspectives, Global Knowledge* is an important contribution to the discipline, particularly to the dialogues germane to world anthropologies. This collection's emphasis on world anthropologies as they are situated and grounded *in practice* is a timely complement to the existing literature, which is extremely rich in critiques of hegemonic formations of the discipline, histories of national and regional anthropologies and theoretical visions and methodological mappings for interculturality and pluriversality – cornerstones for remaking anthropological knowledge. The contributors to this volume reveal what the practice of world anthropologies involves at this twenty-first century moment. Although the focus is on present-day crises and concerns, most of the authors situate the problems they address in appropriately historicized contexts. Such useful contextualization of both local histories and shifts in global, macrostructural conjunctures allows readers to better understand the trajectories of continuity and discontinuity that have shaped the contemporary issues that the contributors interrogate in their research and social analyses.

This collection's analyses bring to readers' attention a fascinating array of concerns, which include the shifting struggles of labour movements under conditions and regimes of neoliberalism; new flows of migration and mobility; diverse enactments, exhibitions and uses of intangible cultural heritage; the role of salvage ethnography in post-disaster recovery efforts; the tensions erupting from the interplay of universal human rights, cultural/religious pluralism and gender; protests over ecologically friendly, humanitarian toilets that conflict with subaltern ideas of citizenship and human dignity; models and strategies for transforming a long-term security crisis into sustainable peace; and the cultural politics of reincarnation and time in minoritized and indigenous communities' claims to autochthony and sovereignty vis-à-vis the state-level polities in which they are disjunctively embedded.

The chapters include studies of unexpected, geographically distant comparisons, as in the case of the political deployments of religious precepts among the Syrian Druze and Australian Anagu and the case of new union movements in Nepal and South Africa. These comparative studies were achieved through collaborations between anthropologists who specialize in different parts of the world in the first instance and, in the second, through individual research done over time in two different field sites. Collaborative work also informs some of the single-site or single-country studies, as attested in the chapters on a South African township's toilet protests and Thailand's southern regional security crisis. In the age of globalization and multi-sited ethnography, the chapter on Brazilian expatriate football or soccer players is an exemplar. It examines patterns of 'motility' dispersing professional athletes across the hierarchically tiered, global market characterized by differential conditions for accumulating celebrity and 'football capital'.

Overall, the contributions to this volume address important questions of heightened interest among anthropologists and the audiences interested in what the discipline has to say about the state of the contemporary world and the ways it is being reconfigured. The volume also presents some degree of disciplinary self-reflection. For example, one of the chapters presents an auto-ethnographic account of salvage anthropology conducted in the aftermath of the 2011 Great East Japan Earthquake and Tsunami. Another chapter examines migration studies based in increasingly neoliberal, corporate-controlled universities, where radical paradigms that take the logic of capital accumulation into account are eschewed.

This collection gives us a valuable glimpse of today's world from a variety of prisms. It should inspire us to think more boldly about the anthropological work that remains to be done.

Faye V. Harrison, IUAES President

–1–

Introduction: A Global Community at Work

John Gledhill

... every time we speak of the 'anthropology of the South', we are talking, in fact, in the plural: the anthropologies of the South are as manifold as the different 'schools' or 'currents' which are acknowledged within the anthropology of the North, or even more so. However, just like the latter, they share certain characteristics. These are not very clear yet, but naturally they have to do with the situation of having been traditionally the place of the 'object' of the original anthropology and with the principal worldwide inter-civilizational conflict that in our day divides the planet into two different and in a certain sense opposing spheres: the North and the South.

Esteban Krotz (1997: 247–8)

The chapters in this book are based on papers presented at the Seventeenth International Congress of Anthropological and Ethnological Sciences (ICAES), held in Manchester in August 2013. Although the very first of these meetings was in London in 1934, the UK anthropological community had not hosted another since then, and the ASA generously postponed its own decennial conference to ensure that all our national energies were focused on ensuring its success. This volume extends the ASA's commitment, as an association now welcoming members from all countries, to strengthening communication and mutual understanding within a global community of anthropologists.

The congress has a separate historical origin to the organization that now sponsors it, the International Union of Anthropological and Ethnological Sciences (IUAES), which was founded in 1948 as part of the United Nations Educational, Scientific and Cultural Organization (UNESCO's) drive to create international scientific networks that would transcend not only cultural and language barriers but also the Cold War divide. The two organizations did not merge definitively until the ICAES was held in Tokyo in 1968, and what became five-yearly congresses supplemented by smaller inter-congresses are not the only activities that IUAES sponsors. Besides giving anthropology a voice in multidisciplinary international forums such as the International Council for Science (ICSU) and International Social Science Council (ISSC), IUAES promotes international collaboration between anthropologists working on particular issues through networks called commissions. IUAES commissions are often very lively international organizations in their own right, organizing their own conferences, and some papers in this book were presented in commission-sponsored panels at the World Congress.

It is ironic that the IUAES does not have a high profile among UK anthropologists today, given that its secretary-general from 1978 to 1998 was the distinguished biological anthropologist Eric Sunderland, who was a professor and later Pro-Vice-Chancellor at Durham University before he returned to his native Wales to become Vice-Chancellor of Bangor University and play a central role in the creation of devolved government through the Welsh Assembly. The relative marginality of IUAES might be simply a consequence of the dominance of social anthropologists in British anthropology and relatively small number of departments pursuing the four-field approach including biological anthropology, archaeology and linguistics that IUAES embodies. I suspect, however, that it reflects something else. Although much of the initial impetus to create IUAES came from Europeans and from North American scholars such as Sol Tax, founder of the journal *Current Anthropology*, and organizer of the 1973 congress in Chicago, IUAES-sponsored congresses became less important for Europeans and North Americans and especially important for anthropologists from countries in East and South Asia, Latin America, Russia and eastern Europe. A Mexican friend once told me that he always went to IUAES meetings precisely because anthropologists from the US and western Europe did not dominate them.

This speaks to one part of what is now a well-established debate, to which I return in the next section, about what it should mean to talk about 'world anthropology' in the twenty-first century, and whether we should speak of 'world anthropology' in the singular or 'world anthropologies' in the plural. The ICAES and IUAES were created to advance a project of building international relations between anthropologists that many contributors to the new debates of the late twentieth and early twenty-first century would consider rather naïve, because they have focused our attention on inequality and exclusion within the so-called 'world community' of anthropologists and on the strong institutionalization of the dominance of 'hegemonic anthropologies' located in the North Atlantic world, especially the anthropology of the United States. The lessons learned from these debates were very much at the forefront of the thinking of the organizers of the 2013 congress and of the many participants in it who have occupied senior positions in the anthropological associations of the countries and regions considered 'hegemonic' in these critiques, as well as those who represented the anthropological communities of 'non-hegemonic' countries and regions.

Bringing this congress back to the UK was one of a number of actions that reflected coordinated attempts by a recent generation of professional leaders to take concrete steps to act on these lessons, many of them promoted through the work of the World Council of Anthropological Associations (WCAA), which also sponsored several panels and a plenary session at the Manchester congress. Given the recent emphasis on 'hegemony' and a more questionable tendency to locate hegemony in particular countries as distinct from transnational power networks, there is a potential difference in meaning between an 'international congress' and 'world congress' that aims to promote a more plural and inclusive global community of anthropologists. We therefore decided to abandon the old (and without knowledge of the history, rather confusing) ICAES name and call the 2013 event the Seventeenth World Congress of the IUAES.

With delegates from more than sixty countries representing all the regions of the world, the Manchester congress was a truly global event in terms of participation. I also hope that all delegates felt that they enjoyed equality of voice during the congress. But, although plenty of younger scholars from many different countries participated as well as more senior colleagues, I cannot feel totally satisfied with what we achieved in terms of inclusiveness. We succeeded in keeping registration and accommodation costs very low for a UK-hosted event, but, despite the generous support of the Wenner-Gren Foundation, we could not begin to compete with the level of subsidization of participation that funding from the Chinese government had made possible at the previous congress in Kunming, held in 2009. To my shame as chair of the organizing committee, British immigration officials refused entry visas to a small but significant number of delegates, despite my efforts, supported by the British Academy and my local Member of Parliament at the time, John Leech, to get what in every case seemed both unreasonable and discriminatory decisions reversed. Cost constraints in the UK's semi-privatized public universities also made it impractical to provide simultaneous translation, so, although a few panels were conducted in other languages, the only official congress language was that which was the second language of the greatest number of delegates: English. Yet, despite these constraints, we did succeed in hosting a genuinely 'global' event. The presentations reflected the existence of different and conflicting paradigms in the discipline both globally and within different countries, and a wide range of stimulating work was presented across the full range of anthropology's sub-fields.

A single book can only include a tiny sample of the 1,283 individual papers presented at the congress, a figure that excludes the contributions to plenary debates and distinguished lectures, which are published separately, as are some of the panels. Because this book is an ASA monograph as well as an IUAES book, the contributions chosen are from social and cultural anthropologists, and, because it is a record of a world congress, I have had to ensure that regional representativeness complements the ASA's usual norms of achieving gender balance and including younger as well as more senior scholars. Some colleagues suggested that I attempt a kind of 'best of IUAES 2013' selection. But this kind of logic is much easier to apply to collections of reissued pop songs than an academic publication of record, especially given the now lively debate about how anthropologists based in the global North decide on what is 'good' or not (Mathews 2010). So, given that it is impossible to represent the full range of issues debated at the congress and acknowledging the certainty that my choices reflect personal and probably structural biases, I have selected a group of papers likely to interest most anthropologists living and working in different countries at the present time, which reflect particular concerns and vantage points but also address some cross-cutting themes and engage with contemporary issues.

Although many other papers presented at the congress would have been equally worthy of inclusion, each of those that I have chosen offers a stimulating contribution in its own right, and together they provide as good a reflection of what made the event worthwhile as any other selection that I might have made.[1]

This book is not, therefore, another programmatic contribution about the principles that should shape the future of world anthropology/world anthropologies. It aims instead to provide a snapshot of some of the things that anthropologists in different countries are concerned about in the second decade of the twenty-first century. It exemplifies what anthropologists working in different global locations have to say about important issues, drawing on accumulated disciplinary knowledge and new ideas and inspirations. Given the amount of debate on principles that has already been published, more attention to exactly what anthropologists are actually doing and saying now seems essential to advancing the project of the world anthropology/anthropologies movement in practice. It is, however, clear that major political questions still need to be addressed, collectively, in relation to the promotion (and defence) of anthropology in different national settings, and in relation to more global issues. These include the role of the market in academic production, and the challenges of financing the global mobility necessary for all anthropologists to enjoy face-to-face dialogues on equal terms. Another mobility-related point that has emerged in the course of the debates about how material inequalities within our communities might affect its intellectual achievements is how it might be possible for more anthropologists from the global South to do research on the societies of the global North without being restricted to an 'ethnic ghetto' or inevitably sucked into a 'brain drain'. There are also significant epistemological issues to be considered in thinking about whether world anthropology should be singular or plural, whether or not, as Paul Rabinow (1986) argued, epistemology is another peculiar flower of European history. Before I go on to introduce the contents of the book, I will therefore devote a little more space to discussing the case for welcoming the pluralism in building a global anthropological community that is implicit in the book's title.

World Anthropology or World Anthropologies?

The IUAES was in the business of building a world community of practicing anthropologists long before the late twentieth and early twenty-first century developments that produced the multi-lingual World Anthropologies Network, with its online journal and other publications, and the Wenner-Gren International Symposium that gave birth to the edited book *World Anthropologies: Disciplinary Transformations Within Systems of Power* (Ribeiro and Escobar 2006). The Wenner-Gren Foundation has provided consistent support for both earlier and later efforts to construct a world community of anthropologists, as Leslie Aiello illustrated in her opening address to the Manchester congress.[2] It is worth revisiting the earlier vision promoted by major

IUAES figures such as Sol Tax and Cyril Belshaw (who succeeded Tax as editor of *Current Anthropology* and was also an IUAES President).

As Greg Acciaioli (2011) points out, much of what Sol Tax stood for anticipated more recent efforts to create a decolonized and engaged anthropology that is serious about dialogue between people with different conceptions, including our own research subjects. The book publication programme associated with the Ninth ICAES in Chicago in 1973 sought to encapsulate the current state of anthropological knowledge on a world scale. Although that proved over-ambitious in the sense that the project bankrupted the Dutch publishing company Mouton, it did demonstrate a strong desire to let a hundred flowers bloom. Tax's vision of world anthropology was undeniably that of a political liberal in the US sense and his approach to 'decolonizing' anthropology populist, as even sympathetic critics have pointed out. One of them, Douglas Foley (1999) used the pages of the journal that Tax founded, *Current Anthropology,* to re-appraise his 'action anthropology' paradigm, which used 'clinical science' as a metaphor for its proposed fusing of academic and applied anthropology in efforts to solve the practical problems of residents of a Native American community while simultaneously contributing to the development of anthropological theory. Foley's research on a project carried out in the region where he himself was raised showed that most of the community projects of Tax's team of students had little lasting impact; their interventions and efforts to broker relations with whites probably hindered rather than helped the Mesquaki become independent political actors. Foley also argues that although Tax's populist stance did break with past styles of applied anthropology, the Mesquakis themselves rejected the idea that the white men could 'save' them by using their science to 'cure' a 'culture' that had become 'dysfunctional'. He concludes that although Tax did question the then dominant paradigm of 'acculturation' to a degree, his 'action anthropology' did not produce a profound theoretical questioning of his era's conceptions of 'science' and 'culture' because it did not institute a process in which the researchers could actually learn from their research subjects and understand what *they* thought was important for perpetuating their culture (ibid.: 183).

Nevertheless, Foley also emphasized that Tax was a very open scholar, who was self-reflexive about his achievements. As Acciaioli points out, the *Current Anthropology* (CA) format of articles with published commentaries and author's response that is another of Tax's legacies represented a crucial move towards a critical anthropological practice based on dialogue. Tax's efforts to 'decolonize' the fieldwork situation may not have been successful, but his journal provided 'an interdiscursive space that Tax never limited due to his own reticence to intervene as editor to limit speakable perspectives' (Acciaioli 2011: 39). His contributions to the development of the IUAES furthered a conception of anthropology as 'group of intercommunicating scholars' as distinct from 'an integrated knowledge system'. Acciaioli argues that this anticipated the kind of 'decentering' of dominant metropolitan paradigms called for by Ribeiro and Escobar (2006) in their introduction to the *World Anthropologies* edited volume, and by Restrepo and Escobar (2005) in an article published in the journal *Critique of Anthropology* that was also subjected to a CA-style discussion by a series of other anthropologists.

One of the anthropologists that *Critique* invited to respond to the Restrepo and Escobar article, João de Pina-Cabral, was strongly critical of the idea of world anthropologies in the plural (Pina-Cabral 2005, 2006). Writing as a Portuguese social anthropologist trained in Johannesburg and Oxford, who has made his career in both Portugal and the UK, has done field research in Macau and Brazil as well as his native country, and played a central role in the development of the European Association of Social Anthropologists (EASA), Pina-Cabral finds Restrepo and Escobar's discussion US-centric. He even asks if there might not be a contradiction in making the argument using the conceptual tools currently fashionable in a 'dominant anthropology' that he finds excessively given to discourse analysis (Pina-Cabral 2006: 467–8). Neither Restrepo and Escobar nor Ribeiro and Escobar are unduly discomforted by the latter kind of charges. They cite Bengali historian and postcolonial theorist Dipesh Chakrabarty: transcending European modernity by 'provincializing Europe' cannot be based on 'an out-of-hand rejection of modernity, liberal values, universals, science, reason, grand narratives, totalizing explanations, and so on', since without Enlightenment universals, in Chakrabarty's words, 'there would be no social science that addresses issues of modern social justice' (Ribeiro and Escobar 2006: 4). European obsessions about how we know what we think we know seem to be the very basis of critical movements that rest on a reflexive approach to social science. It is also difficult not to welcome such recent practical developments within the supposedly globally 'hegemonic' anthropology of our day as the AAA's creation of a Permanent Committee on World Anthropologies, along with a regular special section of *American Anthropologist* dedicated to reflexive articles written by colleagues working in 'subalternized' academic communities such as Irish or French-Canadian anthropology (Saillant 2015).

Nevertheless, Pina-Cabral offers other arguments against insisting on the plurality of anthropology. One is the danger of reifying 'national traditions' that often express sharp internal paradigm clashes, and generally have their own internal academic hierarchies and 'centres' and 'peripheries'. In responding to Pina-Cabral, Restrepo and Escobar (2006: 488) firmly plead 'not guilty' to that charge, and those issues were also addressed in historical depth by various contributions in the Ribeiro and Escobar collection. Yet Pina-Cabral (2005: 125) also worries that 'insistence on the plurality of anthropology' runs the risk of unwittingly reinforcing borders and embracing a 'politically correct' respect for difference that impedes the pursuit of the kind of frank and constructive dialogue that could promote mutual learning and development. This seems a significant line of objection, especially if we also see listening to our research subjects (and maybe arguing with them too) as important to improving our analysis and theory building as well as our professional practice. Pina-Cabral insists that it is now outmoded to think of anthropological thought as divided into four 'great traditions', German, British, French and American, the model for the important series of lectures that celebrated the opening of the Max Planck Institute in Halle (Pina-Cabral 2005: 119–20; Barth et al. 2010). He suggests that we are all now participants in a global 'meta-tradition' based on 'the global interbreeding of the many strands of modernistic anthropological thinking' that nevertheless remains 'permeated by a plurality of sub-traditions'. Sub-traditions correspond to language differences but also constitute 'local intellectual universes' that absorb ideas from the outside without losing their capacity to function as 'spaces of intellectual reproduction' that can 'carry on in relative independence of global hegemonic voices' and 'play an important role in a more globalized inter-action now conducted largely in English' (ibid.: 120–1). Yet accepting this account is to risk ignoring much that is important to understanding the politics of these 'local intellectual universes'.

Proponents of a pluralized view of world anthropologies do not see them as intel-lectually isolated entities. This would be an historical absurdity for countries with long-established anthropological traditions of their own such as Brazil, India, Japan and Mexico. The pluralizers want to do something about the way that global power relations 'invisibilize', or to use the term adopted in an earlier classic contribution to the debate by the Mexican anthropologist Esteban Krotz (1997) from which I quoted at the beginning of this introduction, 'silence' non-dominant anthropologies, a process that is not, as Francine Saillant demonstrates for the relationship between Canadian and Metropolitan French anthropology, restricted to the English-speaking world.

The pluralizers' focus on power relations does not privilege geography, although capacity for mobility and the consequences of mobility are important. Nor does it necessarily privilege national space either. But it does force us to look more closely at how 'local intellectual universes' articulate to both states and transnational power networks in the course of the discipline's development, today as in the past. Transnational power relations could prove a serious problem even for anthropolo-gists with heterodox ideas from the traditional 'hegemonic' centres of anthropology, as illustrated by what happened to the youthful Ruth Landes when she did fieldwork in Bahia at the end of the 1930s (Corrêa 2000). Landes's conclusions displeased both Arthur Ramos, godfather of studies of black Brazil at that time, and from 1949 the director of social science at UNESCO in Paris, and Melville Herskovits at Northwestern University. These two senior men's coordinated campaign affected her career, which only stabilized after she moved to Canada in 1965, although it did not prevent her from producing what is now recognized as a classic book (Landes 1994 [1947]). Yet as William Roseberry (1996) pointed out, there are many other dissident figures that we do not know about because their careers were blocked completely.

A concern that can be both ethical and political about the responsibilities of foreign anthropologists working abroad is once again hardly new, as is shown by the circumstances that led to Franz Boas's censure by the AAA (American Anthropological Association) for denouncing colleagues for espionage. Nor is concern about foreign anthropologists' responsibilities to the local scholarly community that hosts them (Adams and Jones 1971), although it remains common for local researchers to fear that foreign visitors may appropriate the results of their work without citation or acknowledgement. Yet one of the principal complaints of colleagues who have not been incorporated into the international circuits of the 'dominant anthropologies' is that they have different understandings of the social and political realities of their countries or regions that foreigners simply refuse to take seriously.

Nobody has illustrated this problem more forcefully than Susana Narotzky (2006) in her discussion of the reactions of Anglophone researchers to what they see as the 'epistemological nativism' of politically committed Spanish anthropologists such as Isidoro Moreno, who, as an Andalusian, found himself marginalized by one famous Anglophone critic as a resentful 'peripheral nationalist' even relative to Spanish anthropologists based in Madrid. Narotzky is a politically engaged scholar who has made her career in Madrid and Barcelona but had family as well as educational ties with the United States, and has derived lasting inspiration from theoretical ideas that she encountered on the other side of the Atlantic. She makes a compelling case for the deeper kinds of international and intercultural dialogues that the pluralists advocate, that is, for expanding a 'conversation' that recognizes the stimulus that different perspectives can bring to debate, whether one agrees with them or not (Narotzky 2014). We can accept Pina-Cabral's contention that the 'dominant anthropologies' of the past constitute a widely shared professional patrimony while recognizing the creative potential of taking diversity seriously without, in Restrepo and Escobar's words (2006: 485), lapsing into a reactive politics of '*ressentiment* or nativism' or imagining that 'anthropology otherwise' is only possible on the basis of a radical epistemological break with anthropology's past.

Old ideas and paradigms always need placing in their historical context of production, but they sometimes prove worth revisiting. Comparative analyses and theoretical generalizations are, as Eric Wolf (2001: 53) maintained against the postmodern turn, simply impossible if we do not agree, provisionally, to share some concepts and ways of describing the world, and agree on what kinds of answers are 'good enough', for the moment, to direct further observations and attempts at explanation. The cumulative development of anthropological knowledge, along with our commitment to reflexivity, guarantees that whatever answers, explanations, and epistemological positions we come up with will not be considered 'good enough' at a later date. The world anthropologies movement simply seeks to enhance the likelihood that current ideas will be subjected to the widest possible range of questioning from the diversity of perspectives that the global anthropological community can offer. Even if the institutional and practical challenges to doing this remain daunting, Sol Tax's vision of a decolonized anthropology as a community of intercommunicating scholars does remain alive in a practical way through the networks and conferences of the IUAES, WCAA and other more recent initiatives, including expanding south–south networks.

It is, however, important not to allow the politics of knowledge production to be erased in talking about that metaphoric 'community'. In the light of European history, many European social anthropologists become nervous at the very mention of the word 'ethnology', for example. Yet it is worth remembering that some social anthropologists in the German-speaking world closely connected with British colleagues proved eager to offer their services to the Nazi state, while some of the nationalists who dedicated themselves to the folkloric kind of ethnological studies classified as *Volkskunde* refused to become complicit in genocide, as André Gingrich documented in his compelling account of the German tradition at the Halle conference (Barth et al. 2010). History offers plenty of alarming lessons about where prioritizing 'advancing our professional interests' may take us.

The 2013 Manchester Congress did succeed in attracting delegates representing a variety of orientations *within* as well as between particular national traditions. Some British participants who were apparently not very aware of these differences expressed shock at the 'old-fashioned', and for them ideologically unacceptable, nature of some of the concepts and arguments that they heard being presented by some panellists. Yet it seems essential that we do talk about these differences. We also need to recognize the more mundane reality that there are parts of the world in which people with anthropology degrees may not be allowed to teach or research what anthropologists based in the higher education systems of other countries would consider anthropology, either because of financial constraints or because anthropology is considered an unredeemable colonial subject.

One of the most challenging moments in the recent history of the IUAES was the Chinese government's decision to postpone the sixteenth congress, due to be held in 2008, because of sensitivity over unrest in Tibet. Some colleagues decided not to attend the 2009 meeting to make their own protest against Chinese government actions in Tibet and Xinjiang (Hann 2009). These were principled decisions that I would not dream of criticizing. But, speaking for myself, I think that engagement did prove more productive, not only because it allowed those of us who went to Kunming to appreciate the diversity of contemporary Chinese anthropology better, but also because it gave us the chance to understand China itself, however superficially, just a little bit better than we did before. This has always been what IUAES is ultimately about.

An Introduction to the Chapters

This book is divided into four sections, each of which contains three chapters that address related issues. The congress was held in Europe at a time of deepening economic crisis. Renewed interest in what US anthropology often labels 'political economy' was very much in evidence in the large number of delegates who attended sessions on these themes. The first two chapters focus on politics and organized labour, offering case studies from countries in the global North and global South, respectively, but also bringing out global processes that cross-cut these regions, posing similar challenges to working people wherever they live. They therefore provide a perfect initial illustration of the significance of the book's subtitle.

Susana Narotzky uses the steel industry in Spain as a window onto what has gone wrong with the European project. From the perspective of Spanish politicians and intellectuals such as the philosopher Ortega y Gasset joining the European Economic Community was the 'solution' to what they perceived (often with racist undertones) as a problem of Spanish 'backwardness' relative to northwestern Europe. The working classes of southern Europe have now become disenchanted with Europe and increasingly alienated from the social democratic parties to which they initially looked not only for social rights but also political freedoms. Narotzky's incisive analysis, which takes us from the era of 'indicative planning' and the triumph of technocracy through to the current crisis, charts the decay of the 'dream of Europe' as trade unions were forced to adapt to new economic realities produced by neoliberal capitalist globalization. Her analysis documents how clear lines of class solidarity tend to be erased when a language of profitability and productivity becomes hegemonic even in the responses of union negotiators, and provides insights into the emergence of new forms of politics on both the left and the right.

Increasing precarianization of the livelihoods of working people in a world of increasing wealth inequality may be increasing global discontent, but anthropologists have an important contribution to make towards explaining why the expressions and consequences of this discontent are so variable.

Malikka Shakya considers cases that run in the opposite direction to Spain's shift away from heavily 'political' trade unions, using Partha Chatterjee's reworking of Gramsci's distinction between political and civil society, an important example of diasporic Indian scholars' efforts to distinguish the postcolonial and European worlds. Decentering North Atlantic fascination with that region's new manifestations of 'resistance to neoliberal capitalism', such as the Occupy movement, Shakya provides us with an analysis of working-class movements that complements the efforts of a few anthropologists in the UK and USA as well as Europe to explore change in organized labour, such as the development of community unionism, rather than simply its decline. Comparing the cases of the Nepal garment industry and the developments behind the massacre of thirty-four striking miners by the security forces of the post-Apartheid state at the Marikana platinum mine in South Africa, her exploration of the broader political implications of new trade union movements also shows how the specific forms in which neoliberal capitalism is being resisted relate to the undemocratic pasts of these two postcolonies.

Winnie Lem also takes up the question of labour under neoliberal capitalism, but this time the relatively disorganized labour of professional academics comes under the spotlight as well. Her focus is on how shifting 'global power geometries' shape scholarly agendas, arguing that if scholarly activity is understood as a labour process, the topics, methods and theories that we deploy at any historical moment are shaped by national and global forces that operate inside and outside the academic field. Taking studies of migration as her example, Lem argues that the migration and transnationalism literature has become contoured by liberal values that focus on the issue of turning migrants into citizens in a way that mirrors the order and stability-focused response of Durkheimian sociology to another epoch of capitalist transformation. Lem questions the radicalism of the 'post' paradigms of a neoliberal capitalist era that is also the era of the neoliberalized university (such as post-feminism, post-structuralism, post-development, and enthusiasm for 'post-capitalist' autonomist movements), advocating stronger reconnection of migration studies with the analysis of capitalist accumulation and crisis.

The second section of the book goes on to provide two innovative ethno-graphically grounded case studies of migrant populations by scholars based in Latin America. **Carmen Rial** shows how anthropology deepens understanding of particular sectors of the contemporary global economy by examining the circulation of Brazilian football players in overseas club networks. Her ethnographic quest has not only taken her to Europe and countries in the BRICS group (Brazil, India, China and South Africa) but to the United States, where Major League Soccer has enjoyed growing popularity, and Morocco, one of the newer markets for Brazilian footballers overseas. Her comparative study reveals important differences between these circuits, including the social origins of the players in the case of the Major League Soccer (MLS), and includes players who were relative unknowns in Brazil and do not play for clubs with global reputations. Emphasis on the heterogeneity of a flow of migrants with specialized talents not only helps us to understand how a global industry works but also broadens our understanding of the contemporary culture of 'celebrities' by looking at how 'celebrity' works on the margins rather than just at the centre of a globalized market.

Cristina Amescua discusses Mexican immigrants in the southeastern United States. Although Mexico–US migration is a well-established anthropological topic, her approach is distinctive and the social heterogeneity of the study population once again important. Focusing on the cultural practices of the migrants, seen as intangible cultural heritage in the sense defined by UNESCO, she places Mexican migration to Georgia in a longer-term political-economic context that shows how past migration influences the present while also showing why it is normal for intangible cultural heritage to change. Offering a complementary perspective to studies that stress conflict and discrimination alone, Amescua shows how immigrants reshape their intangible cultural heritage to project a positive sense of who they are and to build new social ties not only among themselves but also with members of the receiving society, many of whom have developed a genuine appreciation for Mexican 'tradi-tions'. Yet taking the Day of the Dead and cult of the Virgin of Guadalupe as well as Mexican cuisine as examples, Amescua shows how 'tradition' is a living product of responding to social change both at home and in the migrant context.

In the third group of papers, we return to the politics of culture and heritage. It seemed fitting that a chapter from China should represent the longstanding engagement of IUAES with museum anthropology, since China has recently experienced a dramatic 'boom' in museum construction. **Pan Shouyong** charts the history of museums in China from their beginnings in the nationalist republic through the adoption of the Soviet model of the museum as a propaganda institution to this recent boom and the museological innovations associated with it. Established Chinese national museums have abandoned historical narratives designed to foster socialist nation building in favour of exhibitions of art and national treasures. At the same time a plethora of new regional and local museums now tell local stories that are deeply appreciated by the communities that they serve, as the author illustrates with two case studies from among the various projects in which he has participated personally. China has been an enthusiastic adopter of UNESCO's intangible cultural heritage programme, but as we might expect, its implementation on the basis of a hierarchy of inventories has distinctly Chinese characteristics, and the author also explores the growth of ecomuseums and private museums. His analysis questions some recent Western ideas about the relationships between 'history identity' and 'place identity' on the basis of Chinese experience, and uses the further example of the Anji county ecomuseum project to underscore why social history matters.

In a paper originally presented to one of the panels convened by the IUAES's Legal Pluralism Commission, **Shalina Mehta** takes up the apparent contradiction that the universalizing concepts of the rights of women embedded in the UN Declaration of 1947 appear to conflict with commitments to respect differences of cultural practice, prompting opponents of legal measures to establish equal treatment for all women nationally to argue that the universal rights of minorities are being ignored. These problems are of broad comparative significance, but Mehta focuses on the particularly controversial issue of women and Islam, which she explores both in her native India and the comparative context of Iran. In highlighting that there is as much debate within Islam as debate between Islam and followers of other religions and advocates of a completely secular national order, along with the ways in which the politics of universal versus minority rights have increased the vulnerability of Muslim women in India, Mehta uses self-critical reflection on her own prejudices as a non-Muslim not only to advance a devastating assessment of where the rights of all women actually stand in contemporary Indian society but also to challenge the negative images of the position of women in Iranian society that dominate Western media.

Mehta's use of comparison to advance her analysis echoes the approach of a number of contributors to this volume, but none deploy the comparative method more boldly than **Maria Kastrinou** and **Robert Layton** in the chapter that ends the third section. Bold cross-cultural comparisons are not as common as we might expect in contemporary social anthropology, perhaps because of fear of critique from other social scientists whose 'controlled comparisons', often of a quantitative kind, might at least superficially appear more rigorous. In comparing reincarnation among the Syrian Druze and Australian Anangu, Kastrinou and Layton compare two historically unconnected human groups on the basis of their profound ethnographic knowledge of the cases. In writing comparatively about reincarnation, they are adding to a tradition pioneered by other scholars in search of generalizations that might be applied to different instances of the phenomenon, such as Gananath Obeyesekere. Their discussion adds further nuance to the global picture and proposes a new way of understanding what reincarnation can be about. The authors argue that reincarnation belief allows minority groups encapsulated by larger state systems to stake powerful political and economic claims of autochthony, sovereignty and belonging. But they do not claim that this is all reincarnation is about, taking the theoretical short cut of functionalist reductionism. Instead they document in detail ethnographic grounds on which we could interpret practices in both these societies as the making of 'political and geographical claims to time', and in doing so offer a fascinating example of what anthropology gains by exploiting the theoretical potential of studying human similarities as well as human differences.

The final section of the book offers papers on anthropological engagement with major public issues: health, development and racial and social justice in South Africa; security and conflict in southern Thailand; and disaster relief in Japan. **Peter Redfield** and **Steven Robins** discuss controversies related to the improvement of sanitation in low-income communities in South Africa. Although it might seem self-evident that tackling the issue of the disposal of human bodily waste is a crucial issue for any programme of human betterment, they demonstrate that the issues are more complicated and contested than they appear at first sight. Alternatives to flush toilet technology that reduce waste of scarce water resources might seem good for both people and the planet in general, and aspirations to recycle human excrement safely and productively are longstanding. Yet the humanitarian global designs of the Gates Foundation came unstuck when they conflicted with other kinds of meaning-making processes that are important for black South Africans in poor neighbourhoods in a post-Apartheid era that many continue to find disappointing. Why should only white middle class folks have flush toilets? Contrasting the politics of sanitation within spatially segregated South African cities with the nineteenth-century 'Great Stink' crisis that forced the British elite to take radical measures to tackle London's sanitation problems, the authors explore issues of social and individual 'dignity' that lie at the heart of many contemporary development dilemmas, while also highlighting issues relating to the alternatives of private and public sector provision of solutions.

Paul Chambers, **Napisa Waitoolkiat** and **Srisompob Jitpiromsri** use the ideas of Johan Galtung, the father of peace studies, to discuss how an end might be brought to the long-running violent conflict in the southern provinces of Thailand, bordering Malaysia and inhabited by a Malay Muslim majority. They focus on the relations between all the stakeholders involved in this conflict, including the Thai military and international agencies and actors. Close analysis of the structure of the conflict reveals differences of interest and perspective within these groups (again including the military), while a historical perspective reveals not only how colonialism prepared the ground for it, but the complex politics at national and regional level that have undermined past initiatives to build peace. The authors draw historically and ethnographically grounded conclusions about what it will be essential to do if a lasting peace is to be secured, including the need to involve the military in any new conversation about a settlement, taking up Galtung's emphasis on the centrality of intercultural communication in conflict resolution.

We saw earlier in the book that intercultural communication is important to conflict resolution in the very different context of Mexican migration to new areas in the United States. The final chapter returns us to the issue of intangible cultural heritage as a means of expressing valued identities as well as an element in intercultural dialogue. **Hiroki Takakura** reflects on his experience of a 'salvage' survey project on the intangible cultural heritage of rural communities devastated by the Great East Japanese Earthquake and Tsunami of 2011. Although many Japanese anthropologists asked themselves what they might do as anthropologists in response to this disaster, conducting participant observation fieldwork on how people were coping in emergency shelters was seen as presenting serious ethical challenges. Takakura accepted a commission from local government to carry out a survey of local performances and dances that was not only consistent with Japanese government ideas about what social and cultural anthropologists are useful for but turned out to be welcomed by the survivors despite their difficult circumstances. He argues that this favourable reception suggests that salvaging intangible cultural heritage can contribute to social recovery after disasters and to the future resilience of reconstructed communities. 'Salvage anthropology' should therefore be defended against the charge that it always represents an exoticizing colonial move: far from freezing culture in temporal otherness, its recording strategies are necessary precisely because culture is always dynamic and changing.

In making an argument in favour of close collaboration with government as well as local communities, Takakura is careful to recognize what is specifically Japanese about the relationship between anthropologists and the state, accepting that other kinds of collaboration might be more appropriate in other contexts. In doing so he reminds us that different types of relations between professional anthropologists, government and society remain central to the plurality that characterizes anthropology worldwide.

Notes

1. Thirteen scholars originally accepted the editor's invitation to contribute to this book. Unfortunately, two of them, a distinguished senior Afro-American colleague and a young anthropologist from Sudan completing his doctoral thesis in Germany, were not able to complete their chapters by the tight deadline, as a result of illness and family commitments respectively. Because these contributors withdrew at a very late stage, it was impossible to invite other authors to take their places.
2. Videos of this keynote and all the other congress plenaries can be viewed on the congress website at http://www.iuaes.org/congresses/2013/plenaries.html [accessed 20 May 2015].

References

Acciaioli, G. L. (2011) 'From World Anthropology to World Anthropologies: Continuities in the Project of Decolonizing and Internationalizing Anthropology', in G. L. Ribeiro (ed.) *Global Anthropologies,* Beijing: The Intellectual Property Publishing House.

Adams, R. N. and Jones, D. J. (1971) 'Responsibilities of the Foreign Scholar to the Local Scholarly Community', *Current Anthropology* 12 (3): 335–56.

Barth, F., Gingrich, A., Parkin, R. and Silverman, S. (2010) *One Discipline, Four Ways: British, German, French, and American Anthropology,* Chicago, IL: University of Chicago Press.

Corrêa, M. (2000) 'O mistério dos orixás e das bonecas: raça e gênero na antropologia brasileira', *Etnográfica* IV (2): 233–65.

Foley, D. E. (1999) 'The Fox Project: A Reappraisal', *Current Anthropology* 40 (2): 171–92.

Hann, C. (2009) 'Of Conferences and Conflicts: 16th Congress of the IUAES, China, Summer 2009', *Anthropology Today* 25 (6): 20–3.

Krotz, E. (1997) 'Anthropologies of the South: Their Rise, their Silencing, their Characteristics', *Critique of Anthropology* 17 (3): 237–51.

Landes, R. (1994 [1947]) *The City of Women,* 2nd edn, Albuquerque, NM: University of New Mexico Press.

Mathews, G. (2010) 'On the Referee System as a Barrier to Global Anthropology', *The Asia Pacific Journal of Anthropology* 11 (1): 52–63.

Narotzky, S. (2006) 'The Production of Knowledge and the Production of Hegemony: Anthropological Theory and Political Struggles in Spain', in G. L. Ribeiro and A. Escobar (eds) *World Anthropologies: Disciplinary Transformations Within Systems of Power,* Oxford and New York: Berg Publishers.

Narotzky, S. (2014) 'Weaving Knowledge Histories Around Political Engagement: A Story of Anthropological Understanding', *American Anthropologist* 116 (3): 668–72.

Pina-Cabral, J. de (2005) 'The Future of Social Anthropology', *Social Anthropology* 13 (2): 119–28.

Pina-Cabral, J. de (2006) 'Response to "Other Anthropologies and Anthropology Otherwise: Steps to a World Anthropologies Framework" by Eduardo Restrepo and Arturo Escobar (June 2005)', *Critique of Anthropology* 26 (4): 467–9.

Rabinow, P. (1986) 'Representations are Social Facts: Modernity and Post-modernity in Anthropology', in J. Clifford and G. E. Marcus (eds) *Writing Culture: The Poetics and Politics of Ethnography,* Berkeley, CA: University of California Press.

Restrepo, E. and Escobar, A. (2005) 'Other Anthropologies and Anthropology Otherwise: Steps to a World Anthropologies Framework', *Critique of Anthropology* 25 (2): 99–129.

Restrepo, E. and Escobar, A. (2006) 'Responses to "Other Anthropologies and Anthropology Otherwise: Steps to a World Anthropologies Framework" (June 2005)', *Critique of Anthropology* 26 (4): 483–8.

Ribeiro, G. L. and Escobar, A. (eds) (2006) *World Anthropologies: Disciplinary Transformations Within Systems of Power,* Oxford and New York: Berg Publishers.

Roseberry, W. (1996) 'The Unbearable Lightness of Anthropology', *Radical History Review* 65: 5–25.

Saillant, F. (2015) 'World Anthropologies and Anthropology in the Francophone World: The Lausanne Manifesto and Related Initiatives', *American Anthropologist* 117 (1): 146–50.

Wolf, E. R. (2001) *Pathways of Power: Building an Anthropology of the Modern World,* Berkeley, Los Angeles, CA and London: University of California Press.

Part One

Anthropology in an Age of Crises

2

'Spain is the Problem, Europe the Solution': Economic Models, Labour Organization and the Hope for a Better Future[1]

Susana Narotzky

Introduction

The Spanish philosopher Ortega y Gasset (2004 [1916]) coined a sentence that was to become a leitmotiv in the process of Spain's integration into the European Community: 'Spain is the problem, Europe the solution.'[2] In 2006, for example, celebrating the twentieth anniversary of Spain's entry into the European Economic Community (EEC), the sociologist Emilio Lamo de Espinosa, then Director of the Think Tank Real Instituto Elcano de Estudios Internacionales y Estratégicos, after referring to Ortega's original statement, added:

> The desire to Europeanize Spain, that is, to modernize it and move with the times, was not so much one of several elements in the political project of contemporary Spain, but its central core, the best summary, a project that brought together equally the left and the right, center and periphery, rich and poor. To Europeanize was to modernize and to modernize was to change. … Our Europeanism was incoming and not outgoing … We are European for reasons of domestic politics, not as an instrument of foreign politics. (2006)

We must recall, however, that Ortega (2005 [1922]) sees the 'problem of Spain' in terms of a lack of internal cohesion paradoxically predicated in the incapability of generating an elite that can lead the 'masses' away from endangering the nation's continuity. For Ortega, the problem of Spain manifests itself as 'particularism' (of the workers – *obrerismo,* and of the regions – *separatismo*). Particularism is seen as a pathological trend that endangers the continuity of the Spanish organism by tearing it apart. It is a 'congenital weakness of its unity'.

Therefore, when experts today use Ortega's dictum 'Spain is the problem, Europe the solution' they point to the core relational meaning of Europe for Spain. Europe will be the cure for internal fragmentation expressed in national identities and class interests and will provide the basis for modernization. In the post-Francoist rendering that became hegemonic during the Transition, Europe became once again a 'unifying project' for Spain, oriented towards the overcoming of the famous 'congenital particularism' that had caused the Civil War. It is worth noting that overcoming national and class conflict was also at the core of the European Coal and Steel Community (ECSC) at the origin of the EEC.

This paper ethnographically explores what Europe meant for steel workers' expectations of future wellbeing and how the accession to the EEC first, and later the advent of the global firm, affected their practical capabilities of organization. Focusing on the relationship between the global market, the nation state and the steel industry, it unpacks the centrality of particular models of economic development and political belonging in the production of workers' understandings of their individual and collective agency. After two sections that provide a historical context, the following sections centre on the arguments and logics that union members of the Arcelor-Mittal steel plant in Asturias develop as they strategize to defend the plant and their jobs. In particular, I seek to unravel the spatial dimensions of labour organization and the drive to anchor responsibility in place.

Peace and Europe

After the Second World War the aim of a peaceful future between the nations of Europe became synonymous with economic integration, centred on the creation of an open market for coal and steel. The Schuman declaration (9 May 1950), considered as the founding bloc of the EEC (1957), proposes:

> The pooling of coal and steel production should immediately provide for the setting up of common foundations for economic development as a first step in the federation of Europe, and will change the destinies of those regions which have long been devoted to the manufacture of munitions of war, of which they have been the most constant victims. *The solidarity in production thus established will make it plain that any war between France and Germany becomes not merely unthinkable, but materially impossible.*[3] (emphasis added)

The constitution of an economic community tied to the production and distribution of coal and steel was thus a political economic project where market integration around two key sectors was meant to prevent war and promote peace. The idea was to avoid conflict through promoting industrial collaboration and free trade. Production and the unification of the market of member countries were the centrepieces in the project. At the same time a particular free-trade model of the 'good' economy was proposed, one that was being pushed forward by the United States in its reconstruction policies, through the Bretton-Woods institutions, American economic aid (Marshall Plan) and the General Agreement on Tariffs and Trade (GATT) rounds. An additional aim was 'the equalization and improvement of the living conditions of workers in these industries' (Schuman 1950). Therefore, while the creation of a common High Authority was aimed at curtailing national intervention in these markets for the common good of attaining durable peace, this free-market aspect was often overpowered by the national preoccupation with full employment and class unrest, what Harvey (2005) calls 'embedded liberalism'.

Both Europe and Spain came to envision economic union as a form of political integration and pacification. The idea of becoming part of Europe, as the 'solution' to Spain's internal conflicts following Ortega's idea, was a central argument for the implementation of neoliberal policies in Spain after 1975. I will focus on the industrial restructuring of the Spanish steelmaking industry in the context of Spain's transition to democracy and its integration into the EEC. But I will try to make a wider point about the incorporation of the neoliberal economic model that came with it and its consequences for industrial working-class people in Spain.

The central idea I want to put forward is that working-class people were asked to make huge economic (and political) sacrifices – by political leaders – in order to join Western democracies in Europe during the transition years (1975–82). The hope for democracy that had guided an entire generation of industrial workers became a real possibility, and entry into Europe (meaning the EEC) was to be its final accomplishment. But democracy and Europe, tied in this meaning to economic policy, soon became the way a neoliberal economic model was packaged for the consumption of the Spanish public.

Before Europe: The American Model Under Franco

The nationalist economy of the early Franco regime was a peculiar mix of repression and paternalism for the working class (Babiano 1993; Molinero and Ysàs 1993). Repression was extreme but employment stability during the regime was a reality especially in the large strategic industries such as steel or shipbuilding. This was coupled with a closing of the labour market to women whose main calling was defined as housework.

Two different periods of trade closure can be defined in the first twenty years after the Spanish Civil War (1936–39). First, 'Autarky', a Falangista model of self-sustaining economic autonomy (1939–46). Second, an import substitution model aimed at developing industry in order to achieve competitiveness (1946–59). This second period led to a third period of progressive liberalization after 1953 and the Madrid treaties with the United States (Viñas 2003). In 1963 the International Bank for Reconstruction and Development (IBRD, later World Bank) prescribed for Spain the articulation of monetary stabilization policies, the deregulation of the labour market and the liberalization of trade and foreign investment, while it opened the door to credit aid (IBRD 1963). Starting in 1959 economic policies of the Spanish Francoist governments will follow the model of development that the US had exported to the rest of western Europe after the Second World War, one based on growth, open trade, productivity and competitiveness.

This liberalization model was at the time deemed compatible with state intervention intended to regulate the excesses of the market but not to substitute for it. 'Indicative planning' was a model of economic regulation initiated in France after the Second World War and linked to postwar reconstruction (Ramos Gorostiza and Pires Jiménez 2009). One of its major proponents was Jean Monnet the first president of the High Authority of the ECSC and one of the founders of the EEC. 'Indicative planning' was a technical device based on macroeconomic data (input–output tables, national accounting) that would enable economic actors to make rational decisions. The state's role was to gather and make available this macroeconomic information and to coordinate the national economy and its different sectors in relation to long-term economic development targets. The state had to interfere minimally with market forces, but it had to make decisions as to which sectors of the economy should receive incentives because they were thought to represent the ground base of any further development. The state also aimed at guaranteeing social peace through targeting full employment. Spain followed the French 'Development Plans' centred on 'key' industries (steel, energy, shipbuilding) that would be given preference by the state. In its 1963 report, the International Bank for Reconstruction and Development supported the adoption of 'indicative planning' as a way to liberalization and economic development for Spain (IBRD 1963: 3). The 1960s Spanish industrial development plans have subsequently been strongly criticized on various grounds, with most critiques stressing their inefficiency and continued constraints on full liberalization (Ramos Gorostiza and Pires Jiménez 2009). However, other European nations were implementing similar policies of intervention and subsidizing of heavy industry throughout the 1950s and 1960s, in blatant contradiction to ECSC open market objectives. Even later on, the 'Davignon plan' of 1977, and approval of the 'manifest crisis' clause in 1981 in the second Davignon plan that installed production quotas, expressed the collective support within the ECSC for strong political intervention in times of sectoral crisis, in an attempt to guide restructuring of the sector (Alter and Steinberg 2007).

Indicative planning had two fundamental consequences that are central for the discussion of this chapter. First, it introduced a particular technical language into economic practice, one that seemed to supersede the political language that had infused economic thinking and decisions up to that moment. Macroeconomic data were to be the guides for economic policies and they appeared as devoid of political intention. In Spain, the economists that came to power with that project were aptly called 'technocrats'. Macroeconomic language would eventually become such a hegemonic force as to pervade the discourse of the democratic trade unions and put an end to the politicized, often revolutionary, aspect of the unions that had re-emerged during the Franco regime (Martínez-Alier and Roca Jusmet 1988). Second, however, indicative planning favoured key sector industries that could benefit from economies of scale and Fordist modernization, and gave workers in these industries a job that was protected not only through labour laws but also through long-term economic policies. As a result the workers' position within these sectors was strengthened, which eventually enabled the reconstruction of class-based trade unions.

Under the governments of Francoist 'technocrats' a model of governance emerged where economy substituted for politics, and economic 'modernization' was the argument overpowering the realities of exploitation, oppression and repression. As Maier has put it for post-Second World War: 'In the last analysis, the politics of productivity that emerged as the American organizing idea for the postwar economic world depended upon superseding class conflict with economic growth' (1977: 629; see also 1981). This was presented as a natural force, a logical necessity, requiring sacrifices for a better good. This American model was embraced by Spanish 'technocrats' as early as 1957.[4] With this move, the Franco regime decidedly turned towards a form of 'modern' liberal capitalism that would fully develop after the Transition.

The Ethnography in Context: Images of Europe in the Transition[5]

What were the hopes of steel workers during the Transition? During Francoism there was one, quite straightforward, political hope: the end of the dictatorship, the attainment of 'freedom' and 'democracy'. Freedom was interpreted as 'freedom' of association, of speech and of movement, mostly referring to political freedom (free unions, free parties). Europe was the expression of this longing. Europe was also seen through the narratives of Spanish migrants coming back home for vacation with consumer goods. Consumption of goods such as household electrical appliances and cars increasingly became an expression of wellbeing. These images of Europe contrast with the memories of the Civil War, the realities of repression, the very low salaries, hunger (*los años del hambre*) and precarious social benefits, and the image of Spain as being isolated from Western democracies, being 'different' in a negative way: 'Spain is different' was the self-deprecatory saying.

The image of the economy of that period was constructed as one of 'backwardness' by liberal and social democrat economists alike. The former decried state inter-vention, tariff barriers and the rigidities of the labour market. The latter pointed to corruption, oligopolies and corporativist relations of production. However, if we look at the economic policies and decisions being made for the 'key' industry of steel after the Second World War within the ECSC by Western democratic states, there is little difference from Spanish policies: dirigisme of national industry and protection of jobs through prices, tariffs, subsidies, cartels and bailouts. As in other European countries, private industrialists were often those investing less and maintaining obsolete facilities and being 'protected' by the state, while public industries in these sectors were often the more technologically advanced. Thus, the perception that settled in the minds of workers in the steel industry, of Spain having policies that were hugely different from those simultaneously occurring in Europe, is not clearly sustained by a comparative analysis of facts.[6]

The transition period brought workers great expectations: the hopes of political freedom, fair economic distribution and social rights that had been lost during the dictatorship. These hopes could be summarized as: 1) having a Western-style multi-party democracy (for most workers the appeal of real existing socialism had dwindled); 2) having strong and free-trade unions and the right to strike; and 3) having a better life through increased salaries, consumption of goods and the expansion of public health, education and a reliable social security system. All of this, in a way, was expressed in the image of Europe as a 'social market economy'.

Very quickly, however, the transition discourse gave way to a *realpolitic* based on permanent agreements between the different parties, and between unions, businessmen and the state. The *Pacto de la Moncloa* (1977) was the first of a series of agreements generally compliant with the macroeconomic technical projections and objectives of mainstream economists: curbing inflation, stimulating growth, increasing productivity and competitiveness. The politics of 'agreement' [*concertación*] were described by some as neo-corporativist because they incorporated trade unions into the increasingly neoliberal policies of democratic governments and 'because macroeconomic orientations become the basis of social agreements' (Martínez-Alier and Roca Jusmet 1988: 59). Conversely, the UGT (Unión General de Trabajadores) leader Justo Domínguez perceived it as a new form of 'trade unionism which is inserted in the State's institutions, a trade unionism of participation, that is or tries to be where decisions are made' (Domínguez 1990: 98).[7] This situation produced a discursive hegemony that would frame industrial workers' protests and struggles in a particular 'language of contention' that was that of the dominant groups but appeared to be neutral, technical and universal (Roseberry 1994). Often, this was interpreted as a move towards an advanced form of European unionism, based on negotiation rather than on confrontation as had been the case during the dictatorship, one not based on ideology but on technical realities and rational economic decisions.

Here a note on Spanish unionism is necessary because memories of the strong politicization and social transformation aims of the labour movement during the long years of clandestine re-organization are a constant referent in workers' discourses (Narotzky 2014). Although the trend towards bureaucratic unionism became, as I have pointed out before, a mark of 'modernization', of what being a union in Europe meant for many leaders, there remained a strong rank-and-file commitment particularly in the heavy industry sectors. Because during the dictatorship claims had always been both 'economic' and 'political' the component of what has been described as community unionism was always important and one would find the same people involved in union activism and in neighbourhood association activism in industrial areas. In many heavily industrialized areas, moreover, what happened in the factory was very much a part of what the community's life was about and unions' activism addressed issues such as housing and infrastructure facilities (Collins 2012; Kasmir and Carbonella 2008).[8] In the 1980s, for example, the first restructuring of heavy industry resulted in high unemployment and an epidemic of heroin abuse among the younger cohort and of alcohol abuse among the older. Neighbourhood associations, often organized around union activists, were key to the development of community clinics and rehabilitation centres as well as to furthering claims of general public services provisioning. Retraining courses were also one of the central claims of the unions after the transition 'agreements', especially in areas hit by restructuring redundancies. Finally, unions were attached to parties and were 'political', until the 1980s allegedly aiming at a radical social transformation. The separation between the socialist (social-democrat) and the communist parties and, respectively, the UGT and the Comisiones Obreras (CCOO) unions was part of the 'modernization' and 'Europeanization' of both unions and parties after the Transition.

After the Transition to Democracy, the first socialist government of Felipe González started a restructuring of heavy industry preparing Spain for incorporation into the EEC and the 'challenge of competitiveness'. This trend has continued until the present through various moments of restructuring and job loss and the present period of structural adjustment.

New Business Models: The Struggle for Investment and Profitability

The process of restructuring the Spanish steel industry that began in the early 1980s has not yet ended. The public steelworks ENSIDESA had incorporated several private factories from 1973 to 1993 (UNINSA, AHV) making it the largest plant in Spain. This process was meant to create a restructured and financially healthy company (CSI) ready for privatization. During the 1990s the process led to privatization through various stages of foreign capital takeover: first Aceralia (1998), then Arcelor (2001) and finally Arcelor-Mittal (2006).

Restructuring in the 1980s was considered a necessity stemming from the low profitability of the Spanish industrial fabric that was a consequence of the Francoist policies. This was admitted by the workers, and it was understood as part of the economic sacrifices needed to become part of 'modern' Europe. So investment and profitability became the key logics in the union leadership's strategies, and a hallmark of their being a form of 'modern' European trade unionism that some workers resented. In the words of Antonio, a union representative for CCOO:

> The issue of profitability [rentabilidad] is hard to take on [by union members]. Normally you think of resistance unionism [sindicalismo resistente] and really what you have to do is participatory unionism [sindicalismo propuesta], [otherwise] we would bring in bankruptcy. So we had to close some plants and not others, so why close one and not another? The answer is based on profitability [rentabilidad]. [...] We learned this quickly. We were not like 'European trade unionists' [sindicalistas europeos] because we had come out of Francoism and clandestinity ... but we soon learnt. (2010)

For Juan, a former anarcho-syndicalist rank-and-file worker, this was the expression of a defeat: 'Unions in this kind of firm do not exist. They are like a department of the firm' (J. R. 2011). Indeed, the porosity between union leadership and Human Resources departments that has been pointed at in other cases (Mollona 2009) could also be found in this plant at least in one case. But, generally, workers tended to admit that the new environment required a new form of unionism that was able to understand the challenges of globalization.

The emphasis on profitability became central in the first restructuring period tied to the global steel crisis, the reduction of overcapacity and the accession to the EEC.[9] Here the relational understanding of Spain vis-à-vis Europe is central. Spain's industry was backward because of the policies of the dictatorship. Support of inefficient private companies and corrupt management had been lethal. In some accounts we also find the idea that while all of Europe had been restructuring heavy industry since the 1960s, Spain was not following suit and got left behind. Yet this is incorrect. Mining was partially restructured in the late 1950s in the European Community, but also in Spain. Steel did not enter crisis until 1974, with restructuring really taking place in Europe after 1980, which is when it started to get underway in Spain as well. Nevertheless, the widespread understanding is that what Europe had done, Spain had to do in order to 'catch up'.

> Here we had a dictatorship and that's why the situation is the way it is – that's why we didn't restructure earlier like the rest of Europe … more than blaming Europe, I think we blamed ourselves. Blamed the dictatorship for this – people realized that under Franco you were producing basically just to produce. (2010)

Simultaneously the model of the large 'public enterprise' is described as being created 'to give work' (2011), and it did give direct work to some 27,000 men before restructuring began in the 1980s. It was an 'untenable model … [but] one that made sense in that period when the primary concern was that people have work, social peace, and everybody happy … . There were none of the expectations of management that we have today, profitability, productivity, competitiveness, all those terms we use nowadays' (2011).

The idea of 'not missing the train' [*no perder el tren*] of Europe and modernity was repeated by political, economic and union elites as an 'argument' for restructuring industry and for adopting a particular increasingly neoliberal economic model based on open markets, competitiveness and profitability. For the steel industry in Europe, the problem of competitiveness was often not so much one of profitability but of overcapacity as a result of the worldwide optimistic expansionary forecasts of the late 1960s that led to investment and increased capacity just as the crisis of 1973 dramatically reduced demand (Hudson and Sadler 1989). As a result, plant closure became the mandatory industrial policy all over Europe but often with profitability as the main argument given to the local unions, which were coopted into saving their plant through restructuring.

But betting on profitability meant increasing productivity, which in turn meant redundancies. The plant in Asturias went from 26,000 to its present 6,000 workers mostly during the first (1983–6) and second (1993–6) restructuring periods. To Arturo, a CCOO union representative now working in the Human Resources department, profitability is always a term for personnel reduction: 'When you speak of restructuring processes you know what you are talking about, you are talking about productivity, you are talking about staff … . And when you talk about staff you know you are talking about reducing it' (2011).

Further structural transformations became apparent during the privatization process in the 1990s. There was a moment when *distancing* between workers and management increased in such a way that there was a qualitative change. And this process is expressed in an opposition between foreign national interests and local regional ones. In a narrative of the privatization process Arturo recalls:

[after the final privatization that produced Arcelor] when we have the Belgians, the French and ourselves [the Spanish], then we can see a breakdown between the model of the public enterprise [local, paternalist] and that of the private enterprise [global, profit-oriented] in the bad sense.[10] We can observe that decisions are made very far from Asturias, and you lose control of the decision making process. … (2011)

There is a sense in which this "*you* lose control" is both a class term and a regional term that refers to the 'public' interest of the industry in terms of its weight in the area's gross domestic product (GDP) and the wellbeing of many locals. This distancing and loss culminates with the selling of Arcelor to Mittal in 2006. Arcelor-Mittal is a multinational, and business plans are designed at the level of the firm, not at the level of each individual plant. This is understood by workers as a break of responsibility links, where central managers do not care about what happens to any individual plant, nor, obviously, to its workforce. But this also creates a terrible dilemma for union representatives. Mittal headquarters are in Luxemburg, and representatives of local unions have to go there to negotiate. They must show a united front if they want to save their plant, and there is no room for nuances. As Ismael (a UGT representative) said:

You might think sometimes that [here in Spain] UGT and CCOO [originally attached to the socialist and communist parties respectively] confront each other … but the focus of Europe changes everything […]. In Europe people speak of the Spanish delegation, nobody argues and we don't show different viewpoints. We eat together, we design the lines of action. We had to overcome the [old] image when central union committees […] were 200 meters from the factory management, there you had the one who was in charge and you didn't have to look further. You went there and you said 'no, we are not going to accept this, and we stopped the factory, but now what would we be stopping? We do not amount to more than 4 per cent of Arcelor-Mittal. A speck on a map. This requires a change of mentality and of strategy. Some things we can negotiate at the local level because the managers here have authority on the subject, other things you cannot. The forum is in Luxemburg; there you have the general management. […] Now you have to pressure for the rights of workers but you [also] have to defend your plant … . (2011)

This contradiction is something that is extremely central in union representatives' discourse and it relates to the crucial theme: the need to be competitive, to be profitable, not only in terms of the global market for steel, but also in terms of internal competition with other plants in the same firm. And, as a consequence of this, the union's insistence on the importance of the firm's investment in the plant as a working-class strategy, leading to a form of 'economic nationalism'. At the same time, unions are trying to develop a common front in face of the global firm through European and International union committees. Ismael further explains:

> Because firms are organized in terms of competitiveness and competitiveness makes enemies. [...] As part of the European [Union] committee you have to defend that [closings] do not occur [...] but automatically you are thinking of *your* blast furnaces. It is important to have a good communication [among the European Union committee]. But what is good news for me might be bad news for you, and this has to be debated at the union level, and it is a long debate. *This is the global firm.* (2011)

But Mittal is not only any other global firm. It is the largest steel company in the world, which makes it possible for it to control prices in the steel market, in order to capture a larger share of the market. This, however, has negative consequences for many of its less profitable companies – with higher costs and lower demand, mostly those situated in Europe – in that they are forced to sell below their production cost. So that the firm's global profitability is endangering the profitability of local plants, and it is also forcing them, through the market, to increase their profitability. In Arturo's words:

> You sell underneath the production price because Mittal is forcing market prices to change, by dumping in the market products with a lower cost of production, he gets more profitability but he also leaves you with your pants down [*con el culo al aire*]. This is a global world and competition is internal [to the firm]. It is like a family with lots of siblings where we all fight to eat the soup while it's hot [*por comer la sopa caliente*]. (2011)

For the unions, the contradiction created by this logic is that between the objective to save the local plant and employment locally, the need to be responsible towards steelworkers at home but also in the global firm, and the crucial understanding that there is no responsibility towards any locality or people on the part of general management or the firm. While unions are driven to frame solidarity first in local terms, their bosses are acting in global terms (Kasmir 2014). And they know it. Competitiveness, the key concept of the neoliberal discourse, then also becomes the key concept in the unions' leadership strategy to save the local plant. Competitiveness, productivity and profitability become reconfigured as a bastion of regional economy. But this has two unavoidably negative results: 1) that productivity is always tied to personnel reduction; and 2) that in-company competition between plants destroys the solidarity of the working class in the globalized firm (see also Hudson and Sadler 1989). To quote the socialist union representative Ismael once more:

> Arcelor-Mittal represents 11% of the GDP of Asturias. There are 100,000 people living in Asturias. Somebody thinks that the hand of Lakshmi Mittal would tremble [if he thought of closing the plant]? We only can fight with results. You have to show results, to be competitive, and it is a one-way journey, because Mittal's present politics is that Mittal does not believe in Europe, he does not believe in European steel because of the European tradition of social policies that do not exist in other parts of the world. That becomes a handicap[11] and so there is no interest, the interest is in investing in Brazil, Mexico, China, India, but not in Europe. [...] When Mittal bought [the Arcelor plant in Asturias] there was a deficit in the world steel market [2006]. With the crisis everything collapses and now we see the truth of Mittal's politics: 'I need plants that can equally produce 5 tons or 2 tons, depending on the market'. .... The best situation [for Mittal] would be to subcontract work personnel to external firms when needed. This is the industrial politics of the future, and it is true panic. You are never going to be as competitive as China or Mexico, you won't make it. ... *First products fall, then workshops fall, and then plants fall, no way we are going to stand the pull.* (2011, emphasis added)

In terms of the European strategies of multinational firms, it seems to be the case that there is almost no investment in integrated steel plants anymore. A major reason for this seems to be European environmental legislation setting maximum CO_2 emission quotas for steel plants that have to be attained or traded for at a cost. The European 'Emission Trading System' for steel has been described by the president of the Consultative Commission for Industrial Change as 'diabolic'.[12] It has driven the European business steel association Eurofer to go to court – with union support – in order to change the benchmarking of emission capacity set by the Commission. The threat being that plants will relocate to free emission countries. Moreover, as transportation costs increase, it becomes again a rational move to get plants closer to raw materials (iron or coking coal). So union leaders are in the paradoxical position of siding up with European business in order to ask for less environmental regulation from the EEC in order to save their plants, without really knowing if firms, which are mostly multinationals, are really interested in saving European plants in the long run, or are just trying to eschew their social responsibilities once more (for a related double bind situation of union leadership see Mollona 2009).

Territories and Nations

Since the 1980s' need to restructure in order to become 'competitive', the unions understood that the regional aspect was a crucial instrument of struggle, a situation that continues up to the present. The struggle became a struggle between regions in Spain (during the first restructuring phase), and then between plants within regions of Europe. It was also, very crucially, a struggle for investment. Antonio (CCOO) explains:

> [For political reasons] we saw the impossibility [for the state] of destroying *all* the industrial fabric of the country: in Asturias, we realized right away that closures were inevitable and this is when we began to raise the issue of investing – investing in the plant and making it more modern in order to make it more profitable. That we were demanding investment was shocking when everyone was talking about [overcapacity] cuts, about saving money. I think this was a good move because we managed to secure investments that are modern and profitable [*rentable*]. [...] The unions [*sindicatos*] were the ones proposing this. I think the [initial] idea was to close the steel industry and instead we got them to invest.
>
> We did have an advantage too [in Asturias], because the crisis in steel coincided with the crisis in mining [*la minería*] and we also had the shipyards [*la Naval*] [...] So, the defense of steel [*siderurgia*] was embedded in that of the regional industry and *was turned into the defense of a region*. Mobilization in the 1980s had the slogan '*salvar Ensidesa y salvar Asturias*' ['save Ensidesa and save Asturias'] – and that [regional situation] worked in our favor. [...] We had an advantage, *making it a regional problem and not just a company problem meant that people helped us, people who normally wouldn't have helped.* (2010, emphasis added)

The national or regional delimitation of an economic space that has to be defended becomes a moral instrument that unions have been using in order to make local and national governments responsible, as well as the managers of local plants of multinational firms or the owners of small and medium enterprises (Beynon, Hudson and Sadler 1994). It expresses the entanglement of so-called bureaucratic and community unionism, but it does so by defining a space, a territory, which makes sense to a large constituency. In parallel, the regional or territorial delimitation of economic destinies is reinforced through the EEC territorial units (NUTS) that are used as statistical areas for the compilation of macroeconomic data and are the focus of structural and cohesion funds. These, in turn, contribute to the interest on the part of firms or entrepreneurs to locate particular 'projects' in particular areas that can opt for subsidies from these European funds.[13] As funds are often linked to retraining schemes in de-industrializing areas, and as vocational training is often controlled by unions, the regional aspect is also a central aspect in union's strategies. Thus, territorial economic identity gets reconfigured through the particular relations of specific regions to European subsidies.

It would seem, then, that the hegemonic language is that of neoliberalism, and unions are at pains to take the struggle into a different framework. Their struggle is trapped in the immediacy of fighting to keep jobs, to keep the local plant going and to keep the region alive (Herod 2001; Sanchez and Strümpell 2014). They lack an alternative framework in which to analyse economic processes after the generalized dismissal of political and revolutionary unionism during the Transition, and the adoption of a 'modern' European neo-corporatist unionism. However, there is a sense in which they do not give in and keep on struggling and the struggle is real (Kasmir 2009). There is, undoubtedly a sense of defeat in the face of global competition, often in-firm globalized competition. A sense of awkwardness because the promise of Europe has been a deadly trap: European regulations, such as the Emission Trading System and environmental and security regulations, are collective social benefits that turn into poison in a neoliberal framework that defines territories in terms of their profitability or competitive advantage, in the abstract. This explains why territory, proximity and an attempt to produce responsibility outside abstract models are increasingly successful in these corners of Europe, as the example of economic nationalism or regionalism shows here. This explains why a return to new forms of corporativism based on national identity and inter-class responsibility are substituting for the 'old' class confrontation, and often stirring racist and chauvinistic attitudes among the working class (see Kalb 2011, 2009). This is a deadly trap within a struggle for life.

Conclusion

So where does Europe stand now? Has it been dissolved by global markets? Has it been dissolved by financial capitalism where production doesn't matter any longer? For many steelworkers in Asturias, now, Europe was the beginning of this global nightmare of perpetual competition and layoffs. It was the beginning of the neoliberal turn, but the Transition in Spain glossed over these new realities in a perverse manner. Admittedly, Europe provided a defence, for a while, through the subsidies aimed at convergence. But that 'gift' also proved to be a double bind in the end, for it was premised on the dismantling of the industrial fabric, initially with generous subsidies for early retirement, unemployment funds and retraining. As Spain entered the EEC, the welfare Europe of the 1950s, 1960s and early 1970s, was quickly disappearing. The peace project enclosed in the original ECSC treaty of Paris (1951) that was based on *production* – the union of industrial interest and workforce welfare – within Europe now seems superseded by the circuits of *financial* capital.

For Asturian steelworkers, this neoliberal reality is experienced as an imposition of abstract models that do not take into account human beings, human relations and personal responsibilities. Abstraction and distancing are the hallmark of this form of capitalism, which has been creeping in for a long time. The last turn of the screw is expressed for these workers as the substitution of industrial capitalism by financial capitalism where profits become increasingly unrelated to production. As Antonio describes it: 'Before, investing to make a company profitable was linked to production … what is happening today is that now it is linked to "profits" [*ganancias*] which is a different concept, a completely abstract concept because profits are not produced in factories but in the stock exchange market, and this is another thing altogether' (A. B. 2010).

Moreover, while abstraction in profit making becomes hegemonic, distancing produces another kind of abstraction, namely the total loss of responsibility of the employers towards workers they don't know. Workers, moreover, lose the material ability to pressure the boss, who is not linked to a particular territory either materially or in any other way. Workers try to 'de-globalize globalization' and re-embed it in proximate networks of concrete responsibilities, in a context where capital is increasingly mobile and increasingly abstract. But many, as Ismael, feel this is a lost battle: 'First products fall, then workshops fall and then plants fall, no way we are going to stand the pull.'

In any case, the Europe that these steel workers were aspiring to was a different one. In their imagination, it was a Europe where workers had rights that were inexistent in Francoist Spain. But they got trapped in the hegemonic macroeconomic technical language of incipient neoliberal capitalism from the beginning, in order to consolidate democracy. Although, for many in Spain, the solution is still Europe, an imaginary [Northern] Europe that knows the mechanisms of economic success,[14] many voices, sensing the loss of common purpose among the founding European nations, are beginning to raise doubts.

In January 2010, as Spain was starting its turn in the EU presidency, José Ignacio Torreblanca, then Director of the Madrid office of the European Council on Foreign Relations pointed out:

> [T]he evolution of the European political project which has led to the 27 member EU has cast doubt on Ortega y Gasset's virtuous circle ('Spain is the problem, Europe the solution') which up until now had dominated our foreign policy. If 'more Europe' does not necessarily mean 'more Spain', the Europeanism which has guided our European policy for the last twenty five years is no longer the automatic answer to each new challenge. Indeed, rather the opposite would seem to be the case; in the new context, it is completely legitimate to ask how much Europe Spain needs to achieve its ends, on a case-by-case basis. (Torreblanca 2010: 1–2; see also Elordi 2012)

On the one hand, the present-day reconfiguration of neoliberal capitalism within lines of unlimited competition is reproducing in Europe the same divisive territorialized conflicts that the EEC was set up to prevent. In Spain, a form of economic nationalism (or regionalism) is understood by different agents as forwarding their aims. The language of cooperation between local economic and political actors is used by workers as a bulwark against globalized firms' attack on labour, while it is used by firms as a means to force labour to comply with internal restructuring and to press their claims against environmental and labour regulations negatively affecting costs in Europe.

On the other hand, in a conjuncture of unprecedented wealth polarization, lines of class solidarity are not well defined. They are being erased by flexible production structures that have resulted in subcontracting many tasks to small firms, often spin-offs of the main firm. In this context temporary contracts prevail, creating an increasing differentiation among 'permanent' in-firm labour and 'precarious' subcontract labour (Parry 2009; Narotzky 2015a; Sanchez and Strümpell 2014). But the so-called stable workers in the main firm are themselves struggling to keep their jobs in the global firm. Here, lines of class (solidarity of all the workers in the firm and in the sector) are obscured by the dominant hegemonic language of profitability and competition that has captured workers' logic in their struggle for survival (see Kasmir 2001 for a different kind of shaping of the worker's self to further the firm's interests).

Simultaneously, a form of localized, non-ideological politics is emerging as a grassroots response to the overt collusion of economic and political elites with a neoliberal programme eroding those social rights that were envisioned as the expression of being part of Europe. Parts of the 15-M social movement that expressed this rejection of a political system perceived as unrepresentative of ordinary people's needs is in a process of institutionalization.[15] They present the main political opposition to a ruling 'caste' of colluding economic and political interests that oppresses 'decent people' (Monedero 2013), paradoxically setting the conflict in moral terms rather than in political economic terms (Narotzky 2015b). In contrast, other voices stemming from a reconfiguration of the class perspective still speak of the 'world of work' as inclusive of many different experiences and positions within the capitalist structure but fundamentally based on its members' common lack of economic and political power, where the struggle against financial capital (in its diverse impact on powerless economic agents) would become a new rallying point (Narotzky 2015a; Collins 2012).

It is difficult to guess, in the wake of an increasing global discontent caused by precarious livelihoods all over the world, what will be the emerging identities that will take industrial workers' struggle beyond a neoliberal language of contention and ordinary people beyond moral claims. However, what seems to be losing force in southern Europe is the expectation that becoming a member of the European Union was a project for the benefit of the world of work. The spatial reconfigurations of hopes, claims and politics expresses the demise of a dream of wellbeing tied to an imagination of a Europe oriented, as Robert Schuman's (1950) declaration expressed it, towards the 'equalization and improvement of the living conditions of workers in these industries', at least within Europe itself.

Notes

1. *Acknowledgements*. The European Union Cooperation Research Programme FP7- CT-2009-225670 supplied the funds for the research project 'MEDEA. Models and their Effects on Development Paths: An Ethnographic and Comparative Approach' on which this paper is based; special thanks go to Victoria Goddard for coordinating the project. I would like to thank all the participants in the project for their insights and debate, although I alone

am responsible for the contents of this paper. I am particularly grateful to Claire Montgomery and Elena González-Polledo who conducted interviews in Asturias and to Irene Sabaté who was also part of the Spanish team. The ICREA Academia Programme of the Generalitat de Catalunya provided a five-year fellowship that enabled me to dedicate more time to research. I also wish to thank Sharryn Kasmir and Gavin Smith for their comments on a first draft.

2. In an excellent critique of Ortega's dictum, Gustavo Bueno, the Asturian philosopher, underlines the racist assumptions that are enclosed in it: 'Ortega is saying here: Europe is the Spirit; Spain, separated from Europe, is close to Africa, is barbarian, is Nature […] Europe is, for Ortega, the Spirit, Culture par excellence, raising above the barbarian Nature, represented by Africa. Europe is the fruit of the "divine inspiration" of the peoples created by the Roman Empire. The four or five great European nations come from this origin (France, Germany, England, Italy, Spain) that have followed their destiny of world expansion without ever losing their unity. A unity which is not only spiritual ("cultural") but is also political.' He stresses as well the point that Ortega sees the 'problem of Spain' in terms of a lack of internal cohesion paradoxically predicated in the incapability of generating an elite capable of leading the 'masses'. 'In any case the problem of Spain is diagnosed as a "congenital weakness of its unity", as "invertebrate" will be regularly expressed as a chronic illness […]. In our days Spain's illness […] manifests itself as particularism: particularism of the guilds, "particularism of the workers", particularism of the regions and separatism of the provinces. From its congenital illness emerge the pathological trends that endanger the continuity of the Spanish organism, tearing it apart.'

3 The declaration also included 'the equalization and improvement of the living conditions of workers in these industries' among the tasks with which this common High Authority was charged.

4. It is important to know that the major economic advisors of the regime were intellectual brokers of American models. This was the case of personalities such as Antonio Garrigues Díaz-Cañabate, married to the daughter of one of the first ITT representatives in Spain (an influence that would be taken up by his sons Antonio and Emilio), the Urquijo family bank – an Urquijo is now the president of Arcelor-Mittal Spain and the president of the Spanish steel business association – also originally involved with ITT interests, Andrés Moreno, director general of the Banco Hispano Americano during twenty-five years and the main interlocutor with the American banks extending credit, Fermín de la Sierra, Managing Director of the Comisión Nacional de Productividad Industrial (CNPI; the Spanish centre of productivity, established in 1952) who had a grant in 1946 to study at the University of Chicago under Milton Friedman, returning to the INI in 1947, Javier Benjumea, founder of Abengoa one of the main engineering infrastructures companies, the Aguirre family founder of Agromán one of the main construction companies involved

in the US military bases construction, etc. It is also important to recall that American-style business schools were founded through the public CNPI directed by de la Sierra with strong American support as well as that of the INI president Suanzes – EOI and EAE – in 1957 with the support of Suanzes (INI), the private Business Schools supported by the Jesuits (ICADE and ESADE) and by the Opus Dei (IESE) in 1958, and exchange programmes that were directly addressed at acquiring business management techniques in American universities (Puig and Álvaro 2003).

5. Fieldwork in Asturias was carried out by Claire Montgomery in 2010 and Elena González-Polledo in 2011 under my direction, for the Project 'Models and their Effects on Development Paths: An Ethnographic and Comparative Approach to Knowledge Transmission and Livelihood Strategies' (MEDEA), FP7-CT-2009-225670, coordinated by Victoria Goddard. Transcription of the interviews was done by Diana Sarkis and Jaime Palomera at the Universitat de Barcelona. The ethnography consisted mostly of interviews with steel workers, union representatives and other institutional actors. A qualitative survey of households comprising fifteen households in Galicia and forty-four households in Asturias was conducted respectively by Irene Sabaté and Elena González-Polledo. Results were formalized so as to be comparable with results in other field sites (in Argentina and Slovakia).

6. The 'backwardness' of the Spanish economy in the key industrial sector of steel was not a result of applying a different analysis or policies. The main difference in Spanish political economy was the state of repression and fear that affected workers' claims for better salaries and working conditions. This enabled a higher rate of exploitation that provided rents from labour that inhibited private investment, a situation of absolute surplus value extraction in Marxian terms. Another difference was that private heavy industry firms, often related to the banking sector, were in the hands of elites often supporting the regime. State intervention protected them not only from external competitors but also from internal competitors sustaining a situation of oligopoly in the sector (Clavera et al. 1973; Buesa and Pires 2002). In fact, the creation of large public steelworks in the 1950s was an attempt to create some internal competition that would drive private firms to invest and increase productivity. However, this contradicted the personal support networks that were essential to the maintenance of the regime. As a result, the state inhibited investment in public industry to the benefit of private firms during the Planes de Desarrollo in the 1960s, enabling the continuity of small private and inefficient steel mills. These competed for public funds with the large and potentially profitable public integrated steelworks. Political and economic elites were entangled in patronage networks that produced benefits through the sacking of public funds and the obstruction of internal competition.

7. Justo Domínguez adds: 'In a not so distant future, scholars will have to admit that the great contribution of the UGT to Spain's democratic life and

very saliently to industrial relations, has been the understanding of reality, superseding its own history and tradition without renouncing it, with UGT commemorating its centennial as the largest union in Spain. In order to get there it was necessary to design a trade union model based on negotiation and pressure, open to all workers, without losing because of it its character and conscience as an instrument for the transformation of society' (1990: 103).

8. This might also be the result of the industrial paternalist phase of the large heavy industries where the firm (public or private) provided housing, education, health services, leisure and religious services to families of workers (Bogaerts 2000; Sierra Álvarez 1990).

9. Profitability, however, seems to have been more of a rhetorical argument used by management to explain the need to close plants to reduce overcapacity which was the real aim. See Hudson and Sadler (1989: 70–2) for the Consett (BSC) steelworks in the UK in the early 1980s.

10. The meaning here is that of a public, paternalist, enterprise that 'cares' for the workers, and an abstract private enterprise that does not care.

11. On 11 June 2013 the European Commission issued an Action Plan for Steel in which the negative consequences of some environmental regulations for the steel industry (European Emission Trading System for $CO2$) are considered and calls for a reassessment of regulation (European Commission 2013).

12. Forli (Italy), July 2011.

13. Galicia is still a region receiving 'structural funds' (meant to help towards convergence) while Asturias has been redefined as a phasing-out region, meaning that it would be eligible for 'structural funds' in a EU15 but it is not in the enlarged EU27.

14. After the financial crisis of 2008, with an unemployment rate of 20 per cent, the social-democratic Prime Minister (PSOE), José Luis Rodríguez Zapatero, commemorating Spain's twenty-five years of membership in what is now the European Union declared: 'From the Spanish perspective, over the course of twenty-five years, we have had to make considerable efforts in order to restructure our productive sectors, to take advantage of European funds, and to meet, on time, the requirements for entrance into the Euro, and to accept, definitively, the requirements of supra-nationality when making decisions. And it has always been worth it: always.' (12 June 2010, Royal Palace, Madrid)

15. The Podemos party had a spectacular success at the European elections of 2014.

References

Alter, K. J. and Steinberg, D. (2007) 'The Theory and Reality of the European Coal and Steel Community', Buffet Center for International Comparative Studies, Working Paper 07-001, Northwestern University.

Babiano, J. (1993) 'Las peculiaridades del fordismo español', *Cuadernos de Relaciones Laborales* 3: 77–94.

Beynon, H., Hudson, R. and Sadler, D. (1994) *A Place Called Teesside. A Locality in a Global Economy*, Edinburgh: Edinburgh University Press.

Bogaerts, J. (2000) *El mundo social de ENSIDESA*, Asturias: Ediciones Azucel.

Bueno, G. (2002) 'La Idea de España en Ortega', *El Basilisco* (Oviedo) 32: 11–22. Available online: http://filosofia.org/rev/bas/bas23202.htm [accessed 20 October 2011].

Buesa, M. and Pires, L. E. (2002) 'Intervencionismo estatal durante el franquismo tardío: La regulación de la inversión industrial en España (1963–1980)', *Revista de Historia Industrial* 21: 159–98.

Clavera, J., Esteban, J. M., Mones, M. A., Montserrat, A. and Hombravella, J. R. (1973) *Capitalismo español: de la autarquía a la estabilización*, Madrid: Edicusa.

Collins, J. (2012) 'Theorizing Wisconsin's 2011 Protests: Community-based Unionism Confronts Accumulation by Dispossession', *American Ethnologist* 39 (1): 6–20.

Domínguez, J. (1990) 'Diez años de relaciones industriales en España (1977–1987)', in A. Zaragoza (ed.) *Pactos sociales, sindicatos y patronal en España*, Madrid: Siglo XXI.

Elordi, C. (2012) 'Europa ya no es la solución sino otro problema', *El Diario.es*, 31 October 2012. Available online: http://www.eldiario.es/miradaalmundo/Europa-solucion-problema_6_63753626.html [accessed 16 August 2014].

European Commission (2013) *Action Plan for a Competitive and Sustainable Steel Industry in Europe*. Available online: http://ec.europa.eu/enterprise/sectors/metals-minerals/files/steel-action-plan_en.pdf [accessed 5 January 2014].

Fantasia, R. and Voss, K. (2004) *Hard Work. Remaking the American Labor Movement*, Berkeley, CA: University of California Press.

Harvey, D. (2005) *A Brief History of Neoliberalism*, Oxford: Oxford University Press.

Herod, A. (2001) 'Labor Internationalism and the Contradictions of Globalization: Or, Why the Local is Sometimes Still Important in a Global Economy', *Antipode* 33 (3): 407–26.

Hudson, R. and Sadler, D. (1989) *The International Steel Industry: Restructuring, State Policies and Localities*, London: Routledge.

International Bank for Reconstruction and Development (IBRD) (1963) *Report of a Mission Organized by the International Bank for Reconstruction and Development at the Request of the Government of Spain: The Economic Development of Spain*, Baltimore: IBRD / The Johns Hopkins Press.

Kalb, D. (2009) 'Conversations with a Polish Populist: Tracing Hidden Histories of Globalization, Class, and Dispossession in Postsocialism (and Beyond)', *American Ethnologist* 36 (2): 207–23.

Kalb, D. (2011) 'Headlines of Nation, Subtexts of Class: Working-class Populism and the Return of the Repressed in Neoliberal Europe', in D. Kalb and G. Halmai (eds) *Headlines of Nation, Subtexts of Class*, New York: Berghahn Books.

Kasmir, S. (2001) 'Corporation, Self, and Enterprise at the Saturn Automobile Plant', *Anthropology of Work Review* 22 (2): 8–12.

Kasmir, S. (2009) 'Toward an Anthropology of Labor', *City and Society* 21 (1): 11–15.

Kasmir, S. (2014) 'The Saturn Automobile Plant and the Long Dispossession of US Autoworkers', in S. Kasmir and A. Carbonella (eds) *Blood and Fire. Towards a Global Anthropology of Labor*, Oxford: Berghahn Books.

Kasmir, S. and A. Carbonella (2008) 'Dispossession and the Anthropology of Labor', *Critique of Anthropology* 28 (1): 5–25.

Lamo de Espinosa, E. (2006) 'Presentación del segundo informe Elcano', *Real Instituto Elcano de Estudios Estratégicos*. Available online: http://www.realinstitutoelcano.org/publicaciones/libros/presentacion%20informe%20europa.pdf [accessed 16 August 2014].

Maier, C. S. (1977) 'The Politics of Productivity: Foundations of American International Economic Policy after World War II', *International Organization* 31 (4): 607–33.

Maier, C. S. (1981) 'The Two Postwar Eras and the Conditions for Stability in Twentieth-century Western Europe', *The American Historical Review* 86 (2): 327–52.

Martínez-Alier, J. and Roca Jusmet, J. (1988) 'Economía política del corporativismo en el estado español: del franquismo al posfranquismo', *Revista Española de Investigaciones Sociológicas* 41: 25–62.

Molinero, C. and Ysàs, P. (1993) 'Productores disciplinados: control y represión laboral durante el franquismo (1939–1958)', *Cuadernos de Relaciones Laborales* 3: 33–49.

Mollona, M. (2009) 'Community Unionism Versus Business Unionism: The Return of the Moral Economy in Trade Union Studies', *American Ethnologist* 36 (4): 651–66.

Monedero, J. C. (2013) *Curso urgente de política para gente decente*, Madrid: Seix Barral.

Narotzky, S. (2014) 'Structures Without Soul and Immediate Struggles: Rethinking Militant Particularism in Contemporary Spain', in S. Kasmir and A. Carbonella (eds) *Blood and Fire. Towards a Global Anthropology of Labor*, Oxford: Berghahn Books.

Narotzky, S. (2015a) 'The Organic Intellectual and the Production of Class in Spain', in J. Carrier and D. Kalb (eds) *Anthropologies of Class. Power, Practice and Inequality*, Cambridge: Cambridge University Press.

Narotzky, S. (2015b) 'Hope for Change: The Problem With Podemos', FocaalBlog, April 20. http://Available online: http://www.focaalblog.com/2015/04/20/susana-narotzky-hope-for-change-the-problem-with-podemos [accessed 3 May 2015].

Ortega y Gasset, J. (2004 [1916]) 'La pedagogía social como programa político', in *Obras Completas, Tomo II*, Madrid: Fundación José Ortega y Gasset / Taurus.

Ortega y Gasset, J. (2005 [1922]) 'España invertebrada. Bosquejo de algunos pensamientos históricos' in *Obras Completas, Tomo III*, Madrid: Fundación José Ortega y Gasset / Taurus.

Parry, J. (2009) '"Sociological Marxism" in Central India: Polanyi, Gramsci and the Case of the Unions', in C. Hann and K. Hart (eds) *Market Society. The Great Transformation Today*, Cambridge: Cambridge University Press.

Puig, N. and Álvaro, A. (2003) 'International Aid and National Entrepreneurship: A Comparative Analysis of Pro-American Business Networks in Southern Europe, 1950–1975', *Business and Economic History On-line* 1: 1–31.

Ramos Gorostiza, J. L. and Pires Jiménez, L. E. (2009) 'Spanish Economists Facing Indicative Planning in the 1960s', *Storia del Pensiero Economico* 6 (1): 77–108.

Roseberry, W. (1994) 'Hegemony and the Language of Contention', in G. Joseph and D. Nugent (eds) *Everyday Forms of State Formation. Revolution and the Negotiation of Rule in Modern Mexico*, Durham, NC: Duke University Press.

Sanchez, A. and Strümpell, C. (2014) 'Sons of Soil, Sons of Steel: Autochthony, Descent and the Class Concept in Industrial India', *Modern Asian Studies* 48 (5): 1276–1301.

Schuman, R. (1950) 'Schuman Declaration. Declaration of 9 May 1950'. Available online: http://europa.eu/abc/symbols/9-may/decl_en.htm [accessed 13 October 2011].

Sierra Álvarez, J. (1990) *El obrero soñado. ensayo sobre el paternalismo industrial: Asturias, 1860–1917*, Madrid: Siglo XXI.

Torreblanca, J. I. (2010) 'Una España confusa en una Europa desorientada', *Estudios de Política Exterior*, Vol. 133 (January/February 2010). Available online: http://www.politicaexterior.com/articulos/politica-exterior/una-espana-confusa-en-una-europa-desorientada/ [accessed 3 June 2015].

Viñas, A. (2003) *En las garras del águila. Los pactos con Estados Unidos de Francisco Franco a Felipe González (1945–1995)*, Barcelona: Crítica.

3

Labour Militancy in Neoliberal Times: A Preliminary Comparison of Nepal with South Africa[1]

Mallika Shakya

Neoliberal policies of the 1990s put the rights and freedoms of markets and consumers over workers' rights to collectively bargain for fairer wages and better working conditions. The Structural Adjustment Programs imposed by the World Bank and International Monetary Fund in developing countries helped build a neoliberal platform on which we saw the unfolding of a global geopolitik of capitalism that Fukuyama called 'the end of history'. However persuasive it sounded to many at the time that the collective bourgeoisie were taking over the world, the financial crisis of 2008 put a question mark on the idea of neoliberal capitalism as the 'last man standing'. Even as contest-ations grew against the trumpeting of the victory of neoliberalism, inter-national media gave wide coverage to anti-neoliberal movements such as Occupy in New York and London, thus generating a certain idiom of resistance that went viral. Other uprisings outside these cosmopolitan capitals, some of them more grounded in reality and concrete in terms of agendas for change, were either misunderstood or went unnoticed. Drawing on my decade-long ethnography of the garment industry union in Nepal and a comparative study of the Marikana massacre developed during my two-year residence in South Africa, this paper looks at two labour movements in the early twenty-first century that emerged out of the acute economic and political crises of our times and, in their local vicissitudes, generated nuanced discourses on the neoliberal capture of democracy. Focusing on two of these cases, this chapter shows that the extent of militancy in new unionism was markedly similar, and asks, 'Why?' Attention is drawn to the perceived and real complacency of the mainstream unions in these countries, the contradictions of democracy and neoliberalism, and the embeddedness of industrial relationships within the broader social and political orders.

A Shared Crypto-Colonial History

Nepal and South Africa both had a major paradigm shift in the 1990s, at a time when neoliberal ideology was gaining ground globally. I argue that this paradigm shift was rooted in their common postcolonial experience in the mid-twentieth century, which saw new dictatorial regimes – Panchayat in Nepal and apartheid in South Africa – take over these national polities just as their neighbours embarked on democracy and independence. Both these countries' experiences with colonial history deviate from a standard trajectory of external powers consolidating their bureaucratic apparatus of rule earlier and then vacating once it became untenable. In Nepal, for example, the British acknowledged Nepali sovereignty early on while recruiting mercenary Nepalis to suppress the mutiny of colonial Indian soldiers. In South Africa, the distinction between the colonizers and the colonized was messier than elsewhere, as the British, the Dutch and the Africans embarked on a series of wars to consolidate a form of settler colony. Emergent racial ideology was one that addressed the contradiction between the capitalist mode of production and the pre-capitalist economies through the two faces of segregation and reproduction of cheap labour (Wolpe 1972).[2]

Michael Herzfeld has called such countries crypto-colonial. Being either the buffer zones or having overlapped geographies on the frontiers of colonial empires, these countries were either doubly colonized or compelled to acquire an independent political status at the expense of massive economic dependence on colonialism. Local elites in crypto-colonies then dealt with such paradoxical situations by taking up 'iconic guises' of aggressive nationalism. The subalterns in these geographies thus became 'doubly victimized': having suffered lateral effects of colonialism itself, they then found themselves excluded from the global struggle against both bureaucratic and hegemonic colonialism. Caught in the exclusionary logic of Cold War oppositions, crypto-colonies have been squeezed between the imperial powers and their officially recognized victims, and this has allowed continuation of an elite grip on power in ways that proved untenable elsewhere. Such enduring paradoxes did give rise to subversive popular movements in the late 1970s, of which the student uprising in Nepal calling for political freedom and the Soweto uprising in South Africa against the oppression of the blacks are just two examples. But these need to be differentiated from the independence movements in the colonies in that the demon being wrestled with by the students and young activists of Kathmandu and Soweto was homegrown and hence more difficult to overcome.

Crypto-colonial uprisings have their roots in complex economic and political histories that may not be technically colonial but crisscross in multiple ways with its boundaries. Nineteenth-century Nepal was one where the ruling elites made economic compromises for upholding sovereignty against colonial intrusions, but the very situation that cajoled or coerced them into choosing such paths may have been part of the colonial grand design. A case in point is the episode where the Shah dynasty was forced to open up its southern borders for trade with the British East India Company after its defeat in the Anglo-Nepal war of 1816. Although the border was forced open corporeally, the Shahs continued to block the import of Company goods by putting up lengthy bureaucratic battles about interpretation of the 1816 Anglo–Nepal Treaty.[3] The Shahs' unwillingness to cooperate with the British eventually led to their downfall, triggering the rise of the Rana dynasty, whose members intermarried with the Shahs and ruled Nepal for 104 years through a parallel monarchy. The Ranas' military loyalty to the British was evident especially during the time of the Indian Sepoy Mutiny of 1857, now known as the 'first war of Indian independence'. Jung Bahadur Rana, the founder of the Rana dynasty's rule, came out to the battlefields in person to fight against the Indian rebels to defend the British crown. In appreciation, the British awarded him with some of the territories earlier lost in the Anglo–Nepal battle, and the two embarked on business ventures in collaboration with common mediators.[4] A democratic mass uprising ousted the Rana regime just three years after the British left South Asia. Unfortunately, democracy was annulled when King Mahendra Shah seized power to build a new polity in the name of *vikas* (development), which nurtured a mono-ethnic Nepali national identity associating the state with his own ethnicity, that spoke the *khas* language, wore *daura suruwal* attire and followed Hindu religion (Burghart 1984: 121). Panchayat was ousted eventually in 1990 through a popular uprising, following which Nepal adopted a multi-party parliament system and the Shahs were confined to constitutional monarchy.

While the Nepali people's periodic struggles for democracy were not strictly about colonialism despite having an anti-colonial twist, the history of black uprisings in South Africa is also bigger than anti-colonialism. The rise of the Shaka–Zulu kingdom in the early nineteenth century and the continuation for another decade of *difaqaane* (conquest and forced migration among the black Africans) altered the black power equation in South Africa fundamentally. The blacks were further weakened by the arrival of British settlers and their shrewd mediation of the disputes between the Xhosa and the Boer in the 1820s. The messy history of nation-state building is reflected in the formation and dissolution of several polities within half a century: the Boer Republic of Transvaal was created in 1852 and later became the South African Republic in 1881. As a rising power, Zululand was annexed by the British in 1879, the Union of South Africa pact was signed between the British and the Dutch in 1910. The forging of the nation states was, of course, marked by violence, including the Battle of Blood River as well as the two Anglo–Boer wars, not to mention Shaka–Zulu encounters. The second Anglo–Boer war essentially turned the dispossessed Boers into de facto proletariat for the British, who were set to capitalize on the mineral revolution of the late nineteenth century. The making of the poor working class among the whites lay the ground for the rise of a racist, workerist politics against the black South Africans (Sharp 2014). Just as anti-colonial struggles were gaining momentum elsewhere in the world, South Africa found itself trapped in an apartheid apparatus after the Nationalist Party of the Boers won the election in 1948. The black uprisings since then – the Sharpville massacre of 1960, the African National Congress's (ANC's) armed revolt and peaceful struggles thereafter, and the Soweto uprising of the 1976 eventually led to an acclaimed victory against apartheid in 1994.

Beyond Postcolonial: Spirit of Neoliberalism in Nepalese Garments and South African Platinum

In discussing national transformations in Nepal and South Africa, I concern myself with the central problem; that is, the rise of neoliberalism under a democratic ethos during the early twenty-first century, and the popular uprisings against neoliberalism that followed. How do we understand the making of these uprisings? Who are the protestors and what are their protests about? I borrow the term 'political society' from Partha Chatterjee (1986) to discuss those living on the border between legal and illegal and who must corporeally mobilize their own bodies to gain access to resources and services that should have been provided naturally by the state. The 'political society' marked for its vernacularity is different from the 'civil society' whose rights are legally constituted even if they may at times put pressure on the state for expedited access or alteration of the set priority. From a political economy perspective, the former is the space of management of non-corporate capital whereas the latter is a space where corporate capital is hegemonic. The divide was pervasive in colonial India. Speaking of what emerged half a century after the end of colonialism,[5] Chatterjee went on to claim that the rising wave of neoliberalism (or the retreat of the state) has brought forth a situation where the bulk of the population now lives outside the orderly zones of civil society and that a new subalternization process is in the making. To this, Amita Baviskar and Nandini Sundar (2008) responded that the state has not only withdrawn from citizens' legitimate demands for public services but has at times come down firmly on one side of the socio-economic divide, militarizing large swathes of the countryside to clamp down on subaltern resistance in the interests of the corporate elite, and then generating distorted media discourses that legitimize such heavy-handed interventions.

Do trade unions belong to political society or a civil society in Partha Chatterjee's framework? For several decades, unions in both South Africa and Nepal were part of the broader political struggle against racial and ethnic dictatorships, which did not allow them space within civil society. They were granted their legitimate spaces within mainstream civil society once these countries became democratic. Congress of South African Trade Unions (COSATU) in South Africa formally forged an alliance with ANC and the South African Communist Party (SACP) to join the government after apartheid. The largest union federation in Nepal, the General Federation of National Trade Unions (GEFONT), part of the Left alliance that joined the democratic government following the popular uprising, consolidated its bureaucratic apparatus substantially in the 1990s. But this was happening at a time when neoliberalism was globally mobilizing nation states to undermine unions and other messy forms of protest.[6] There is an inherent tension between democracy and social justice within neoliberalism that takes deregulation of labour (along with liberalization of capital and commodification of land) to be a central tenet of economic governance. Its proponents strive to justify the neoliberal notion of the free market by claims that it pre-empts 'rent-seeking' thereby allowing release of resources from less to more productive applications even if in reality we have seen neoliberalism unleash financialization that takes rent-seeking to levels not seen since the eighteenth century (Harvey 2005). Two specific implications of this for national union movements should be noted. New industries will pre-empt unionization, whereas already existing unionized sectors may see withdrawal of state regulation or a fundamental restructuring of labour markets, thereby giving the corporates the freedom to either coopt unions or sideline them.[7] Both scenarios give rise to a situation where unions lose their legalized status and begin to operate in zones messily scattered between formal and informal. I discuss how the new (and more militant) unions operate outside the legally protected civil society domain through the case studies of ready made garment industry in Nepal and the platinum belt in South Africa.

The readymade garment industry was a 'fruit' of neoliberalism in Nepal. It came into being in the early 1980s, in response to America's Multi-Fibre Arrangement (MFA) of 1974, which privileged exports from smaller countries in order to counter Chinese penetration of the American market.[8] But it took roots only in the 1990s, after Nepal opened up its economy as part of its democratic promise to its people. This industry was built almost entirely on flexible labour functioning under a 'piece rate' system that comfortably circumvented the minimum wage rates determined by the state while avoiding having to offer workers longer-term contracts allowing some degree of job security. Businesses found this system flexible and cost-effective, and the workers considered it beneficial because they believed 'hardworking' piece-raters could make more money than others and also that they were made to feel empowered about being able to choose their own employers and change jobs when wanted. A capitalistic work ethic was implanted on the shop floor. Workers poured in from all over the country to work on the garment shop floors, and recruiting was done anonymously and in bulk to suit the extreme seasonality of the industry. Unlike South India where middlemen played a central role in labour recruitment, the Nepali garment industry eliminated all intermediaries as factories grew in size and sophistication (De Neve 2005; Shakya 2004). Work was 'Taylorized'; that is, workers were placed in the managerially controlled assembly lines where each carried out just one small task of the bigger manufacturing project thus requiring very little skill per se.

As far as unionizing was concerned, the democratic Labour Act of 1991 made union registration mandatory in Nepal but its neoliberal premises sidelined unions immediately. Although all garment factories went on to set up unions, there was a widespread view among the workers that the union was an unnecessary burden (*nachahine tanta*) and not only tedious to maintain (*jhyau*) but also potentially dangerous. Not surprisingly, therefore, the number of dues-paying members was extremely low in the garment industry. In one extreme case, the factory proprietor put himself up as the 'elected President' of its union, taking advantage of the fact that the law was extremely vague. In other cases, the union was a façade for local mafia who took orders from owners. For these reasons, the national trade union federation hesitated to establish a separate wing for the garment industry; it was posited as a branch of an older textile industry even though the new garment industry employed approximately 100,000 workers while the textile industry had barely 10,000 workers (Manandhar 2009).

A major crisis hit the garment industry in 2004, fundamentally changing the nature of class consciousness among the workers and with it, the structure of its union. The expiry of MFA in 2004 had meant that the United States ended its duty subsidies for Nepali garments, triggering a sharp fall in Nepalese garment exports: so much so that the industry shrunk to one-tenth of its previous size just a year later (Shakya 2004). But the crisis also had its roots in the fetishized notion of trade among the global buyers who took no interest in the human implications of their mercantile country hopping. 'It is all the matter of demand and supply,' one besuited garment buyer told me, going on to elaborate his case with an unsettling analogy: 'We are like fleas on the dog. When a dog dies, we don't sit around doing a postmortem, we fly to catch the next in line.' By early 2005, most buyers had abandoned Nepal and moved on to more competitive countries, namely China and Bangladesh, among others. The tragedy of exports was a lesser one compared to the tragedy of state policy: the Nepali government followed the neoliberal gambit of making the industry responsible for its own demise, claiming that it was never competitive in the first place and that its demise was only to be expected. Workers – tens of thousands thrown out to streets as factories shut down one after the other and businessmen either distanced themselves from workers or left the country altogether fearing labour wrath – were all left on their own under tremendous pressure to 'compete and adapt'. Let alone a full-fledged social security scheme, even simple cushioning measures did not come forth to help workers who lost their jobs. That the garment workers were responsible for their own fate and so they must help themselves out of this crisis was the ruthless rhetoric the policymakers maintained throughout. It is in this moment of despair that a new resistance emerged among the garment workers in Nepal.

Garment workers initially knocked on the doors of GEFONT, which accepted the enormity of the crisis but was not prepared to alter its byelaws that considered contract labour less eligible for union support. It was ironic that the union byelaws had assumed conventional employment contracts for the working class whereas the garment industry had grown precisely by selling neoliberal dreams to workers that being a precariat meant being free. However, as grievance and disillusionment intensified among the garment workers, a select few leaders from within GEFONT came out of the rank and file to lend support to garment workers even if the union byelaws did not allow for representation of the casual workforce. This conundrum took on a new meaning once the workers established contacts with the revolutionary Maoist movement of Nepal. Krishna Hachhethu (2004) has argued that the Maoists were considering a directional shift after having adopted the 'Prachanda path' in 2001 with two key elements: targeting operations towards the Kathmandu Valley and searching for forms of protest other than armed combats. It was in and around 2003 that the previously marginalized unions on the garment shop floors established contacts with the Maoists and renewed their energy. Altered forms of camaraderie and solidarity were central to union resurgence: the new union embraced not only the casual workers but also those who had been made unemployed after their factories shut down. It was asserted that unions should not be bound by the possession of company papers in deciding who was a comrade and who was not.

As the divide widened between the new and the old, the radicals split from the old federation GEFONT and launched an All Nepal Federation of Trade Unions (ANTUF) under the Nepali Maoist party. The two clashed on over fifty occasions between 2006 and 2008 (Manandhar 2009). This twisted saga made ANTUF the new leader among the garment workers but also offered Nepali Maoists an urban foothold through labour. Especially after the Maoists signed a peace agreement with an alliance of democratic parties in 2006 and joined mainstream politics, ANTUF marched not only on issues of jobs and wages but also on a whole gamut of national political agendas including an end of the Hindu monarchy, ethnic inclusion and the federal restructuring of the state. The new union clearly lost its 'civility' and went 'political' following the garment crisis, and fed into urbanization of the Maoist movement in Nepal.

Broadening of politics among the unions of the crisis-ridden garment industry in Nepal can be likened with what Bjorn Beckman (2004) and Sakhela Buhlungu (2001) noted about union commitment to the anti-apartheid cause in South Africa. Especially in a political conjuncture of instability, unions may act more like an element of political (as opposed to civil) society by broadening their social base and infusing it with new legitimacy drawn from making connections between union activity and broader popular demands and concerns (beyond the repre-sented economic sector and indeed purely economic relations as such). In this sense, unions are macro-social organizations capable of not only contributing to workers' bargaining capacity for better wages and working conditions but also a basis for establishing a broader culture of rights. There are practical reasons why such seemingly unconnected issues do come together, and the synthesis of issues and identities might have disruptive effects at times. Studies of violent confronta-tions between rural workers living in the factory hostels and urban workers from townships have shown how collective identities are not determined solely by shop floor relations but are permeable to identities forged beyond workplace (Von Holdt 2002). In this sense, apartheid-era union activities were never isolated from the broader social and political issues within which class identities were embedded. The same holds true for post-apartheid South Africa.

The Marikana crisis that violently erupted in the platinum belt of South Africa in 2012 is one such case where mines became the battlegrounds for confronta-tions rooted in deeper tensions. The story of forty-four workers being shot in the London-listed and World Bank-supported platinum company Lonmin's Marikana site reminded the world how inextricably enmeshed the issues of class and culture are in the way union rivalries play out in modern industries. At the heart of the strike that provoked the police shoot-out were the miners carrying out the lowliest paid but hardest job of drilling the rock underground. The rock drillers earned

US$ 500 a month in a country of over US$ 7,000 per capita, and they wanted this salary to be increased three-fold to make it comparable to better-paid miners. There was little or no support for this demand from the National Union of Mineworkers (NUM), which commanded a vast membership of 360,000 members and boasts an impeccable record of anti-apartheid struggle in the 1980s. Marikana rock drillers attributed this to NUM's revolutionary past getting 'unforgivably rusty': its founding father Cyril Ramaphosa now sat on the board of Lonmin weighing the monetary value of company shares, and its general secretary Frans Baleni, who earned a comfortable salary of US$ 13,000 a month, allegedly likened striking miners to 'sharks attacking under water' and hence needing 'dewatering'.

Beyond the immediate factory shoot-out, Marikana quickly turned into a battleground for politics of class and culture. To start with, rock drillers were mostly uneducated people from the rural Eastern Cape and the mountains of Lesotho whereas the elected NUM leaders were usually educated and 'shrewd men from townships'. Many of them lacked the necessary documentation at work even as the NUM maintained the rhetoric on salaried jobs now increasingly sidelined under a neoliberal regime. The subaltern workers, earlier waging resistance on their own, later came to be represented by the Association of Mineworkers and Construction Union (AMCU), a faction that broke away from the NUM in 1999 when it tried to dismiss a chair of a local branch, Joseph Mathunjwa, alleging financial misconduct.[9] In a bitter confrontation a decade later, Marikana miners dismissed NUM leaders as sell-outs whereas the latter spoke of AMCU as ignorant hillbillies with a ready appetite for roughness and violence. By this time, AMCU had garnered over 20,000 members among the platinum belt's mining workforce of 30,000 or so, mostly among the lowest rank of rock drill operators with poorest documentation and job security. Trevor Ngwane (2015) argued that labour casualization was achieved by allowing shanty towns to grow in the Rustenberg mining area that would absorb the semi-unemployed miners instead of companies housing them in hostels as was the case during the apartheid era. Ironically, while the hostel system was used as a form of near totalitarian labour control during the apartheid regime, these had actually vouched for the companies' contract with labour and went on to function as the 'organizational fulcrum' of many of NUM's activities (Bezuidenhout and Buhlungu 2008). A few decades later, the further the Marikana miners distanced themselves from NUM's unwillingness to represent workers not clearly documented[10] and its muddled rhetoric on how class had now posited itself within the teleology of market gains, the stronger became their affiliations with an emerging social-political movement rooting for an alternative to ANC. In the days that followed the Marikana shoot-out, when ANC's firebrand (if controversial) youth leader Julius Malema[11] visited the platinum belt his call for nationalization of mines was readily welcomed with cheers. These were the same workers who had earlier boycotted the Marikana memorial service chaired by President Jacob Zuma and went on to listen to Malema instead.

Militancy's Roots in Labour Histories

Race is inextricably woven into class in South Africa as elsewhere (Wolpe 1972; Burawoy 1974). Social movement unionization, or unions' broader alliance building along political fault-lines, has a much longer history in South Africa than in Nepal. As early as 1928, South Africa's communist party had received a mandate from the Communist International to join hands with ANC on protests against racial exploitation. Even then, the industrial councils found it hard to get white-dominated councils such as the Mechanics', Unions Joint Executive (MUJE) to work in harmony with the overall union. Inter-union unity deteriorated decisively in South Africa when the Nationalist Party took power in 1948, waving the flag of Afrikaner separatism. Fissures were already running deep between the white and the black South Africans but the Afrikaner-dominated unions formally broke away just as the Native Labour Act of 1953 denied black and coloured South Africans any participation in the collective bargaining system.

Ironically enough, it was in this racialized context that the South African Trade Union Council or SATUC was founded in 1954 to pursue 'non-racial' unionism. It was later consolidated as TUCSA in 1962, after it opened up its membership to African trade unions, even if it lost some of its biggest white affiliates in doing so (Coupe 1995). In any case, TUCSA maintained an ambivalent position of 'tolerating but not embracing' its black affiliates. Disillusioned black workers then went on to found separate associations, of which the NUM was one key example. Three years after establishment, NUM affiliated itself with COSATU in 1985 and emerged as a mighty force against the anti-apartheid struggle. A memorandum was signed among the union leaders after two years that an industry would have only one union, so as to avoid union rivalry, especially in preparation for a unified struggle on national race politics.[12] After victory was acclaimed in anti-apartheid struggle, COSATU went on to join ANC's cabinet under a 'tripartite alliance' that also involved the SACP.

While ANC continues to rule South Africa today, and COSATU remains the largest trade union, with friends in the Union Buildings, in the seat of government where cabinet offices are located, fissures are growing on multiple fronts. The wine-making industries of the Western Cape, retail manufacturing in Gauteng and construction workers elsewhere have at times challenged the dominance of ANC's union allies. In the Marikana case, agitating workers openly called NUM representatives sell-outs and kept them out of mine premises during their ill-fated strike. The lines between political and civil societies blurred time and again as the rival unions violently clashed. NUM defended its legitimacy in the platinum belt through the legal-bureaucratic apparatus and mobilized its contacts in the government to secure material gains; its rival AMCU mobilized bodies to chant against the state and the corporates to invoke the morality of protecting the livelihoods of ill-paid workers working hard.

Union trajectories in Nepal and South Africa offer interesting points of comparison for understanding how neoliberalism functions in differing contexts. At the height of the anti-Rana movement, the Nepali Congress had established contacts with factory workers in the eastern border towns in the 1940s, but an All Nepal Trade Union Congress (ANTUC) could be convened only after the Rana regime was ousted a decade later. The union movement came to a halt when King Mahendra suspended democracy in 1960, banning both unions and political parties. Parties operated underground or from cross-border India, and unions took the same track. One agreed with the other that political dictatorship was the 'central enemy' to be dealt with before getting to the specifics of power, be it about governance or class. This is reflected in Nepal's first ever strike of 1975, in Biratnagar Jute Mills on the eastern Nepal–India border town, where workers walked out in solidarity with the Nepali Congress's call for democracy.[13] The Left alliance founded its own federation GEFONT in 1989, which again maintained a dual status as a democratic ally and a trade union. The culmination of party–union alliance could be seen in the popular uprising of 1990, when they joined hands with civil society associations such as the teachers' association, students' association and doctors' association, etc. This movement reached its culmination with King Birendra disbanding Panchayat and lifting the ban on parties and unions. The democratic Labour Act 1991 went on to make unions mandatory for all industrial units, following which the largest party, Nepali Congress, also founded its own Nepal Trade Union Congress (NTUC).

After democratization, NTUC distanced itself from GEFONT on the degree of capital-friendliness and politicization of labour. NTUC shared with the Nepali Congress the vision that economic growth was a common democratic aspiration including for workers. This led NTUC to adopt a strategy of 'de-linking', implying that unions would refrain from hard politics and keep an 'equi-distance' from its host party, the Nepali Congress, as well as from civil society organizations such as the Chamber of Commerce. This was clearly a capital-friendly move, and NTUC became the preferred union among the business community. Most factories registering new unions under the Labour Act 1991 chose to register with NTUC even if GEFONT had a wider spread in terms of individual members paying dues. In 2009, GEFONT had over 300,000 members and NTUC just over 220,000 members, but the largest union was ANTUF, affiliated with the Communist Part of Nepal (Maoist), which boasted of somewhere between 500,000 to one million members at this time.

Union Movements and the Third Wave of Marketization

This article has followed Partha Chatterjee (1986; 2008) in comprehending union transformations by juxtaposing two urban settings with comparable trajectories of labour unrest. For Chatterjee, democracy entails the incorporation of political society into civil society, while modernization may unleash a new subalternization process. But what happens when democracy is trumped by neoliberalism, or the two collide? Amita Baviskar and Nandini Sundar (2008) have suggested a double-edged outcome: state withdrawal from concerns of social justice on the one hand

and policy sledgehammering for protection of corporate interests on the other. The resulting social and political movements may give rise to a new subaltern, hit doubly by the double-edged sword, and possibly committed to resist both, triggering what Karl Polanyi (1944) might have called a 'double movement'. The soil seems fertile for such movements especially in countries that embraced liberal democracy at the height of the neoliberal era. Michael Burawoy (2010) called this phenomenon of evasive social disembedding of markets 'the third wave of marketization', succeeding two earlier waves that had given rise to proletarianization of labour in the eighteenth century and the rise of national capitalism in the former colonial peripheries two centuries later.

At the heart of the disembedding phenomenon in Nepal and South Africa lies the state apathy to labour grievances against the double jeopardy of neoliberal hegemony and social oppression. New proletariat classes were being formed in new industries in Nepal following the new wave of marketization. As the neoliberal crisis of MFA hit one of these industries, workers became disillusioned and went on to build a collective movement almost from the scratch. While the mainstream unions remained indifferent to concerns of the new proletariat, the state adopted the heavy-handed approach of dismissing labour grievances as the sour grapes of incompetence. The responsible ministry's blunt response to the demise of the Nepalese garment industry that 'it fell because it was not competitive enough', almost echoed the global buyers' disembedded mercantilism, that buyers are like 'fleas' who abandon dogs when they fall sick. This political vacuum was eventually filled by a new labour militancy that took up the Maoist banner and challenged the 'old regime' (*purano satta*) as a whole, thus connecting labour concerns with a wide range of social-political demands including a secular republic and a federal structure to recognize cultural diversity.

Why were existing unions indifferent to the calls of the new proletariat? Buhlungu (2001) called this a 'paradox of victory', a reflection of the way that the old notions of sacrifice and the collective ethic of the days of struggle in South Africa have been replaced by a new individualist ethic of material gain. Union activists and leaders either took up public offices or joined the neoliberal wave to amass personal wealth. A case in point is Cyril Ramaphosa, one of the founders of the NUM, and a key figure in negotiating a political settlement to end apartheid. He went on to be the deputy president of ANC and deputy chair of the National Planning Commission. Benefiting from Black Economic Empowerment (BEE), a post-apartheid policy to create a new black business elite class, as I noted earlier, Ramaphosa actually became a director of Lonmin that owned the Marikana mines. His role during the Marikana massacre was deeply controversial, since miners alleged that he had put pressure on the state to shoot their striking comrades.[14]

What do we make of the new unions voicing the grievances of those victimized by new marketization? In Nepal, they took the 'broadening' road under the Maoist banner, a trajectory bearing an uncanny resemblance to the political unionization of 1980s' South Africa, which spoke of a broader culture of rights (Beckman et al.

2006). Ironically enough, however, post-apartheid South Africa seems to have moved away from this to embrace what Viswas Satgar (2014) called 'Afro-indigenization' of transnational neoliberalism. A bizarre reflection of the perverted character of the kind of indigenization that the new black South African elite is engaged in was provided by media reporting circulated by the state-sponsored media during the Marikana disaster, on how the striking miners had consulted *sangomas* (witch doctors) in the immediate days leading to the shooting to ask for *muthi* (mystic substances) that would protect them from bullets. Their misplaced sense of invincibleness, according to the state media, was what had provoked the striking miners to charge on the police with their spears, obliging them to open fire in self-defence. There was a critical response to this story by activist-sociologist Peter Alexander (2013), who pointed to the glaring inaccuracies of this account and questioned the footage showing the group of workers supposedly 'charging at the police' which had been widely circulated by state media. The alternative account that emerged from this heated debate was that the workers might actually have been fleeing the 'killing koppies', since the police had shot at striking workers from behind and out of sight, forcing them to run towards the only narrow exit, which was on camera. Consistent with this hypothesis, the number of bodies recovered from behind the hill heavily outnumbered bodies recovered at the so-called frontline captured in the footage.

Towards a Synthesis of Forces

This chapter has conveyed a general picture of new union movements in Nepal and South Africa confronting general apathy in their efforts to secure redress for their grievances in the face of a corporate offensive. I have demonstrated how new unionism originates from the fissures developing in old unions, linking it to issues of complacency and rigid bureaucracy, but above all to the individualistic ethic of material gain promoted by neoliberal capitalism. Any substantial effort to comprehend what is happening to labour in these crypto-colonial geographies would have to acknowledge a global paradigm shift at the turn of the century, when neoliberalism coopted democracy and questioned its credibility for the groups left behind. Yet most of the explanations given by labour sociologists and anthropologists are caught up in the assumption that there is a clear-cut dichotomy between 'political' and 'shop floor' unionism, or between political and civil societies. I have emphasized how neoliberalism blurred the lines between political and civil – a repetition of what had happened just a few decades ago in both Nepal and South Africa during the unified union–party struggles against Panchayat and the apartheid regime.

Following the new labour militancy at the turn of this century, which splintered existing unions, a synthesizing trajectory is emerging in both Nepal and South Africa. A vanguard ANTUC had inserted itself into the union scene by challenging GEFONT as the gatekeeper of the old regime (*purano satta*) that chose to overlook the striking workers. Fifty or so violent clashes erupted between the two in the following decade, but now the two have become collaborative partners in the Joint Trade Union Coordination Committee (JTUCC), originally founded by GEFONT as an anti-ANTUC alliance with its lesser rival NTUC of the Nepali Congress. A kind of synthesis is in the making in South Africa too, but on a somewhat different basis. Although founded as an 'apolitical' union, the AMCU of the platinum belt has distanced itself even further from its adversary NUM and opened itself to sympathizing with other political forces, including the Economic Freedom Front (EFF) newly founded by Julius Malema, the ousted head of ANC's Youth League who has called for the nationalization of mines. While NUM remains a formidable union apparatus, and ANC's hold in power remains strong, AMCU's success is significant in that it did achieve a strong presence on the platinum belt, and eventually gained acceptance from the Lonmin board for negotiations on labour rights and welfare, thereby reversing the insistence of COSATU during its anti-apartheid struggle on the principle of 'one industry, one union' (Pillay 2014).

I have argued that the new labour militancy triggered by a third wave of marketization gained counter-legitimacy by targeting mainstream unions and by forging broader alliances that go beyond the immediate calls of collective bargaining. In doing so the meanings of 'political' and 'civil', and indeed trade unionism itself, were continually redefined while the boundaries of company and nation blurred time and again. Nepal and South Africa offer a useful point of comparison for a critical anthropology on new social-political movements of the twenty-first century and the role of workers within them.

Notes

1. I am grateful to Keith Hart, Jonathan Hyslop and Vito Laterza for their constructive comments on an earlier draft.
2. Hyslop (1988) extended Wolpe's framework to examine the Bantu education system under apartheid, and to revisit Hindson's (1985) earlier argument that the cheap labour apartheid reproduced was not as homogenous as superficial reading of Wolpe's framework might suggest, but differentiated.
3. Many of the operational barriers were imposed invoking a discrepancy noted in the Nepali translation of the English text in Article 6 of the Nepal–EIC trade and transit treaty of 1792, which specified that the free movement of goods was meant to be not only for Nepal–EIC trade but EIC's trade with a third party via Nepal. See General Bogle and Francis Buchanan, quoted in Mahesh Chandra Regmi (1971).
4. See Shakya (2014) for a discussion on the rise of Marwari traders in Nepal and India just as the British East India Company consolidated itself in the Raj. In India, the Marwaris facilitated the British businesses of tea and opium, whereas in Nepal they launched jute and sugar mills in partnership with the

Rana elites. The formerly impenetrable border between Nepal and India was gradually opened up for trade through Marwari social networks that enabled the construction of viable business networks and complex financial instruments, thus making inter-country trade possible and desirable.

5. Akio Tanabe (2007) used the expression 'post-postcolonial' to indicate the time when the struggle for independence was decisively over and the postcolonial polity has had the time to institutionalize itself adequately.

6. Although this paper deals with the issue of labour, it acknowledges that neoliberal hegemony has weakened the state's appetite for broader wealth redistribution programmes in South Africa and Nepal that some might allege reneges on the spirit of the public uprising. See Bond (2000) for a discussion on ANC's shifting positions on the promises of anti-apartheid movement on redistribution of economic power along the racial lines. See Shakya (2013) for a discussion on how the neoliberal notions about market forces automatically guaranteeing social progress left untouched several structural problems concerning social discrimination along the ethnic, gender regional lines in Nepal.

7. The 'Doing Business' indicators of the World Bank, which became one of the most powerful policy instruments through which to monitor progress in its debtor countries, considers corporate freedom to hire and fire workers as a necessary precondition for industrial growth. This has become one of the ways through which labour has been casualized under neoliberalism, thus pre-empting union legitimacy.

8. See Shakya (2004) for a detail discussion on the Multi-Fibre Arrangement (MFA), which was initially signed in 1974 for three years but renewed multiple times with a declaration in 1994 that a final closure will be achieved in December 2004. MFA mandated that every piece of garment entering American soil from outside must show a 'visa' or permit to qualify for a generous subsidy on import duties. Large countries considered potential threats to the United States, e.g. China, were issued a smaller quota for 'visas' whereas smaller countries such as Nepal were offered generous quotas, thereby altering the platform on which the international trade of garments could proceed.

9. NUM dismissed Joseph Mathunjwa in September 1999 over allegations of financial misconduct but reinstated him after 3,000 or so workers protested, occupying the mine's underground section for ten days. Mathunjwa was then reinstated but was called to a disciplinary hearing under the union's General Secretary Gwede Mantashe, which he refused. NUM then terminated his membership and the entire workforce of 3,000 members under his leadership also resigned their membership and founded AMCU.

10. See Barchiesi (2007) for a broader discussion on the neoliberal labour restructuring in South Africa. He argues that further casualization and structural high unemployment has been somehow missed by mainstream unions that keep on focusing on work as salaried work even though this is in steep decline in South Africa.

11. Malema was once described as 'the future leader of South Africa' even by Jacob Zuma along with other senior ANC leaders but the ANC later expelled him owing to an embittered saga of hate speech against the white Afrikaaners in March 2010, followed by a number of tax disputes. Malema went on to found his own party Economic Freedom Fighters (EFF) in August 2013.

12. The slogan chanted in the late 1980s was that of 'one industry, one union, one federation'. Each industry would recognize the majority union as its negotiating partner. It was considered a successful negotiating strategy because it successfully pre-empted industrialists from dividing the workers and instigating rivalry. But, equally, many considered that this led to unions becoming too complacent about accommodating themselves to industrialists' interests.

13. This strike was led by Nepali Congress stalwart Girija Prasad Koirala, who went on to become the Prime Minister of Nepal few decades later. But his affiliations with labour hardly went beyond the initial strike he led in his home-town Biratnagar. It was a noted Congress intellectual Hari Sharma who played a key role in the founding of NTUC after Nepal became democratic.

14. See Buhlungu (2005) for a discussion of how the new democracies of the neoliberal era give rise to a culture of individual gain that turns collective bodies into 'exclusionary cartels' simply facilitating the distribution of the fruits of power among insiders.

References

Alexander, P., ed. (2013) *Marikana: A View from the Mountain*, Johannesburg: Jacana Press.

Barchiesi, F. (2007) 'Privatization and the Historical Trajectory of "Social Movement Unionism": A Case Study of Municipal Workers in Johannesburg, South Africa', *International Labour and Working-Class History* 71: 50–69.

Baviskar, A. and Sundar, N. (2008) 'Democracy versus Economic Transformation?', *Economic and Political Weekly* (November 15): 87–9.

Beckman, B. (2004) 'Trade Unions, Institutional Reform and Democracy: Nigerian Experiences with South African and Ugandan Comparisons', in J. Harris, K. Stokke and O. Tornquist (eds) *Politicising Democracy: The New Local Politics of Democratisation*, New York: Palgrave Macmillan.

Beckman, B., Buhlungu, S. and Sachikonye, L. (eds) (2006) *Trade Unions and Party Politics: Labour Movements in Africa*, Pretoria: HRSC Press.

Bezuidenhout, A. and Buhlungu, S. (2008) 'Union Solidarity under Stress: The Case of the National Union of Mineworkers in South Africa', *Labour Studies Journal* 33 (3): 262–87.

Bhattarai, B. R. (B.S. 2063) *Raajniitik Arthashastrako Aankhijyaalbaata* [*From the Window of Political Economy*], Kathmandu: Janadhwani Publications.

Bond, P. (2000) *Elite Transition: From Apartheid to Neoliberalism in South Africa*, Sterling, RSA: UKZN Press.

Bond, P., Desai, A. and Ngwane, T. (2013) 'Uneven and Combined Marxism within South Africa's Urban Social Movements', in C. Barker et al. (eds) *Marxism and Social Movements*, Leiden and Boston, MA: Brill.

Buhlungu, S. (2001) 'The Paradox of Victory: South Africa's Union Movement in Crisis', *New Labour Forum* 8 (Spring–Summer): 66–76.

Buhlungu, S. (2005) 'Union–Party Alliances in the Era of Market Regulation: The Case of South Africa', *Journal of South African Studies* 31 (4): 701–71.

Burawoy, M. (1974) 'Race, Class, Colonialism', *Social and Economic Studies* 23 (4): 521–50.

Burawoy, M. (2010) 'From Polanyi to Pollyanna: The False Optimism of Global Labour Studies', *Global Labour Journal* 1 (2): 301–13.

Burghart, Richard (1984) 'The Formation of the Concept of Nation-state in Nepal', *The Journal of Asian Studies* 44 (1): 101–25.

Chandravarkar, R. (2003) *The Origins of Industrial Capitalism in India: Business Strategies and the Working Classes in Bombay, 1900–1940*, Cambridge: Cambridge University Press.

Chari, S. (2004) *Fraternal Capital: Peasant-workers, Self-made Men, and Globalisation in Provincial India*, Hyderabad: Orient Blackswan.

Chatterjee, P. (1986) *Nationalist Thought and the Colonial World: A Derivative Discourse?*, London: Zed Books.

Chatterjee, P. (2004) *Politics of the Governed*, New York: Columbia University Press.

Chatterjee, P. (2008) 'Democracy and Economic Transformations in India', *Economic and Political Weekly*, 19 April, 53–62.

Coupe, S. (1995) 'Divisions of Labour: Racist Trade Unionism in the Iron, Steel, Engineering and Metallurgical Industries of Post-war South Africa', *Journal of South African Studies* 21 (3): 451–71.

De Neve, G. (2005) *The Everyday Politics of Labour: Working Lives in India's Informal Economy*, New Delhi: Social Science Press.

Hachhethu, K. (2004) 'The Nepali State and the Maoist Insurgency, 1996–2001', in M. Hutt (ed.) *Himalayan People's War*, Bloomington and Indianapolis, IN: Indiana University Press.

Harvey, D. (2005) *A Brief History of Neoliberalism*, Oxford and New York: Oxford University Press.

Hindson, D. (1985) 'The Pass System and Differentiated Labour Power', *Law Society Seminar Paper*, University of the Witwatersrand.

Hyslop, J. (1988) 'State Education Policy and the Social Reproduction of the Urban African Working Class: The Case of the Southern Transvaal, 1955–1976', *Journal of South African Studies* 14 (3): 446–76.

Manandhar, N. M. (2009) *Industrial Relations and Business Environment in Nepal*, Unpublished Report prepared for UK Department of International Development office in Nepal.

Ngwane, T. (2015) 'Against all Odds: The "Spirit of Marikana" and the Resurgence of the Working-Class Movement in South Africa', paper presented at the 12th International Conference on Alternative Futures and Popular Protest, Manchester Metropolitan University, 30 March–1 April 2015.

Pillay, S. (2014) 'The Marikana Massacre: South Africa's Post-apartheid Dissensus', *Economic and Political Weekly*, 14 December, 32–7.

Polanyi, K. (1944) *The Great Transformation: The Political and Economic Origins of Our Times*, Boston, MA: Beacon Press.

Regmi, M. C, (1971) *A Study in Nepali Economic History, 1766–1846,* New Delhi: Manjusri Publishing House.

Satgar, V. (2014) 'Beyond Marikana: The Post-apartheid State of South African State', *African Spectrum* 47 (2–3): 33–62.

Shakya, M. (2004) 'Nepalisation of an Indian Industry: The Fast Evolving (and Dismantling) Readymade Garment Industry of Nepal', *Contributions to Nepalese Studies* 31 (2): 265–91.

Shakya, M. (2013) 'Nepali Economic History through the Ethnic Lens: Changing State Relationships with Entrepreneurial Elites', in M. Lawoti and S. Hangen (eds) *Nationalism and Ethnic Conflict in Nepal: Identities and Mobilization after 1990*, London: Routledge Politics and International Relations Series.

Shakya, M. (2014) 'Marwari Traders Animating the Industrial Clusters of India–Nepal Border', in K. Hart and J. Sharp (eds) *People, Money and Power: Perspectives from the Global South*, New York and Oxford; Berghahn Books.

Sharp, J. (2014) 'Market, Race and Nation: History of the White Working Class in Pretoria', in K. Hart and J. Sharp (eds) *People, Money and Power in the Economic Crisis: Perspectives from the Global South,* New York and Oxford: Berghahn Books.

Tanabe, A. (2007) 'Toward Vernacular Democracy: Moral Society and Post-postcolonial Transformation in Rural Orissa, India', *American Ethnologist* 34 (3): 558–74.

Von Holdt, K. (2002) 'Social Movement Unionism: The Case of South Africa', *Work, Employment and Society* 16 (2): 283–304.

Wolpe, H. (1972) 'Capitalism and Cheap Labour-power: From Segregation to Apartheid', *Economy and Society* 1: 425–56. Reprinted in H. Wolpe (ed.) (1980) *The Articulation of Modes of Production*, London: Routledge and Kegan Paul.

4

Radical Assertions and Anthropological Practice: A Reflection on Re-framing the Study of Migration[1]

Winnie Lem

At the height of the cultural turn in anthropology, James Clifford and George Marcus (1986) asked us to engage reflexively in our discipline. Such reflexivity must be directed inward to critique, auto critique and to dialogical inquiry, so these authors suggested, in order to enable the rethinking of writing and representational strategies.[2] Their interventions into anthropology drew devotees who lauded their efforts for being revelatory and many channelled their own energies towards autoethnography.[3] These views also drew detractors who raised concerns over the tide of narcissism that was washing over the discipline.[4] The clamour generated by the work of Clifford and Marcus has now dissipated and the debate over its merits relegated to the annals of the discipline. Nevertheless, their entreaties to take a reflective stance, although by no means unprecedented, did much to remind us that visiting epistemological framings of anthropological practice may indeed be fruitful.[5]

This chapter therefore positions itself within this mode of disciplinary self-reflection. My purpose here is to think through how scholarly dispositions towards choices of subject, theory and method in anthropology are formed. To do this, however, the method of reflection that I follow departs significantly from that advanced by Clifford and Marcus and also Marcus and Fisher (1986). Rather than emphasizing inwardness and interiority, this chapter deploys a methodological reflexivity that turns the optics outward. I will focus on the how different forces in the political and economic conjunctures that have prevailed over the last half-century condition anthropological practices. The method also departs by asking how such practices may, in their turn, inform social processes in the world. By focusing on the relationship between anthropological practice and social forces as one of reciprocal conditioning, the form of reflexivity I follow here is less a dialogical engagement than one that is dialectical. I undertake this engagement as an attempt to grapple with the forces that are implicated in the deployment of different paradigms to frame objects of inquiry in our discipline. The anthropology of migration will serve as one example of such an object and I will advance the hypothesis that an analytic that is embedded in a liberal mode of thought has come to occupy a position of primacy. Using this example, I will also consider how this paradigm has become so prominent as to eclipse radical paradigms in this field of inquiry.

I begin this reflection by drawing on the insights of writers who have suggested that the work of scholarship is part of an intellectual labour process. This will be followed by a discussion of the conjunctures of forces that conditioned anthropology and, more generally, the world of scholarship. Then my attention will turn towards the question of how such forces converge on the anthropology of migration to frame its questions. I end by considering the significance of different framings of scholarly work on the social world.

The Intellectual Labour Process

In a critique of the turn towards self-reflection that was current in the mid-1980s and early 1990s, Pierre Bourdieu (1977; 2005) posits that intellectuals should position their work as a practical activity that is similar to the practical activity of other people. Such positioning, he argues, is intellectually responsible because it allows scholarship to transcend what he calls intellectual ethnocentrism and also the conceit that accompanies a focus on the scholar as the subject of scholarly inquiry. In extending this idea, Gavin Smith (2014) suggests that scholars should be seen as workers who make products and that the work of scholarship should be seen as an intellectual labour process (Smith 2008). He further suggests that these products are in fact the outcome of a process that is embedded in distinctive social and political economies in the social world. Informing this world are the intellectual's social origins, her position, trajectories, beliefs, gender and age, as well as nationality. This world, furthermore, is made up of what Bourdieu calls 'fields', and so the scholar is embedded in a field that is constituted by institutions that make the academy. She is, therefore, positioned within the microcosmic field of the discipline. The social world is also made up of a larger field. This is a field of constraints that constitutes and informs the institutions and disciplines in which the scholar is embedded. So fields, according to Bourdieu, are characterized by tensions, contradictory forces and struggles over definitions (Bourdieu 2003). The Bourdieusian field is therefore a field of forces.

To suggest that intellectual production is part of a labour process that is embedded in such a field of forces implies that intellectuals do not make unfettered choices about the form of their work. The scholar's most decisive choices of topic, method and theory therefore depend on habits of thought, mandatory problematics, shared beliefs and commonplaces, rituals, values and consecrations, as well as national traditions and peculiarities.[6] This suggests, furthermore, that scholarly activity is work that is executed within a constellation of forces in specific times. By examining the work that we undertake as scholars through the optic of a constellation of forces, it becomes possible to suggest why within a field of objective possibilities, the form of our work is disposed to taking on particular topics, methods and theory in particular times. Moreover, it becomes possible to assess its significance to the prevailing problems of those particular times.

Anthropology, then, is a field and like all others it is pervaded by tensions and struggles in which different topics and theories have different valences. Such valences have, for example, been present in debates to define key facets of national anthropologies. To use a somewhat autoethnographic illustration, I focus on a field in which I am embedded as a scholar. This is the field of Canadian anthropology. Within it, struggles have taken place over the demarcation of the boundaries of a tradition that might be defined as Canadian anthropology. These tensions and struggles are exemplified by what has come to be known as the Howes–Dunk debate. This debate centred on whether structuralism and cultural theory or political economy could be positioned as distinguishing Canadian anthropology from other national traditions.[7] In that debate, Dunk (2000, 2002) argued that prevalence of one theoretical tradition over the other notwithstanding, the constant in Canadian anthropology is the slavish following of paradigms that have their origins in American, British and French anthropology. This following, he argues, is an expression of the historical power geometries of colonialism and the continuing subordination of Canadian scholarly agendas to intellectual imperialism. This subordination renders autonomous choices of theory and method difficult to pursue. Dunk's insights on such tensions and struggles suggest that we should look towards global power geometries in history and conjunctural forces in order to understand how dispositions in the labour process of scholarly production are shaped in different instances.

Conjunctures

Global power geometries have been the subject of much anthropological writing. William Roseberry (1997), for example, has focused on the conjuncture of forces that informed the production of radical imaginaries and how they were mitigated by Cold War antinomies. He notes that during that period of time, contests for global dominance between superpowers rested on enlarging spheres of influence between the world of capitalism and the world of state socialism. The staging ground for much of this conflict consisted of developing countries that were engaged in the processes of creating postcolonial societies and economies. In those countries, wars by proxy were fought and fuelled divisions within those societies over visions of how to remake former colonies into post-independence postcolonial nations. One such vision was offered by the forms of socialism that were initiated by agrarian revolutions in China, Algeria, Vietnam, Mexico and Cuba. In the anthropological literature, this was written off as the 'peasant wars' of the twentieth century (Wolf 1969). A competing vision for an independent modern capitalist and 'non-communist' society also found its scholarly interlocutors (Geertz 1963).[8]

In the midst of such antinomies and as part of the radical engagement of our discipline, much anthropology turned to addressing the 'the agrarian question' and studies of the peasantry. The 'agrarian question' in classical Marxism focused on the political question of the role that peasants and various segments of the peasantry would play in advancing the development of capitalism, or in resisting it.[9] It occupied a place of prominence in the anthropological agenda during the middle decades of the twentieth century. The imminence of the processes of decolonization and colonial revolutions, not only mandated understanding and envisioning of how newly independent nations were to be formed, but also understanding the past of resistance and revolution. A radical anthropology that focused on these problems was a way of contributing towards the advancement of progressive projects of social transformation.

These thematics in anthropology were not of course limited to the study of peasantry. Radical agendas also focused in different ways on the struggles of first nations/aboriginal peoples and continuing anti-colonial struggles, as well as anti-imperialism and nationalist struggles in the 'global South'. In the 'global North', they also focused on exploring the histories and struggles of labour, exploitation under industrial capitalism, class formation and class struggles. Such practices in anthropology were aligned with calls for the transformation of society and indeed social revolution, that extended well beyond the academy in the liberal democratic contexts of Western industrial capitalist society (Palmer 2009).

But with the emergence of the global recession that followed from the oil crisis in the 1970s, such calls lost traction. This was in a period of time in which the economy of capitalism took a turn that is often discussed as the transition from a Fordist to a post-Fordist regime of accumulation. Its beginnings in the 1970s signalled changes in the prevailing dynamics of capitalist accumulation and reproduction.[10] A dominant dynamic of reproduction premised upon circuits of accumulation through industrial production managed within the nation state seemed to be giving way to a dynamic increasingly premised on accumulation through financialization and the circulation of fictitious capital.[11] Also, in this transition the management and regulation of such circuits was becoming rescaled, to fall within the ambit of supranational regulatory agencies that support the transnational movements of capital. In this period, the application of neoliberalism's set of pro-market, monetarist, economic principles came to prevail in efforts to stabilize economies that were in crisis. There have been many discussions of the features of neoliberalism and its doctrines.[12] The application of these doctrines has become encapsulated in the term 'austerity'. This term reflects prescriptions for fiscal discipline, reduction in public expenditure, tax reform, financial liberalization, market-determined exchange rates, trade liberalization, an open door to foreign direct investment, privatization of public services and state-owned enterprises, deregulation, and secure property rights.[13] These measures were not only seen as remedial, but in fact, were also meant to restore growth and assure increasing quanta of accumulation in national and international economies.

This is the period of time that we refer to retrospectively as the onset of globalization or the beginnings of a new phase of global transformations. It was precisely within this conjuncture that studies of migration gained momentum or, as some scholars have asserted, rightly or wrongly, the era of globalization is also the age of migration.[14]

Anthropology of Migration

This era of globalization, so it is argued, marks the transformation of migration from largely a transatlantic phenomenon to one that is truly global.[15] As borders were made increasingly permeable by strategies of governance that promote economic liberalization, so the mantra insists, people along with capital, commodities and ideas, all flow through. In the literature on migration, these assertions, observations, and also arguments about the nature and historical significance of globalization[16] have provoked much rethinking of the paradigms that prevail in the analysis of the cross-borders movement of populations.[17] Scholars have argued that 'traditional approaches', including the paradigms of neo-Marxism, cannot contend with migration in this era, as they were developed to explain earlier forms of migration that were limited in scope and geographic scale (Massey et al. 1999). So, 'new' perspectives were needed to advance the analysis of the intensified cross-border, multination commitments, activities and orientations of migrants. They included social capital theory and the new economics of labour migration, as well as the transnational framework of analysis that is perhaps most familiar to anthropologists.[18]

Refracted through these theories are a series of topics and debates that represent key subjects in the burgeoning scholarship on migration. These include but are not limited to migrant incorporation, exclusion, integration, assimilation, rights, security, management and control.[19] While it is not possible to be comprehensive in listing recent topics and debates, it is possible to say that many of their concerns revolve around the issue of citizenship, for migration provokes anxieties about citizenship's forms, possibilities and limitations. This is evident in the fundamental functions and meaning of citizenship as a status and identity. As fundamental identity, citizenship helps situate the individual in society, since the status of the citizen is defined by the relation between the individual and the other members of society. It is also defined by the relation between the individual and institutions of government and so situates the individual within the political community (Prior et al. 1995). Notions of citizenship specify the principles according to which these two relations should be conceived in order to realize a good society. In liberal democracies, it is generally held that people who live legally within the state make a social contract with the state to agree to be ruled in exchange for a series of rights. This contract also means that each citizen must perform a set of responsibilities to be a good citizen, however that is defined. This contract, as it has been envisioned in liberal democratic societies, is one that is made with the state as a sovereign unit and a territorially bounded unit.[20]

This model of citizenship has been much complicated by diasporas or transnational communities which challenge the idea that citizenship may exclusively be based on the nation state. It is also complicated by migration in which people are crossing national boundaries and are effectively members of many different states and find themselves facing difficulties, both socially and politically in both the societies of departure and of relocation. So key concerns in the study of migration focus on the problems, processes and limitations of making migrants into citizens as well as on ensuring that the processes of incorporation of migrants adheres to the ideals that are foundational to, and maintain stability in, liberal democracies. These include the protection of liberties and freedoms: respect for legal entitlements and guarantees of free assembly and discussion.

Concerns over how these principles are applied in migration scholarship is not immaterial, for they resonate with the everyday and real concerns of migrants themselves as they circulate through liberal democratic nations and must contend with the challenge of struggles to make a livelihood. For political bodies that must regulate and manage migration, these concerns are also important, since the making of policy often has a determining effect on the movement of people across borders. There is therefore inherent value in the pursuit of agendas that address the issues that contour migrant lives. Moreover, the dedication of intellectual labour towards a politics that critiques regimes in which these principles are not upheld is also inherently valuable. My concern in this chapter is not with the value of such work, but with how such agendas have come occupy a place of prominence to such an extent that alternatives to them tend to appear out of place.

To address this concern, Bourdieu's (2005) notion of habitus is helpful. By examining the habitus of scholarly practice, so Bourdieu tells us, we can get a sense of how agents incorporate a practical sense of what can or cannot be achieved based on their intuitions gained through past collective experience. This sense of what can be achieved constitutes the 'objective possibilities' that are presented through and enacted upon in a field of forces that simultaneously constrain and enable.

The past collective experiences of scholars who work on migration suggests the objective possibility that the transformation of migrants into citizens is achievable. Their research and writing show that migrants can and have been incorporated into liberal democracies, their rights respected and their voices heard. Charting and problematizing such processes and struggles, as well as acting as advocates for them, are therefore apposite. Moreover, the material products that we produce – texts – further conditions the intellectual labour process towards reproduction of questions that focuses on the challenges of citizenship and the problems of incorporation of migrants into liberal democratic societies. This reinforces the possibilities of what can and must be pursued. Yet such agendas also resonate well with perspectives that focus on how societies could maintain their integrity, stability and coherence, ideals that are paramount in the liberal democracies in which many of us live but can be used politically in ways that are deeply disadvantageous to migrants.

As Bourdieu reminds us, fields are characterized by tension and struggle. Scholars have struggled against this dominant paradigm to propose an alternative framing that suggests the necessity of moving beyond a mere critique of the problems of liberal democracy towards envisioning its transformation. This view, which for the purposes of this chapter, I call radical, runs counter to dominant paradigms that are premised on coherence, integration and stability. The framing of migration scholarship as a radical practice does not focus merely on whether liberal democracies live up to their ideals. It moves beyond liberal precepts to confront the forces of capitalist transformation as an intellectual and political project. In other words, it advances a problematic that focuses on a critique of capitalism as the social and economic system that underpins such democracies. Such an alternative sets its analytical sights on questions of how migration, and also the study of migration, may contribute towards the ending of all forms of social injustice.

Scholars who have deployed radical paradigms in the study of migration have focused on exploring the relationship between migration, processes of accumulation and class formation within capitalism (Barber and Lem 2012; Binford 2013). Turning to questions of class necessarily orients its analytics towards questions of agency, conflict and transformation. This turn therefore also implies questioning the possibilities for migrant mobilizations against the depredations of drives towards accumulation under capitalism. For, as I have suggested elsewhere, migration is formed by and in turn informs struggles over accumulation and indeed, the processes of what has become hyper-accumulation in the late twentieth and early twenty-first century (Lem 2012). It is imperative therefore to understand the different manifestations of accumulation that are taking place and its implications for migrants in what Glick-Schiller and Caglar (2011) call the strategic sites in which migration processes occur. These sites are situated at different scales across the globe but are entwined and mutually constituting.

In what follows I illustrate how such a critical analytic optic may shed light on the relationships between migration and accumulation. I focus on questions of gender in migration, and the work of social reproduction, to illustrate how the conceptual architecture of a radical paradigm may advance our understandings of exigencies of capitalist change that inform the dominant economic system we inhabit and, very importantly, its nature and effects on ordinary people and their everyday activities of making a livelihood.

Migration, Reproduction and Capitalism

For many ordinary people, the rendering of rural and urban economies that favour forms of hyper-accumulation by states and the neoliberal doctrines of supranational financial institutions added momentum to the imminent processes that increasingly separated people from the means of sustaining life. Such renderings were in evidence in the programme initiated around 1978 for remaking the economy of China from a command and control regime based on surplus redistribution to market driven regime based on surplus accumulation. In the 1990s, this drive was intensified as

China sought entry into the World Trade Organization (WTO) and complied with its conditions to reduce the role of the state in the economy and to dismantle the iron rice bowl system. This was a system developed in the Maoist period (1949–78) that guaranteed job security and benefits to employees in enterprises run by the state. The closing down of state run industries and enterprises, and their privatization, combined with the dismantling of the iron rice bowl, have effectively created a US-style 'rust belt' in China's North East (*dong bei*), where state-run heavy industry once served as the backbone of the economy (Lee 2007). These closures and privatization drives have created a significant population of contingent workers – a surplus population – as people came to be ejected from the social economy, deprived of their means of making a livelihood.[21]

This contingent labour is often wrenched from its ties to place as people are transformed into migrants who follow trajectories of mobility towards those key spaces of capital accumulation in national and transnational settings. Cognizant of the limits of securing and sustaining a livelihood through transregional migration,[22] many former state workers and employees have relocated transnationally, channelled through diasporic networks towards places where they are reabsorbed into the local social economy. Many have relocated to sites where the finance and service complexes of transnational capital have emerged as burgeoning avenues for accumulation under post-Fordism (Sassen 2005).

Such forces shaped the life course of many migrant women such as Gin Jie, a middle-aged woman who arrived in Paris in 1998 and works in the service economy of the city.[23] Gin Jie worked in the offices of a steel factory in Heilongjiang province but lost her job when the factory closed in 1994. As a mature woman, the experience of contingency and precarity arrived relatively late in her work life during a period when she was caught between caring for children and ageing parents. The shock of the experience of unemployment for many middle-aged women fuelled their fears for the wellbeing of children and parents. For Gin Jie, those fears transformed into panic as social goods, such as education and healthcare became increasingly privatized, and fees for school and hospital visits strained family resources. Such crises of care and crises of reproduction have therefore stimulated the strategic relocation of women and men to transregional and transnational labour markets where possibilities for making a livelihood are pursued in service economies that have burgeoned as forms of accumulation. Those are the economies in which a growing class of managers, CEOs, consultants and executives participate by requiring extra support in their domestic lives in order to maintain households and families.

Many women from China's North East have secured a livelihood by working in the households of Chinese families in Paris. Within the private spaces, such workers were subject to petty tyrannies that inform the structures of exploitation that were hidden within homes (Levy 2005; Lieber 2008). Gin Jie, for example, works as a live-out nanny, helping the stay-at-home mother care for four children. When she was hired, her employer explained that her wage would be higher than what was paid to the previous nanny who was live-in, as it would not reflect a deduction for a room. Gin Jie was pleased with this until her employer mentioned that a small deduction would still be made for the cost of her meals. This brought her wage down to a level that was marginally above that of the live-in nanny. Such petty tyrannies are in fact forms by which surplus value is appropriated by employers whose families are supported by the labour of migrant women.

Transnationalized and feminized flows, then, are often directed towards and localized within the domestic spaces of households to perform the intimate work that is dedicated to reproduction of people. This brief example shows how these forces are embodied in the figure of the domestic, the nanny, the cleaner or the cook, whose labour provides services for employers whose own labour is deployed towards the production and exchange of commodities – real and fictitious – that sustain the current leading sectors of the economies of capitalism.

The primary objective of a critical, radical, framing of the anthropology of migration, then, is to show how such an economy is sustained. This paradigm also responds to what some suggest is the paucity of work that tends to breaks new ground.[24] This paucity is marked by many interventions in which description tends to substitute for theory and in which a tendency towards tautology prevails. In debates regarding citizenship and integration, for example, the parameters of the discussion are constrained by an underlying normative vision of the society as stable, in equilibrium and indeed static. As a norm, it inclines scholarly efforts towards a focus on coherence and stability, reinforcing what is in essence the same functionalist vision of society that Durkheimian sociology offered in another historical era of social change induced by capitalist transformation.

In the present conjuncture, a powerful constellation of political and economic forces is contributing to the effacing of imaginaries that point towards the possibilities for subverting capital. As the example of China has shown, forces that have been dedicated to the remaking of socialist state formation as development based on a market economy have reinforced the perspective that existing alternatives to capitalism had failed to subvert it. This imaginary has also been inhibited by the fall of the Berlin Wall in 1989, which to some signalled the end of a previous phase in history and the triumph of capitalist liberal democracy (Fukuyama 2006). Liberal democratic societies and economies came to be remade into neoliberal formations and many societies into what has been called post-socialist societies. Indeed, in this conjuncture, the emergence of 'post-' in the lexicon of many scholarly interventions became inserted as a doxa within the academy.

Doxa, according to Bourdieu (1990), are the spontaneous beliefs or opinions that shape people's view of the world. These are derived, so he suggests, from a reciprocal relationship between the ideas and attitudes of individuals and the structures within which they operate. The idea of 'post-' became consecrated as a doxa in anthropology and much of the scholarly field. Affixed to a word, 'post-' is a multiple signifier (Genz and Brabon 2009: 3). Not only does it signal the past and something ending, but it also signals transcendence, occlusion, overcoming and irrelevance.

This is the case, for example, in post-feminism and indeed post-socialism. While the ideologies of the terms are contested and their definitions debated, their circulation as a doxa suggests that feminism and indeed socialism has been transcended, overcome and surpassed. Their phase in history has ended (Hawkesworth 2004: 969). To return to the idea of reflection, the point of departure of this chapter, reflexivity on, and as a practice in, anthropology reached its apogee at the fin de siècle, e.g. amidst much thinking about the end of modernity and the modes of modern thought that characterize the modern era. The era of 'Post' modernism had arrived and its invectives against the grand theory of the modernist thrust scholarship towards the cultural turn.

Over the past couple of decades then, not only did the doxa of 'posts' come to occupy a place of increasing prominence on the intellectual landscape, but some of its adherents have also insisted that it has come to represent a new terrain of radical positionality because of the power of scholarly practice to subvert and transcend. Indeed, 'post-' has been affixed to capitalism in work that makes precisely such claims. Post-capitalism purports to transcend and bypass what is called the 'timeworn oppositions between global and local, revolution and reform, opposition and experiment, institutional and individual transformation' (Gibson-Graham 2008). This post-capitalist imaginary emerges, so scholars have suggested, from the multiple movements and pockets of resistance that are launched against global neoliberal agendas. According to Gibson-Graham, The Zapatistas, the World Social e-Forum, and, more recently, the Occupy movement in Europe and North America, are all charting a globally emergent form of localized politics that create autonomous zones of counter power (Graeber 2004). Yet such positionalities and the doxa of 'post-' share a history of having come of age and gained momentum at a conjuncture in which shifts in the global geometries of capitalism favoured neoliberalism as a political and ideological project. So, the imaginary of post-capitalism nestles comfortably with the likely more familiar imaginaries of post-feminism, post-structuralism, post-development and post-socialism.

As the conditions of crisis and adversity prevail in this conjuncture, the analytics of radical paradigms, as I have tried to show, provide an effective lens through which to view people and their entanglements in enduring regimes of domination, marginalization and exploitation. Within this conjuncture, efforts to reclaim the space of critique by using radical paradigms are urgent for they enable us to apprehend and contest the vicissitudes of change as people confront conditions of crisis and adversity that are tending to become ever more profound.

Conclusion

This chapter has focused on conjunctures and fields of forces which condition our practices in what I insist, following the realist tradition, is a world out there that cannot be understood solely as a 'social construction'. I end by turning our attention to the institutions of the academy. This is the particular world that we academics inhabit.

Currently, neoliberal doxa and practice pervade the structures of governance in what has been called the neoliberal university. The neoliberal university is a corporate university, as magnates attempt to assert their influence and control over research agendas, topics and methods of inquiry. Scholarly work has become entangled in the assemblages of neoliberal technologies of governing and as a result often manifests itself as intellectual corruption and betrayal, 'la trahison de clercs'.[25] Such entanglements in the current conjuncture ultimately undermine the role of the intellectual in the intellectual labour process. This is the professional universe that many of us occupy

As Bourdieu reminds us, and perhaps cautions us, decisions and choices for topic, theory and method depend very closely on the location that scholars occupy within this professional universe. Moreover, as Smith (2014) insists, our intellectual labour process is a practical activity that has distinctive political implications in different periods. It is evident that a radical framing inclines our studies towards a vision of society that moves us away from the functionalist vision of society envisioned by Durkheim towards the agonistic one envisioned by Marx, in which class conflict provokes change. I contend, therefore, that the choice to continue to engage radical paradigms in migration studies and the discipline of anthropology as a whole is not merely a practical activity. It is also a praxis that contests the prevailing politics of our times. This is the time to recall Marx's well-known admonition in his eleventh point of critique of the materialism of the Hegelian philosopher Feuerbach, originally penned in 1845: 'The philosophers have only interpreted the world, in various ways; the point is to change it.'

Notes

1. This is a revised and expanded version of a chapter that was prepared for a panel sponsored by *Dialectical Anthropology* at the IUAES Congress, convened by Kathy Powell and entitled 'Producing Political Positions and Political Futures'.
2. See also Marcus (1998: 198).
3. See, for example, Ellis and Bochner (2000); Young and Meneley (2005).
4. See, for example, Fox (1991); Polier and Roseberry (1989).
5. Indeed, the entire project of *Annual Review of Anthropology* undertakes this kind of reflection, while the initial impetus behind *Critique of Anthropology* was to engage in a critical reflection on the discipline by publishing works of radical scholars.
6. See also Lane (2000).
7. See Howes (1992) and Dunk (2000, 2002).
8. Another classic contribution in this vein is Rostow's *The Stages of Economic Growth: A Non-Communist Manifesto* (Rostow 1990 [1960]).
9. See Kautsky (1988 [1899]).
10. See Lipietz (1987). For a discussion in anthropology, see Kasmir (1999) and Baca (2004).

11. See Marx (1981) for a discussion of fictitious capital. Also, see Soederberg (2013).
12. For a discussion of the neoliberalism as a movement, see Mitchell (2005).
13. See Pradella and Marois (2015).
14. This was an assertion made by Castles and Miller (2009) in the first edition of *The Age of Migration* in a statement which was revised and modified in later editions.
15. See, for example, Castles and Miller (2009); Massey et al. (1999).
16. See, for example, Ohmae (1991) and the 'hyperglobalist' school of thought, which insists that globalization represents a new and logical final phase for human development. Friedman (2004: 67) by contrast suggests that it is in fact a configuration of a world system, which is a phase in a larger cycle of expansion and contraction.
17. See, for example, Portes and DeWind (2008) and Portes (1999).
18. Others include segmented labour market theory, world systems theory, and the theory of cumulative causation (Massey et al. 1999: 16).
19. For an overview of topic theories and methods in the interdisciplinary study of migration that is fairly comprehensive and has been updated to adapt to changing times, see Brettell and Hollified (2003: 2015).
20. These include civil rights, such as freedom of organization and expression, political rights, such as the right to vote, and social rights, the right to a minimum standard of living. Many of these ideas are taken from the work of T. H. Marshall (1950) who underscored that citizenship is a differentiated bundle of rights and responsibilities. See also Brown (2009).
21. Smith (2014) refers to a surplus population with reference to Marx's (1976) law of population in Capital Volume 1 that suggests that when labour is not adding value to capital, it appears to be of no use to capital and therefore is superfluous.
22. Labour markets in such centres in China in the late twentieth and early twenty-first centuries had become saturated with contingent labour, as people, mainly peasants, became expelled from the social economy as a result of reform and the restructuring of the agrarian economy. This reform and restructuring involved a programme of agrarian reform that was initiated in the late 1970s with the dismantling of rural collectives and the development of private forms of cultivation. Reform also included the institution of a 'responsibility system', which permitted resources to be contracted to individuals, households or groups of households. The terms of such contracts came increasingly close to de facto ownership. Communes were replaced with local governments and mixed (private and public) forms of economic organization. The reforms also entailed the revival of a market for labour power, thus labour became recommodified and hiring labour became legal. Private marketing was also revived and agricultural products as well as other factors of production were, along with labour, recommodified.

23. This example is taken from my own ethnographic fieldwork, which focuses on livelihoods and Asia-Europe transnational migration.
24. As Castles and Miller (2009) have argued, transnational theory is one exception to this.
25. See http://www.monbiot.com/2013/05/14/la-nouvelle-trahison-des-clercs/ [accessed 20 May 2013].

References

Baca, G. (2004) 'Legends of Fordism: Between Myth, History, and Foregone Conclusions', *Social Analysis* 48 (3): 169–78.

Barber, P. G. and Lem, W. (eds) (2012) *Migration in the 21st Century: Political Economy and Ethnography*, New York and London: Routledge.

Binford, L. (2013) *Tomorrow We're All Going to the Harvest: Temporary Foreign Worker Programs and Neoliberal Political Economy*, Austin, TX: University of Texas Press.

Bourdieu, P. (1977) *Outline of a Theory of Practice*, Cambridge: Cambridge University Press.

Bourdieu, P. (1990) *In Other Words: Essays Towards a Reflexive Sociology*, Palo Alto, CA: Stanford University Press.

Bourdieu, P. (2003) 'Participant Objectivation', *Journal of the Royal Anthropological Institute* (NS) 9 (2): 281–94

Bourdieu, P. (2005) 'Habitus', in J. Hillier and E. Rooksby (eds) *Habitus: A Sense of Place*, London: Ashgate.

Brown, W. (2009) *Regulating Aversion: Tolerance in the Age of Identity and Empire*, Princeton, NJ: Princeton University Press.

Castles, S. and Miller, M. (2009) *The Age of Migration: International Popular Movements in the Modern World*, London: Palgrave.

Clifford, J. and Marcus, G. E. (eds) (1986) *Writing Culture: The Poetics and Politics of Ethnography: a School of American Research Advanced Seminar*, Berkeley, CA: University of California Press.

Dunk, T. (2000) 'National Culture, Political Economy and Socio-cultural Anthropology', *Anthropologica* 42 (2): 131–45.

Dunk, T. (2002) 'Bicentrism, Culture and the Political Economy of Social-cultural Anthropology in Canada', in W. Lem and B. Leach (eds) *Culture, Economy, Power: Anthropology as Critique, Anthropology as Praxis*, Albany, NY: State University of New York Press.

Ellis, C. S. and Bochner, A. (2000) 'Autoethnography, Personal Narrative, Reflexivity: Researcher as Subject', in N. Denzin and Y. Lincoln (eds) *The SAGE Handbook of Qualitative Research,* Los Angeles, CA, London, New Delhi, Singapore and Washington, DC: Sage Publications.

Fox, R. G. (ed.) (1991) *Recapturing Anthropology: Working in the Present*, Santa Fe, NM: School of American Research.

Friedman, J. (2004) 'Globalization', in D. Nugent and J. Vincent (eds) *A Companion to the Anthropology of Politics*, New Malden and Oxford: Blackwell.

Fukuyama, F. (2006) *The End of History and the Last Man*, New York: Simon and Schuster.

Geertz, C. (1963) *Peddlers and Princes: Social Development and Economic Change in Two Indonesian Towns*, Chicago, IL: University of Chicago Press.

Genz, S. and Brabon, B. A. (2009) *Postfeminism: Cultural Texts and Theories*, Edinburgh: Edinburgh University Press.

Gibson-Graham, J. K. (2008) 'Diverse Economies: Performative Practices for "Other Worlds"', *Progress in Human Geography* 32 (5): 613–32.

Glick-Schiller, N. and Caglar, A. (eds) (2011) *Locating Migration: Rescaling Cities and Migrants*, Ithaca: Cornell University Press.

Graeber, D. (2004) *Fragments of an Anarchist Anthropology,* Chicago, IL: Prickly Paradigm Press.

Hawkesworth, M. (2004) 'The Semiotics of Premature Burial: Feminism in a Postfeminist Age', *Signs: Journal of Women in Culture and Society* 29 (4): 961–85.

Howes, D. (1992) 'What is Good for Anthropology in Canada', in W. K. Carroll, L. Christiansen-Ruffman, R. F. Currie and D. Harrison (eds) *Fragile Truths: Twenty-five Years of Sociology and Anthropology in Canada*, Ottawa: Carleton University Press.

Kasmir, S. (1999) 'The Mondragon Model as Post-Fordist Discourse: Considerations on the Production of Post-Fordism', *Critique of Anthropology* 19 (4): 379–400.

Kautsky, K. (1988 [1899]) *The Agrarian Question: In Two Volumes*, Winchester, MA: Zwan Publications.

Lane, J. F. (2000) *Pierre Bourdieu: A Critical Introduction*, London: Pluto Press.

Lee, C. K. (2007) *Against the Law: Labor Protests in China's Rustbelt and Sunbelt*, Berkeley, CA: University of California Press.

Lem, W. (2012) 'Migration, Political Economy and Ethnography', in P. G. Barber and W. Lem (eds) *Migration in the 21st Century: Political Economy and Ethnography*, New York and London: Routledge.

Levy, F. (2005) 'Les femmes du Nord, une migration au profil atypique', *Hommes & Migrations* 1254: 45–57.

Lieber, M. (2008) 'Clivages ethniques, domination économique et rapports sociaux de sexe. Le cas des Chinois de Paris', in E. Dorlin (ed.) *Sexe, race et classe: pour une épistémologie de la domination*, Paris: PUF.

Lipietz, A. (1987) *Mirages and Miracles: The Crises of Global Fordism*, trans. David Macey, London: Verso.

Marcus, G. E. (1998) *Ethnography through Thick and Thin*, Princeton, NJ: Princeton University Press.

Marcus, G. E. and Fischer, M. M. (1999). *Anthropology as Cultural Critique: An Experimental Moment in the Human Sciences*. Chicago, IL: University of Chicago Press.

Marx, K. (1976) *Capital*, vol. 1. New York: Penguin

Marx, K. (1981) *Capital*, vol. 3, London: Harmondsworth.

Marshall, T. H. (1950) 'Citizenship and Social Class', in T. H. Marshall, *Citizenship and Social Class and other Essays*, Cambridge: Cambridge University Press.

Massey, D. S., Arango, J., Hugo, G., Kouaouci, A. and Pellegrino, A. (1999) *Worlds in Motion: Understanding International Migration at the End of the Millennium*, Oxford: Clarendon Press.

Mitchell, T. (2005) 'The Work of Economics: How a Discipline Makes Its World', *European Journal of Sociology* 46 (2): 297–320.

Ohmae, K. (1991) *The End of the Nation State*, London: Harper Collins.

Palmer, B. D. (2009) *Canada's 1960s: The Ironies of Identity in a Rebellious Era*, Toronto: University of Toronto Press.

Polier, N. and Roseberry, W. (1989) 'Tristes Tropes: Postmodern Anthropologists Encounter the Other and Discover Themselves', *Economy and Society* 18 (2): 245–64.

Portes, A. (1999) 'Immigration Theory for a New Century: Some Problems and Opportunities', in C. Hirschman, P. Kasinitz and J. Dewind (eds) *The Handbook of International Migration: The American Experience*, New York: Russell Sage Foundation.

Portes, A. and DeWind, J. (2008) 'A Cross-Atlantic Dialogue: The Progress of Research and Theory in the Study of International Migration', in A. Portes and J. DeWind (eds) *Rethinking Migration Theory*, New York and London: Berghahn.

Pradella, L. and Marois, T. (eds) (2015) *Polarizing Development: Alternatives to Neoliberalism and the Crisis*, London: Pluto Press.

Prior, D., Stewart, J. and Walsh, K. (1995) *Citizenship: Rights, Community and Participation*, London: Pitman Publishing.

Roseberry, W. (1997) 'Marx and Anthropology', *Annual Review of Anthropology* 26: 25–46.

Rostow, W. W. (1990) *The Stages of Economic Growth: A Non-Communist Manifesto*, Cambridge: Cambridge University Press.

Sassen, S. (2005) 'Introducing a Concept', *Brown Journal of World Affairs* 11 (2): 27–43.

Smith, G. (2008) 'Canadian anthropology is a labour process like any other', Paper presented at the 2008 Meeting of CASCA in a panel organized by J. Waldram entitled 'Canadian Anthropology is ...'

Smith, G. (2014) *Toward Intellectual Praxis: Essays in Historical Realism,* London: Berghahn.

Soederberg, S. (2013) 'Universalizing Financial Inclusion and the Securitization of Development', *Third World Quarterly* 34 (4): 593–612.

Wolf, E. R. (1969) *Peasant Wars of the Twentieth Century*, Norman, OK: University of Oklahoma Press.

Young, D. J. and Meneley, A. (2005) *Autoethnographies: The Anthropology of Academic Practices*, Toronto: University of Toronto Press.

Part Two

Extending Perspectives on a Mobile World

–5–

From 'Black Kaká' to Gentrification: The New Motilities of Expatriate Brazilian Football Players

Carmen Silvia Rial

Sport is a field that has been little explored by social scientists and specialists in the studies of globalization, transnationalism and migrations. Of the occasional articles that do appear, many focus on political conflicts generated by mega sporting events such as the World Cup or the Olympic Games, their impact on the host cities, population shifts and the use of new security measures. Nevertheless, historians have demonstrated deep connections between the development of sport – particularly football (soccer in American terminology)[1] – and the processes of economic and cultural globalization. The globalization of football began in the late nineteenth century:

> as the 'games revolution' colonized British imperial outposts (e.g. cricket in Asia and Australasia), the 'global game' of football underwent mass diffusion along British trading and educational routes (in Europe, South America), and distinctive indigenous sports were forged as part of the invention of national traditions in emerging modern societies (e.g. baseball and American football in the United States). (Giulianotti and Robertson 2007: 108)

As Pascal Boniface (1998) noted: 'Football is certainly the most universal phenomenon today, far more than democracy or the market economy, which are said to have no boundaries, but are not as widespread as football.'[2]

Football today 'is an economically significant, highly popular, globally networked cultural form' (Smart 2007). It is an integral part of the consumer culture and focused on celebrities. The global expansion of football is linked to growing interest by the media in the sport and to the development of media technologies, such as satellite TV and the internet. Football games are the most widely watched events in the world.[3]

Sports stars are elevated to an iconic global celebrity status, while they continue to represent local and or national communities. As Smart (2007: 130) puts it: 'The celebrities serve as role models, as objects of adulation and identification, but also increasingly as exemplars of consumer lifestyles to which spectators and television viewers alike are enticed to aspire.' Synthia Sydnor (2000) also offers some interesting reflections on celebrities in sport, showing how they deeply affect the lives of their fans. As Morin (2007) observed, they are capable of breaking this prison-world into pieces.

Football presents features found elsewhere and has been subject to the same process that has influenced sports since the 1970s in the developed capitalist economies and liberal democracies of Europe and America, which has been called the second globalization (Giulianotti and Robertson 2007). One of the central characteristics of this second globalization of football is the adoption of global player recruitment strategies with a consequent growth in the transnational circulation of players.

In recent years, I have been studying the transnational circulation of Brazilian football players, many of whom are celebrities. In this chapter, my goal is to inquire about the homogeneity or heterogeneity of this flow. To do so, I ethnographically analysed three groups of Brazilian expatriated players: celebrities who work in global clubs, the unheralded (obscure or 'infamous' in Foucault's sense[4]) players who circulate among second-tier clubs in distant countries, and the players performing in the US Major League Soccer (MLS). I conclude by emphasizing the heterogeneity of this circulation, a mobility that reveals a variety both from the point of view of the involved subjects (in terms of their social origin and cultural capital) as well as their real experiences in the destination countries, especially in relation to the local, i.e. how they are inserted in the daily life where they live. For many of them, life abroad takes place in protected 'bubbles', where the relations of the protagonists are more translocal than transnational. Among the important factors that determine a greater or lesser permeability of this 'bubble', their insertion in the local, is the rank of the destination club in the hierarchy of the football system, the age of the player when he left, his cultural capital, time of permanence abroad and whether he has children living with him.

Among the nearly three million Brazilians living abroad as immigrants,[5] nearly five thousand are football players. The number of people who have left Brazil to play football has been above one thousand for a number of years – and in 2013 exceeded 1,500 (Chade 2013). The number of countries of destination for these players is also growing: it was seventy-one in 2002 (the year that the Brazilian Football Confederation (CBF) began to divulge its statistics) and reached ninety-five in 2008.[6]

Brazil is not the only large exporter of football players. In Latin America, Argentina and Uruguay export more players per capita, while Brazil leads in absolute numbers. As Cornelissen and Solberg (2007: 295) have shown 'Africa is a primary source for football flows to Western Europe, an aspect that is mostly viewed as exploitative and an extension of neo-imperialist relations between the continent and its former colonial powers. Over the past decade, however, South Africa has emerged as an important alternative destination for many of Africa's departing footballers.'

Brazilian players are found in most of the 208 countries and territories where football is controlled by the International Federation of Association Football (FIFA), in social, political and sporting contexts that often do not have the same security offered by European clubs or the MLS in North America. Even countries that are unlikely destinations for Brazilian workers, such as India and Saudi Arabia, have received football players. So much so that Brazil's Ministry of Foreign Relations recently prepared a pamphlet to warn football players about potentially dangerous ties with unscrupulous managers in countries such as Armenia, Singapore, South Korea, China, Greece, India and Thailand. Despite the brochure's good intentions, and the fact that each of these countries has a different reality, I have been to all those mentioned (with the exception of Armenia) and, did not find anything that could be characterized as human trafficking.[7]

The dissemination of Brazilian football players throughout the world, even if not recent, has heightened in the twenty-first century, presenting a large symbolic impact given football's strong presence in the global media and its colonization of masculine imaginations. In addition to the player-celebrities at global clubs in Europe, there is a numerically significant flow of non-famous players who look for work in countries that are unlikely destinations for other Brazilian emigrants, such as Russia, China, India, Korea and Morocco. There is also a nearly invisible flow of Brazilian women football players who seek the United States and northern European countries to practice the sport within which they have historically suffered discrimination in their home country (Rial 2014a).

Based on multi-site ethnographic research conducted since 2003, I have been questioning categories such as frontier, migration and immigrant/emigrant to see if they still apply to the new mobilities such as those of male and female football players. Like the trajectories of other professionals (such as diplomats, intellectuals and students) football players *circulate* across state borders with periodic returns to their country of origin.

First Scenario – Living in a Bubble

Naldo,[8] whom I met at a Dutch football club, has a special function: he is the 'secretary' for Berto, a young and talented Brazilian player, who as a three-year-old child sold spices from his mother's garden in the streets of Fortaleza to survive. As Naldo explained to me, his work is similar to that done by another 'secretary' who accompanies a world-famous Brazilian player, and has been part of his life, for ten years:

> You know how difficult it is for a Brazilian player when he leaves the country to go abroad. First the language: it's always a very big barrier. The issue of communication is terrible because in Brazil it is not like Europe. Here, the (European) players have the opportunity to study and learn English. In Brazil, some players did not even go to elementary school, so they can barely speak Portuguese. And as a consequence of the

communication issue, the cultural conditions (of the host country) are usually completely different from that of Brazilian culture. People have another type of education, everything is different, it changes everything. Usually they do not come with their family. So it's complicated, sometimes a player with great potential, in Brazil stands out, and when he goes abroad, he ends up not performing what is expected of him because he is lost, he is isolated at home, he has no one to be with him, he does not know how to organize things, he cannot communicate. So, precisely to avoid this kind of problem we were inspired by the work that was done with Silvio, which was successful ... And my role here is exactly to provoke his adaptation so that it is focused only on training and on games, and he does not have any other kind of concern.

Living in Berto's house, being his driver, his translator, accompanying him when he travels for games, mediating his relationships with other players, with the manager, with the medical staff and with any stranger that approaches him, and writing a daily report (that includes images) to his agents located in Switzerland, Naldo's panoptic view delivers a service that blends labour, supervision and friendship, and dissolves the boundaries between work and personal life.

Berto is a good example of the form of human resources administration that led me to characterize the daily life of these athletes as being realized in a *bubble* (Rial 2012) within which athletes are isolated from local social connections – luxury hotels, training centres, physical therapy clinics and residential condominiums. Contact with local common mortals is minimal. Berto's eight-year-old son studies in a local school and is the only one in the family able to say a few words in Dutch. When I accompanied Berto's mother and his aunt on a shopping walk, he insisted on translating dialogs with vendors. His other child, a three-year-old girl, was still living with her mother in Brazil (the couple are separated), but will come to live with Berto when she is old enough to go to school.

During my visit to their house, I was served a good Brazilian meal, made by his aunt, with some imported ingredients, which is quite common among the expatriated Brazilian players I met in the Netherlands and other countries, whether they are stars or not well known (Rial and Assunção 2011). Brazilian restaurants are preferred, and when they do not exist, those that serve dishes considered similar to those at home are chosen instead. With this consumption pattern, Brazilians express a banal nationalism as described by Billig (1995): the presence of their original place is omnipresent in their daily lives.

Berto is perhaps an extreme case of a *bubble* construction (Rial 2014b), so common among the players who are celebrities – the *happy few* who inhabit the global clubs.[9] We find examples of similar bubbles in other professions, such as movie stars during film shooting, and in the higher echelons of politics. Once their credentials are in hand, the subject enters the bubble and becomes isolated from other mortals, only coexisting with other subjects who have the same credentials. Their movements are monitored by security agents who encircle the group. They travel in special aircraft, areas of airports are closed-off for them. Their food needs, transportation and accommodations are all provided for.

Players in global clubs receive similar treatment on many occasions. To move from one country to another, once in the bubble, they do not need a plane ticket or to exchange currency. There will be someone, provided by the club or by their impresarios (as in the case of Naldo), to take care of all the 'minor' details. These mediators wait at the airport when they do not accompany them on the journey, get visas, negotiate with local authorities, open bank accounts, look for homes in enclosed estates (usually those where other Brazilian footballers already live), take their children to the doctor, read restaurant menus for their first meals in the new country, lead them to the training centre until the path is familiar, serve as chauffeur until they get a driver's licence, help get a car (some do not even need to buy one: the global clubs have contracts with luxury car manufacturers that provide 'free' automobiles to their stars).

We know that immigrants (lawful or unlawful) rarely venture without the backing of a known network (Machado 2005) that guarantees basic support in the early days abroad. However, in the deterritorialization process very few of them have the same facilities given to the players of the global clubs.

For the majority of the 232 million[10] people worldwide who in 2013 did not reside in the country where they were born, crossing a border may create a region of opportunities, where they can reinvent themselves and leave behind the burden of a legacy. Simultaneously, the border represents a risk and a progress area, a space of opportunities in new social and political contexts (Hannerz 1996). But not for players inside a football system controlled by FIFA. Their travel involves identified certainties, rather than risks.

The circulation of Brazilian players abroad is carried out in an area (a bubble) consisting of homogenized spaces that are monitored and protected by restricted access. These include airports, stadiums, hotels, training centres, medical clinics, physiotherapy clinics and saunas, which could be designated as globalized non-places (Augé 1992), and places (home, restaurants) marked by Brazilian consumption and lifestyles (Rial and Assunção 2011).

The permeability of the bubble, that is, the degree of 'protection' (an ambiguous term that also involves monitoring) and the quality of the services that are provided, varies greatly depending on the place occupied by the player and the club in the hierarchy of the football system. Nevertheless, even a young unknown player such as Nandinho, who played in Denmark, receives special attention: 'My Danish teacher was waiting for me at the airport, and showed me the city. I lived in an apartment that the club gave me. I was very tranquil there, thanks to God.' In fact, the celebrity players abroad are a small group among the about 500 who work in Europe. Many others are dispersed across other continents.

Second Scenario – Kaká Noir

In the first half of 2013, Latin American countries exported outside the continent about 5,000 footballers with a total value of over US$1.1 billion. Argentina and

Brazil alone exported over 3,000 football players, or US$400 million in football talent. 'As a whole, Latin America exported more soccer players in value in the first half of 2013 than in live animals throughout the year 2011' (Ferdman and Yanofski 2013). Since much of the players' salaries returns home in bank transfers, emigration clearly involves significant financial advantages. Player transfers have become a vital source of financial support, without which clubs would not be able to maintain the high wages paid to their other professionals. It goes without saying that the salaries of the celebrities change enormously when they are transferred abroad.

Alongside these celebrities, there are about five thousand other players in marginal countries of the world football system, like those I met in India, Canada, Belgium, Morocco, China, South Korea, Hong Kong and Uruguay, who often receive little more than twice the Brazilian minimum wage. These are the unheralded and 'infamous' players who each year include an increasingly significant quota of women who leave Brazil to practise a profession in which they have been discriminated against. Many of them live with a certain economic precariousness, and all of them fall far short of receiving the millions of dollars in annual income enjoyed by the celebrities that I initially contacted. They circulate in secondary circuits of the global football system.

Who are these Brazilians who now live in over a hundred different countries, in cities where the presence of other Brazilian immigrants is minimal or non-existent?

Marrakech, November 2009: they came to the Kawba Training Centre, walking together. Kerson, less bulky, light brown hair, green eyes, looking very lively and intelligent, spoke to me with self-confidence, but without pretension. He was wearing plaid shorts that reached below his knees, a red T-shirt with black squares, and had a small backpack, which probably carried his uniform. He was like a young tourist, similar to the many that wander around the Jeemaa Al-Fadar square at dusk, when the world's largest open-air restaurant begins to mount its tables and their kitchens. Kerson is not a typical player: he comes from a family from the interior of Paraná State whose father 'worked with yerba mate, had a good income, a simple life, but honest'. The family was never lacking necessities, a category so often evoked among the player-celebrities who I had contacted. 'Food, fruit [were never lacking], at home, it was a German house ....' Kerson finished high school and it was only then that he had to choose between two options, go to college or begin a professional football career. Kerson was almost the oposite of Heison (who is muscular, with closely shaved hair), whose profile is similar to most of the players I had contacted. Heison came from a 'humble' family in Rio de Janeiro. He had already played in Uruguay, Spain, Tunisia, Togo, Ghana and Malaysia before arriving in Morocco. He had 'spun around', as they say in Brazil: that is, he had circulated through many clubs, which is considered a way of gaining 'experience', football capital. 'At home we are seven and I am the youngest male,' he said, confirming another feature common to many of the players: that of being the youngest in the family (Rial 2008).

They talk about their lives naturally, without embarrassment, answering my questions with my little camera almost glued to their faces to better capture the sound, happy to speak to a Brazilian. Other players (apparently Moroccans) rushed into the Training Centre, already wearing the red uniform of the Kawkab Athletic Club of Marrakech (KACM), a club founded in 1947, which has the honour of being a four-time national champion and six-time winner of the King's Cup (Coupe du Throne). Nevertheless, I was completely unfamiliar with the club, because it remains isolated from the hegemonic global football community. Thanks to the team's good performance in the national championship, Kerson can send his entire salary to Brazil and get by on the monetary compensation for victories. Part is used to support his family, part is placed in a savings account 'to earn a little interest'. He does not earn a high salary, but one that would require 'hard work to get in Brazil', he told me later while sitting on the couch of the apartment that the club offers him, beside Eliana, his young wife, who recently graduated with a degree as a pharmacist, and his fifteen-month-old son, who were visiting him for the first time, after one year.

The Moroccan players heading to the locker room stopped to greet them, jokingly, in French, but mixing some words in Portuguese (*'Tudo bem?'*, 'Legal'). One of them caressed Heison's bald head: *'C'est notre Kaká noir'*, he tells me, resting his head affectionately on Heison's shoulder. I think the phrase ('He is our black Kaká') is doubly revealing. Partly because much of the charisma of players like Heison, scattered among small clubs throughout the world, depends on the success of Brazilian players and mediascape-celebrities like Kaká. Also because, in some way, they are similar to their black ancestors who had traversed the Atlantic to labour in precarious conditions. In the football spectacle, they are the ones who work for low wages, those living in the worst conditions, those who remain unknown to an audience beyond the places where they perform.

Morocco, an unlikely destination for other migrants, is also not an important destination for football players. Only seventeen Brazilian players moved there between 2002 and 2008.[11] Because of its subaltern status in the global football system, Morocco is part of an alternate circuit of exchanges that often includes local clubs vying for secondary championships, which could be designated as part of a non-hegemonic globalization (Ribeiro 2010).

Indeed, most Brazilian expatriated players do not come from first division clubs. For instance, among 1,017 Brazilian players who moved abroad in 2009, less than 15 per cent came from clubs in the A Series or top division. Surprisingly, over 64 per cent of the players were transferred from clubs that do not even dispute Brazil's fourth division championship series. This was also found in India. According to the Brazilian consulate in Mumbai, which I visited in 2011, there were only sixty-four Brazilians in the large region of southern India. None were labourers, but engineers and technical specialists who usually sojourn for one to three months transmitting technology. They come and go without maintaining ties with the country. 'There are no immigrants here,' a consulate diplomat explained to me. 'India has one of the world's cheapest labour forces, cheaper than the Chinese. What would they do here?'

And yet they do come to play football, dozens of them, the only Brazilian residents in India visible in the media. The Brazilian players here do not enjoy the same weight as those in Morocco, as confirmed to me by the president of the Western India Football Association, because football is still a sport 'that is growing rapidly in public popularity' but positioned far behind cricket (the colonial sport introduced by the English, in which in an example of complex postcolonial relations, India now has supremacy over its former colonizers).

Why do the Brazilian players accept the 'sacrifice' (as many described their situation) of living in distant places, far from family and friends, without mastering the local language, for a salary that is not as high as they could earn at home? The first response would be: to have a professional football career that would be threatened by the lack of space in the four main divisions in Brazil, or restricted to semi-amateur clubs, and playing only on weekends.

In short, they are following a dream of becoming celebrities. And, on this difficult quest, some places offer better 'windows', as they say, than others. 'The Moroccan championship is broadcast in the Arab countries,' Kerson told me, seeing his stay in Marrakesh as a springboard for a millionaire market. 'Uruguayan football is followed closely by European clubs, they think the players here are more accustomed to the climate and to their robust style. Often, impresarios come to watch the practice,' one of many Brazilian players I met in Montevideo told me. Many of them play for three months of the year in local clubs of the second division in nearby Southern Brazil, for six months in Uruguay and are unemployed – or, as they put it, 'working at home' – for the other three months waiting for a phonecall to guarantee another three-month gig the next year.

These Kaká noirs, i.e. the players under contract on foreign clubs situated on the lower levels of the global football hierarchy, expose an important feature in the global consumption of South American players: the celebrities exude an aura that casts its light onto unknown players, causing their value to rise in the market as if their national origin give them an ethnic guarantee of good performances.

In a new dynamic created by capitalism in the football system, most of these players were originally under contract with clubs formed with the main purpose of selling them, clubs that do not compete for championships – they are exclusively training centres run by impresarios and geared to export. The real Kaká, who played for global clubs in Europe, made a speedy return to his former club in Brazil in 2014, and then took a path that would be improbable for famous players until a few years ago: he signed with Orlando in the MLS.

Third Scenario – The USA: A Singular Case

Although the United States continues to be the preferred destination for Brazilian emigrants in general, with 60 per cent of them living there, it has never been a destination coveted by male football celebrities.[12] This has changed slightly in recent years, with the consolidation of MLS, which is attracting an increasing number of world football stars, even if most are close to retirement. The MLS seems to have enticed a special kind of Brazilian player that I rarely met elsewhere: middle-class players attracted to the United States by recruitment agencies that combine sports and high school or college education.

As I approached the United States ethnographically, I thought that I would find Brazilian players over-protected by clubs and managers, and subject to rigid hours and discipline, like those in Europe. I expected to find that they would have a lifestyle marked by the consumption of Brazilian products and images, strong nationalist sentiments, and that their transnational circulation, like that of many diasporic groups, stimulates national feelings expressed by the display of the national flag in celebrations and by the consumption of common products from 'home' (Rial and Assunção 2011). I also imagined that they would have the same strong religious values that I found among Brazilians in other countries and that the presence of neo-Pentecostalism would be hegemonic (Rial 2012). I did find these characteristics in the United States, but I also found a pronounced local insertion among Brazilian players in the United States.

Finally, I expected to find athletes from the humble social origins that are common to the large majority of players with whom I had previous contact, celebrities or not. Nevertheless, to my surprise, I found a considerable number of players from middle-class families, which I did not find in any of the other countries where I conducted research. These are the specificities in relation to the global circulation of players that I would like to explore now.

Football does not enjoy the same popularity in the United States as it does in most of the planet, even if the audience for the 2014 World Cup reached unprecedented levels.[13] However, professional football in the United States has a long history and has enjoyed several moments of popularity throughout the twentieth century. Professional soccer leagues were founded in the United States nearly at the same time as football became a sport in England (Elias and Dunning 1986), some as early as the 1890s. Nevertheless, the sport has never caught fire at the professional level in the United States. Soccer leagues have not only been in the shadow of baseball, football, basketball and ice hockey, but with the exception of MLS, a newcomer on the mainstream sporting scene, all of the previous soccer leagues folded within a couple of decades. MLS is in part supported by the tastes of the immigrant population (Apostolov 2012), which is altering the country's social and political landscape.

In contrast with its strong global leadership as a sport, in the United States soccer has a long way to go to catch up with the popularity of Ultimate Fighting Championship (UFC) fights, car racing, baseball and American football. The US sports scene dialogues with the rest of the world but maintains a strong local accent. It has an ethnocentric trait, imaging itself as being global – the annual baseball championship in the United States even dares to call itself a *World* Series.

From a foreign point of view, there are many interesting particularities that distinguish football in the United States such as the large popularity of women's football, the close relation between clubs and ethnic communities and the inclusion of foreign clubs (Toronto FC and Vancouver FC) in a national league. But here I will focus on only two features related to the transnational circulation of Brazilian players: the huge importance of academic sports and the large presence of expatriate players.

In fact, the numbers in the MLS[14] are astonishing: in 2010 there were more than twice as many foreign players (454, of whom twenty-one were Brazilians) than US players (219). This decreased relatively by 2015 when there were 236 foreign (of whom nineteen were Brazilians) and 323 US players. Although it would be easy to find other professions in the United States that include many foreigners (gardeners, home caretakers, taxi-drivers in New York, etc.) it is unlikely that there are any with as wide a variety of foreign nationalities involved (sixty-eight in 2010; fifty-two in 2015), ranging from Norway to Uganda, and a wide range of salaries, with the top talents earning millions.

Not that the United States is different from other countries in terms of the importation of football talents. Studies conducted in Europe's five major football leagues indicate an increasing migration of football players from outside Europe, mainly from South America and Africa (Poli and Besson 2014). This cosmopolitan trend of accepting foreigners prevails mainly among the large clubs in the North, although the issue of national quotas is still present (Gardiner and Welsh 2009).

But let's return to the MLS. As we mentioned, Brazil was the country with the second highest number of foreign players in the MLS in 2010[15] (behind Colombia), and the third in 2015 (behind Argentina and England). The strong presence of Brazilian players in US football is not exceptional. They are also found in Europe, where Brazil has been the country of origin of the largest contingent of athletes disputing the European Champions League, the world's most important club competition.

The football hierarchy and the political economy of nations are not in perfect correspondence. In the world of football, countries such as Greece or Turkey have a better classification than the United States, Canada or Australia. In fact, in the FIFA ranking,[16] the United States is in twenty-eighth place among the male squads, which might be one of the reasons for its absence among the preferential destinations of Brazilian football stars. The US market is still seen by Brazilian football players as a good place to end or begin their careers, although this has been changing in recent years, after the contracting of football celebrities who would still be marketable in Europe.[17]

Of the nineteen MLS clubs in 2010, twelve have at least one Brazilian player and of the twenty clubs in 2015, thirteen have at least one Brazilian player. They are usually quite successful. Two of them were nominated in 2010 for MLS's 'Best Latino' award, although no Brazilian would spontaneously identify him- or herself as Latino.

There is great similarity among the careers, trajectories, projects and lifestyles of the Brazilians in the MLS and other Brazilians who circulate in the global football system. I would like to emphasize here factors that initially appeared to be distinct and particular in the MLS, notably the gentrification of the recruitment process.

A significant portion of the players (19 per cent in 2010) are college graduates who passed through high school and university teams before joining the MLS teams. While the sample is small and this is only four athletes, it is four more than in all of Brazil, where there are thousands of football players. Most of the players I interviewed in Europe, Asia and elsewhere in the Americas had only attended elementary school.

Most of the Brazilian players in the MLS reached the United States in the past two years, but there are players who have been here for nearly ten years – those who were in colleges and universities.

Their place of origin is quite restricted. More than half the Brazilian players in the MLS in 2010 were born in the state of São Paulo, and of these seven come from small cities in the interior of the state. Four were born in the state of Rio de Janeiro and two in Paraná. That is, of the twenty-one Brazilian players in the MSL, eighteen were born in Brazil's south and southeastern regions, which are the most economically developed in the country. There is no player from the municipality of Governador Valadares in Minas Gerais State, the largest source of Brazilian emigrants to the United States. And there are none from Criciuma in Santa Catarina, which has recently become another important source of emigrants.

A surprisingly large number of players, ten in 2010, were either completely or partially trained in the farm clubs of a single Brazilian team, São Paulo FC, which leads me to the hypothesis that this club has a business connection with the MLS. It also appears to be important that Kaká, one of the most popular Brazilian players in the United States, began his career in São Paulo.[18] Moreover, Kaká's younger brother Digão was in the MLS, as was Marcelo, who wrote a biographical note that appears on the team's website:

> [Marcelo] is a devoted Christian, and likes the music of Michael W. Smith … [W]hile they were together at São Paolo, Marcelo lived with Brazilian and Real Madrid star midfielder Kaká and his family … their friendship has remained strong as each served as each other's best man in their respective weddings … while at São Paolo, met his wife Carolina, who was a volleyball player at the club … the couple have a son, Matheus.

Other players' biographies mention that they played with Kaká in São Paulo – but did not say that this was when they were on the youth teams. For most of the Brazilian players in the MLS in 2010, the United States was not their first destination outside of Brazil. Many had worked on foreign clubs in countries such as Mexico, Honduras, Portugal, Spain, Italy, England, Turkey, Greece, Tunisia, Libya, Israel, Switzerland, Malta, South Korea, Russia and Croatia. Some were in youth divisions (U-19) in Europe. As generally occurs with these players, many left their families and Brazil when they were still boys.

Most of the players transferred to the United States from a Brazilian club that was in the second or third division, with the United States being the peak of their careers until now, or started their professional career when they were already abroad. Nevertheless, there are two players (Fio Tilliarz and Kevin Diogo, whom I contacted) who had played for European clubs. They are the oldest, older than thirty-two, and appear to have chosen the United States to end their careers (which was the case of the first player but not the second, who returned to play in an important Brazilian club).

I observed a great proximity between the players in Europe, in other parts of the world and those in the United States. But I also noticed some marked distinctions of tastes and lifestyles. For example, in the USA they did display national consumption preferences but not exclusively. Along with expressions of nationalism and patriotism, I also found expressions of a cosmopolitan taste – social media posts in other languages, references to US music, to Mexican food and American brands (Ben & Jerry's, The Juice Factory), attendance at basketball games and bowling, which in this case appear to correlate more with the players' original social layer (Bourdieu 1979) than with the country where he is found. These tastes are those among the young players who studied in the United States and who certainly come from the middle class. We can thus consider them what Appiah (1997) called 'cosmopolitan patriots':[19] usually middle-class individuals in their nation of origin who become cosmopolitan without losing their national attachments.

How can it be explained that Brazilian middle-class youth are practising a profession in the United States that in Brazil (and in the rest of the world) is mostly occupied by youth from the lower classes? Part of the answer is the way that they were recruited in Brazil. Contrary to the common use of scouts to find players, some of these players were registered in 'exchange' programmes for students that sought to place them in US schools where they could practice the sport and receive a grant to do so.[20]

This form of recruiting young Brazilian players, because of its form and costs, basically affects the middle classes. One agency, 2SV, operates primarily over the internet, a tool that still excludes access by large contingents of the Brazilian population, although its use is growing rapidly in Brazil. It is common for middle-class Brazilians to dream of sending their children to the United States, yet for most the only way to get a visa is through a study programme. But studies in the United States are expensive, usually undertaken only by youth from Brazil's economic elite, rarely by those from the middle classes. When they do go, it is through exchange programmes.

Some of these student athletes are able to find a place on professional teams in the MLS. Ricardo, from Real Salt Lake, was one of those recruited by 2SV. Others return to Brazil to play football, as did Caio – who was unknown in Brazil because he lived in and became a player in the United States, but returned to Brazil, where he played in first division teams such as Botafogo and Internacional (and, in 2015, was playing for Al-Wasl, in Dubai).

The existence of youth training centres in the global South dedicated to preparing athletes for the North is nothing new (Darby 2007). This is one of the forms of recruitment of new players in the second globalization phase (Giulianotti and Robertson 2007). Many of the large European clubs have *soi-disant* philanthropic centres in their former colonies (especially in Africa but also in Indonesia). Because laws in the South are less restrictive than those in the North concerning required schooling, these centres are able to more quickly develop athletic bodies and a player *habitus* (Mauss 1968) among poor youth. With more 'free' time not in school, they can train many more hours. The novelty I found in the US is the existence of centres aimed at the middle classes.

Final Considerations

There is a lot in common between the situation, context, lifestyle and values of Brazilian players abroad, e.g. a strong presence of Brazil in their daily life, as if they were permanently divided between two worlds, as often occurs with transmigrants (Basch et al. 1994). But the heterogeneity of the flow of the transnational circulation of Brazilian players is clear. Even if they all move to do similar work, even if they all move within a football system controlled by FIFA (and therefore are always documented immigrants), the salaries, contracts and club facilities vary enormously from one subject to another. I identified three broad groups of expatriated players: the celebrities, the unheralded 'black Kaká', and the middle-class players of the MLS. Each of which has a different relationship with the experience of living abroad.

For the celebrities, life abroad takes place in protected 'bubbles' with few contacts with the local culture. These bubbles are sanitized, controlled, predictable, repetitive and monotonous. Protected, safe and often comfortable, the star players cross national borders without the emotion experienced by common migrants. But the bubble also exists for other players. It is a characteristic of the football system today, with a permeability that differs according to various factors including the age of the player, their cultural capital, time of permanence abroad and the presence of children. Those who left Brazil at an earlier age, those who had a formal education and those with children establish local ties.

The large majority of expatriate players come from the subaltern classes. However, in a new dynamic of the global football system, there are also players from the middle classes who were captured as youths in Brazil with an educational alibi. The United States appears as a place for 'wealthy' Brazilians to come to train to play football. They must have the financial resources to pay for their travel to the place of the try-outs and if approved, for their initial stay in US high schools or universities. It thus appears not only as a new possible destination, but as a destination with unique characteristics, promoting a sort of gentrification in the transnational circulation of Brazilian players.

Notes

1. Following the advice of the International Football Association (FIFA), I use 'football' to refer to what is usually called 'soccer' in the United States, thus using the name accepted worldwide. Soccer is neither slang nor an idiomatic term for football. It's simply a contraction of the word association – as in association football – and refers to the game regulated by FIFA, a supernational organization that now has 208 member countries and territories. I use the term American football to refer to the game derived from rugby that is played in the United States.

2. *Le football est certainement le phénomène le plus universel aujourd'hui, beaucoup plus que la démocratie ou l'économie de marché, dont on dit qu'elles n'ont plus de frontières, mais qui ne parviennent pas à avoir la surface du football.*

3. Billions of people watched the World Cups, but even a single game of the global clubs can reach a huge audience. In 2015, the Spanish derby between Real Madrid and Barcelona was broadcast to 145 countries.

4. Freely inspired by Foucault's text (1977), by 'infamous' I want to highlight the condition of anonymity, at least in Brazil, of those that circulate in the secondary circuits of the global football system.

5. Brazil's Ministry of Foreign Relations estimated in 2012 that 2,801,249 Brazilians were living abroad, 30 per cent fewer people than in 2008. The figures are imprecise (except for Japan) because they are based on reports sent by its foreign offices, based on estimates. For the numbers by country, see http://www.brasileirosnomundo.itamaraty.gov.br/a-comunidade/estimativas-populacionais-das-comunidades/estimativas-populacionais-das-comunidades-brasileiras-no-mundo-2013/Estimativas%20Brasileiros%20no%20Mundo%202013.pdf [accessed 4 June 2015].

6. Source: http://www.cbf.com.br/php/transferencias.php [accessed in November 2009].

7. The folder is also aimed at models, capoeiristas and Brazilian barbeque cooks, which are professions thus curiously associated as posing threats to Brazilian emigrants.

8. Although I have their authorization to publish the names of the players, agents and family members that I had contact with, to protect the identity of my interlocutors, all names have been changed. I use the real names of players whose information I found on the internet.

9. In an analogy with the category of global city (Sassen 1991; 2003), I mean by global clubs those that transcend the boundaries of their communities, regions and even their nation state. They are nodules of economic, human, media and symbolic global flows, concentrating capital that circulates globally, employing players from different parts of the world. They bring together supporters scattered throughout the world, colonizing the imagination of a planetary, yet mostly male, population. As imagined communities bringing together

supporters scattered throughout the world, one could see them as nations (Weber 2009) with their anthems, flags and a strong sense of belonging.

10. These international migrants account for just over 3 per cent of the world population (*International Migration Report 2013*, Nations Unies, 2013) http://www.un.org/en/development/desa/population/publications/migration/migration-report-2013.shtml [accessed 22 November 2015].

11. The Brazilian Football Confederation (the national FIFA affiliate) currently does not provide open access to its database.

12. Pelé played for the NY Cosmos in the 1970s but this was an unrepeated exception.

13. This was higher than the National Basketball Association finals.

14. See http://www.mlssoccer.com [accessed November 2010 and June 2015].

15. I do not consider Canadians to be foreigners, since there are Canadian teams in the MLS, given the particular political geography of sport that does not always respect national geo-political borders.

16. See http://www.en.fifaranking.net/ranking/ [accessed 4 June 2015].

17. Like Beckham, the world's highest-earning athlete according to Forbes magazine in 2010, or David Villa in 2013, Kaká in 2014, or Lampard in 2015.

18. Although Kaká was playing for Real Madrid in 2010 and arrived in the US only in 2014.

19. 'The cosmopolitan patriot can entertain the possibility of a world in which everyone is a rooted cosmopolitan, attached to a home of one's own, with its own cultural particularities, but taking pleasure from the presence of other, different places that are home to other, different people. The cosmopolitan also imagines that in such a world not everyone will find it best to stay in their natal patria, so that the circulation of people among different localities will involve not only cultural tourism (which the cosmopolitan admits to enjoying) but migration, nomadism, diaspora' (Appiah 1997: 618).

20. One of the channels that mediates trips to the United States is the 2SV, an 'exchange' agency for Brazilian youths to US schools where I found various Brazilian football players in the United States playing as 'amateurs'. The agency said it had the support of Disney and ESPN. It recruits youths through an Internet questionnaire, and football is one of various sports it offers. After undergoing athletic tryouts, youth who pass are registered in US high schools or universities, where they hope to win a place on the school team. The 2012 selection chose 'more than 100 student-athletes'.

References

Appiah, K. A. (1997) 'Cosmopolitan Patriots', *Critical Inquiry* 23 (3): 617–39.

Apostolov, S. (2012) 'Everywhere and Nowhere: The Forgotten Past and Clouded Future of American Professional Soccer from the Perspective of Massachusetts', *Soccer & Society* 13 (4): 510–35.

Augé, M. (1992) *Non-lieux*, Paris: Seuil.

Basch, L. G., Glick-Schiller, N. and Szanton, B. C. (1994) *Nations Unbound: Transnational Projects, Postcolonial Predicaments, and Deterritorialized Nation-states*, London and New York: Routledge.

Billig, M. (1995) *Banal Nationalism*, London: Sage.

Boniface, P. (1998) *Géopolitique du football*, Brussels: Editions Complexe.

Bourdieu, P. (1979) *La distinction – critique sociale du jugement*, Paris: Minuit.

Chade, J. (2013) 'Transferência de Jogadores Bateu Recorde em 2013'. Available online: http://exame.abril.com.br/economia/noticias/transferencias-de-jogadores-bateram-recorde-em-2013-2 [accessed 9 June 2015].

Cornelissen, S. and Solberg, E. (2007) 'Sport Mobility and Circuits of Power: The Dynamics of Football Migration in Africa and the 2010 World Cup', *Politikon: South African Journal of Political Studies* 34 (3): 295–314.

Darby, P. (2007) 'Out of Africa: The Exodus of Elite African Football Talent to Europe', *Working US* 10 (4): 443–56.

Elias, N. and Dunning, E. (1986) *Quest for Excitement: Sport and Leisure in the Civilizing Process*, Oxford: Blackwell.

Ferdman, R. A. and Yanofski. D. (2013) 'Latin America Earns More from Exporting Soccer Players than Live Animals'. Available online: http://qz.com/109317/latin-americas-soccer-player-exports-are-worth-more-than-its-animal-exports/ [accessed 4 June 2015].

Foucault, M. (1977) 'La vie des hommes infâmes', *Les Cahiers du Chemin* 29 (15): 12–29.

Gardiner S. and Welsh R. (2009) 'Sport, Racism and the Limits of "Colour Blind" Law', in B. Carrington and I. McDonald (eds) *'Race', Sport, and British Society*, New York: Routledge.

Giulianotti, R. and Robertson, R. (2007) 'Sport and Globalization: Transnational Dimensions', *Global Networks* 7 (2): 107–12.

Hannerz, U. (1996) *Conexiones transnacionales: cultura, gente, lugares*, Madrid: Ediciones Cátedra.

International Migration Report 2013 (2013) New York: Division de la Population, Département des Affaires économiques et sociales (DAES), Nations Unies.

Machado, I. J. R. (2005) 'Implicações da imigração estimulada por redes ilegais de aliciamento – o caso dos brasileiros em Portugal', *Ilha, Revista de Antropologia* 7 (1–2): 187–212.

Mauss, M. (1968) 'Les techniques du corps', *Sociologie et anthropologie* 58: 363–86. Paris: PUF.

Morin, E. (2007) *Les stars*, Paris: Seuil.

Poli, R., and Besson, R. (2014) 'Football and Migration: A Contemporary Geographical Analysis', in R. Elliott and J. Harris (eds) *Football and Migration: Perspectives, Places, Players*, London: Routledge.

Rial, C. (2008) '"Rodar": The Circulation of Brazilian Football Players Abroad', *Horizontes Antropológicos* 4. Available online: http://socialsciences.scielo.

org/scielo.php?script=sci_arttext&pid=S0104-71832008000100007&lng=en& nrm=iso [accessed 4 June 2015].

Rial, C. (2012) 'Banal Religiosity – Brazilian Athletes as New Missionaries of the Neo-Pentecostal Diaspora', *Vibrant* 9 (2): 128–58. Available online: http://www. scielo.br/scielo.php?script=sci_arttext&pid=S1809-43412012000200005&lng= en&nrm=iso [accessed 4 June 2015].

Rial, C. (2014a) 'New Frontiers: The Transnational Circulation of Brazil's Women Soccer Players', in S. Agergaard and N. C. Tiesler (eds) *Women, Soccer and Transnational Migration*, London and New York: Routledge.

Rial, C. (2014b) 'Circulation, Bubbles, Returns: The Mobility of Brazilians in the Football System', in R. Eliott and J. Harris (eds) *Football and Migration – Perspectives, Places, Players,* London and New York: Routledge.

Rial, C. and Assunção, V. K. (2011) 'As viagens da comida: notas a partir de etnografias de brasileiros emigrantes na região de Boston e com futebolistas que circulam pelo mundo', in S. M. F. Arend, J. M. Pedro and C. Rial (eds) *Diásporas, Mobilidades e Migrações,* Florianópolis: Editora Mulheres.

Ribeiro, G. L. (2010) 'A globalização popular e o sistema mundial não-hegemônico', *Revista Brasileira de Ciências Sociais* 25 (74): 21–38.

Sassen, S. (1991) *The Global City*, New York, London, Tokyo and Princeton, NJ: Princeton University Press.

Sassen, S. (2003) *Contrageografías de la globalización: género y ciudadanía en los circuitos transfronterizos*, Madrid: Traficantes de Sueños.

Sydnor, S. (2000) 'Sport, Celebrity and Liminality', in N. Dyck (ed.) *Games, Sports and Cultures*, Oxford: Berg.

Smart, B. (2007) 'Not Playing Around: Global Capitalism, Modern Sport and Consumer Culture', *Global Networks* 7 (2): 113–34.

Weber, M. (2009) *From Max Weber: Essays in Sociology*, London and New York: Routledge.

–6–

Cultural Practices of Mexican Immigrants in Gwinnett County (USA): Intangible Cultural Heritage as a Space of Conviviality in a Receiving Community

Cristina Amescua-Chávez

Introduction

Mexican immigration to the southeast of the US has shown a massive and sustained increase over the last two decades. The growing visibility of Mexican communities in the Atlanta Metropolitan Area has had a great impact on the social and economic configuration of small suburban communities. Drawing from more than six years of fieldwork in Gwinnett County, this chapter addresses how the Intangible Cultural Heritage (ICH) of Mexican Immigrants in Georgia (USA) is contributing to the construction of complex social and cultural interactions not only among immigrants but also with the local population in suburban areas.

The first part of this chapter introduces the concept of intangible cultural heritage, including a discussion of its reach as a public policy tool and its usefulness from an anthropological standpoint. After a succinct discussion of the methodological approach of this study, I will present a brief historical overview of Mexican immigration to the US in order to contextualize the current trends and the social phenomena that led to the emergence of the Southeast as a new receiving desti- nation. The last part of the text offers an ethnographic account of several cultural practices of Mexican immigrants in Gwinnett County that can be understood as incipient spaces of conviviality. It will discuss the reproduction of Mexican culinary traditions and their reception in the local community. The frictions between tradition and new cultural practices will be addressed through a description of the adaptation of the Day of the Dead festivities and the adoption of Hallowe'en. An analysis of the celebrations in honour of the Virgin of Guadalupe will present the interactions of Mexican immigrants and local religious communities.

Rather than presenting an in-depth analysis of each of the selected cultural practices, I aim to identify a relatively wide array of scenarios where Mexican culture is being re-enacted, negotiated and transformed. This will allow me to discuss how immigrants are reshaping their intangible cultural heritage, both symbolically and formally, to build new social ties not only among themselves but also with members of the receiving society. This is particularly important because the cultural phenomena analysed here are developing within a context where immigrants remain vulnerable and subject to discrimination. Looking at how spaces of conviviality are nevertheless being built though intangible cultural heritage practices may allow a better understanding of the coping strategies that emerge to deal with adverse situations in everyday life.

Intangible Cultural Heritage

The concept of Intangible Cultural Heritage (ICH) was created after over a decade of intense debates by different groups of experts within the UNESCO (1972) framework. Following the implementation of the 1972 Convention Concerning the Protection of World Cultural and Natural Heritage (commonly known as the World Heritage Convention), several claims were made about the underrepresentation in the World Heritage List of countries and regions where culture took an expressive rather than a physical form. Along with what is known as the cultural turn in the social sciences, a worldwide intellectual and political movement advocated the recognition of particular cultural knowledges (in the plural), meanings and practices. Anthropologists, ethnologists, linguists, artists, cultural promoters, lawyers and policy makers participated actively in the debates seeking to build an international public policy instrument to recognize and protect living cultures. In 2003, UNESCO's General Assembly approved the International Convention for the Safeguarding of Intangible Cultural Heritage.

In its second article, this Convention defines ICH as:

> The practices, representations, expressions, knowledge, skills – as well as the instruments, objects, artifacts and cultural spaces associated therewith – that communities, groups and, in some cases, individuals recognize as part of their cultural heritage. This intangible cultural heritage, transmitted from generation to generation, is constantly recreated by communities and groups in response to their environment, their interaction with nature and their history, and provides them with a sense of identity and continuity, thus promoting respect for cultural diversity and human creativity … . (UNESCO 2003)

By 2015, a total of 162 countries had accepted, approved or ratified the Convention.

ICH as a Public Policy Tool

Over the last decade, the Convention has triggered multiple reactions from different actors. One of the most significant current debates is the one that questions the validity of the tangible/intangible dichotomy. To some, it is unnecessary (Giménez 2007: 221), while others recognize its usefulness but emphasize the difficulty of clearly separating both aspects. For example, a pyramid is undoubtedly tangible but the cosmogony behind its construction is not. From a strictly conceptual point of view, I agree with these arguments but from a public policy approach the differences between the tangible and intangible dimensions of culture and heritage are extremely relevant: the same measures cannot be applied to protect and preserve a monument and to safeguard a living cultural practice. Tangible heritage represents past periods of human cultures, so its protection includes the preservation of its original features; while intangible heritage reflects the current and changing reality, therefore its safeguarding mostly means '… its continued practice within and by the relevant cultural community. That is living cultural heritage has to be vital, dynamic and sustainable in order to be considered safeguarded' (Kurin 2007: 12).

Another heated debate focuses on the establishment of lists as the main – or at least the most visible – mechanism for the implementation of the Convention. According to Hafstein (2009), the heritage system is exclusionary because it values some things above others, based on vague and undetermined criteria. Indeed, construction of a list implies a taxonomic view of culture that introduces hierarchies – voluntarily or involuntarily (Villaseñor and Zolla 2012). According to Kirshenblatt-Gimblett, 'Some of those involved in the process of developing the intangible heritage initiative had hoped for cultural rather than metacultural outcomes; they wanted to focus on actions that would directly support local cultural reproduction, rather than on creating metacultural artifacts such as the list' (2004: 56). Indeed, with approval of this procedure, the power to list and thus accord recognition lies in the hands of governments. Inscription, as Villaseñor and Zolla argue, is in fact representative of 'the capacity of institutional actors to identify and manage the expressions they consider outstanding, or those whose promotion is convenient for political or economic reasons' (2012: 73). This is clearly an enormous deflection from the spirit of the convention because from its standpoint:

> It is the dynamic social processes of creativity, of identity-making, of taking and respecting the historically received and remaking it as one's own, that is to be safeguarded. And the arbiters of value – those who might be mindful of variants and yet decide on their relative significance and correctness – are not governments or scholars or collectors or aficionados, but rather members of the concerned communities themselves. (Kurin 2007: 13)

Safeguarding itself is another contested issue (Arizpe 2011; Khaznadar 2011; Van Zanten 2011). Protecting or conserving it (as it is done with tangible heritage) could lead to its objectivation, its fossilization or its extraction from the social and cultural contexts that create and recreate it. That is why safeguarding implies securing the viability of the contexts and conditions for its reproduction, always considering that its dynamism and adaptability are essential components (Lenzerini 2011; Schmitt 2008; Stefano et al. 2012).

Anthropological Perspective on ICH

Despite the debates that still surround this cultural public policy tool, ICH is a concept deeply linked with anthropology, and it is as an anthropologist that I look at it and work with it. From an anthropological standpoint, ICH is a social construction, a process through which communities assign symbolic value and meaning to some of their cultural practices. It is rooted in the past, exists in the present and is projected into the future. It is transmitted from generation to generation. Each generation preserves the tradition but adds new elements – formal and symbolic – that ensure its continuity. It is a form of heritage because people consider it important, because it contributes to building their identity and because it gives them a sense of belonging, allowing them to build the ties that bind them together. But it also builds bridges connecting the collectivity to the outside: by sharing their intangible cultural heritage, human groups identify with it and also show themselves to others. They share what makes them proud, what keeps them alive and gives them meaning: what they are, what they do and what they know.

The main characteristic of intangible cultural heritage is movement and transformation, because adaptation and dynamic change are the key elements that ensure the endurance of the deeply grounded meanings that give a sense to collective life (Amescua 2013: 205). But the communities that create and recreate it are themselves increasingly involved in mobility processes as more and more local communities are becoming sending or receiving places (or in some cases both) for migrants (ibid.: 206). As Levitt (2005) points out, the literature on migration normally overlooks its cultural dimensions and a better part of migration studies are devoted to the quantification of the phenomenon. The number of studies aimed at systematically exploring the impacts of mobility on culture is considerably smaller, and literature devoted specifically to intangible cultural heritage in migratory contexts still scarcer. A decade after the adoption of the Convention, the topic has only been addressed by half a dozen authors (Amescua 2010; Le Bot 2011; Gößwald 2007; Littlefield Kasfir et al. 2004; Machuca 2011; Margolies 2011; Nettleford 2004; Vlachaki 2007).

Methodology for Researching ICH and Migration

Although the ethnographic method is still the main tool for anthropological research, as Federico Besserer states: '… the conventional instruments of "community ethnography" are not entirely useful to understand transnational life' (2000: 20). Social sciences, and particularly anthropology, are faced today with the challenge of imagining new methodological instruments capable of capturing the high velocity transformations of the contemporary world. For my broader research on perceptions and experiences of encounters and frictions between Mexicans and Americans in Georgia, I adopted the methodological model Anna Tsing (2005) calls 'patchwork ethnography':

> … it is impossible to gain full ethnographic appreciation of every social group that forms a connection in a global chain. My experiment was to work my way back and forth between the Meratus Mountains – where I had a long-term ethnographic background – and the places implicated in the chains I traced. My knowledge is variously ethno-graphic, journalistic, and archival, and it is formed in discrete patches. I search for odd connections rather than seamless generalizations, inclusive tables, or comparative grids. (Tsing 2005: x–xi)

My fieldwork started in 2006 and up to 2013 I had conducted nine visits focused in Gwinnett County, particularly in the cities of Lawrenceville and Norcross, although I also followed some interesting leads to the cities of Gainesville in Hall County and Atlanta. I conducted participant observation, indic-ative surveys and interviews within both Mexican and American communities in such diverse settings as commercial areas, religious communities (Catholic and Protestant), schools, the homes of middle-class Mexican families drawn to Atlanta by the city's demand for people with high skills, undocumented immigrants and Mexicans with legal status. Seven main data collection instruments were designed for this Project:

1. Survey of Mexican Immigrants in Norcross – 2006 (EMN)
2. Survey of Mexican Immigrants in Lawrenceville – 2008 (EM)
3. Electronic Survey of Americans – 2009–10 (EAW)
4. Survey of Americans working in the State Bar of Georgia – 2010 (EAL)
5. Interviews with Mexican Immigrants 2006–10 (EnM)
6. Interviews with Americans – 2006–10 (EnA)
7. Interviews with Returned Mexican Immigrants in Morelos (2004–15) (EnMRM).[1]

In the following sections, each time I quote directly from one of these instruments I refer to its particular code and add demographic data (gender, age and ethnic self-identification) when the people interviewed were willing to disclose this information.

Mexican Immigration to the US

Mexican Immigration to the US – historical overview

Mexican immigration to the US is far from being new. The ties that historically bind these two countries are tight and long lasting. The twentieth century shows a fluctuating but rather constant trend. The first two decades were marked by the Mexican Revolution and characterized by strong social turmoil and an intense movement of people, mainly from the borderlands. In 1912, 22,001 Mexicans entered the US, reaching 51,042 by 1920. Between 1910 and 1920, the number of Mexican residing across the border rose from 221,915 to 486,418 (Amescua 2006: 60). Several factors were behind this trend. Aside from the social and political instability and armed conflicts all over Mexico, there was a growing labour demand in the US, particularly for railway construction, but also for the fast growing industrial sector and an agricultural sector that was abandoned by local workers who migrated to the flourishing northern industries.

During the late 1920s and 1930s, there was a notorious decline of Mexican immigrants due to the mass unemployment in the US provoked by the Great Depression. The United States undertook mass deportations of Mexicans in 1921, 1929 and 1939. The 1921 episode can be explained by the homecoming of soldiers from the First World War, which boosted native labour-force availability, whereas the second and third mass deportations were due to the deep economic crisis that made foreign workers not only unnecessary but also a burden to the system (Amescua 2006: 61).

During the 1940s, Mexican immigration started to rise again, propelled by the bracero programme, which started in 1942 and lasted until 1964. The onset of the Second World War made Mexican labour indispensable again, and the governments of both countries signed agreements that allowed Mexicans into the US on temporary agricultural contracts. Alongside them came a parallel wave of undocumented immigrants who took advantage of the accumulated social capital and the social networks built by the *braceros*. Over two decades, more than four million Mexican workers were hired under this programme and the number of undocumented immigrants thought to have reached at least another four million. By the mid-1960s, there was an excess of 'illegal' agricultural workers, which, along with the mechanization of many agricultural processes, led to a saturation of the labour market and end of the bracero programme. But the economic situation in Mexico made it impossible for *braceros* and their families to survive back home, so they kept coming to the US illegally. Although the magnitude of this migration was of some concern for a number of social and political sectors, few efforts were made to implement restrictive policies during these times, mostly because the labour demand remained vigorous. By the mid-1980s, however, Mexican immigration had grown to such proportions that it was inevitable for government at both state and federal levels to seek ways of restricting entry to the US. In 1986, the Immigration Reform and Control Act (IRCA) decreed the illegality of hiring or recruiting undocumented workers, placing responsibility for immigration status verification on employers. At the same time, paths to legalization were offered for two groups of immigrants: 'Aliens who had been unlawfully residing in the United States since before January 1, 1982 (pre-1982 immigrants) were legalized under Section 245A of the Immigration and Nationality Act (INA).

Aliens employed in seasonal agricultural work for a minimum of 90 days in the year prior to May, 1986 (SAWs) were legalized under Section 210A of the INA' (Rytina 2002: 2).

The IRCA had enormous consequences for the future of Mexican immigration to the USA, although the results it produced were radically opposed to those expected. Its main objective was to regulate migratory flows through closing borders, which was supposed to stop new entrances of undocumented immigrants, as well as resolve the legal situation of immigrants already in the US. But legalization created a need to implement a family reunification policy, which consolidated immigrant settlement patterns in the receiving regions and strengthened immigrant social networks, increasing undocumented migration.

It was during those years that immigration acquired its current characteristics. The regions and localities both of origin and destination diversified; the immigrant demographic profile became more heterogeneous with the incorporation of more women, children and indigenous people, along with people with higher educational levels. There was considerable occupational and sectorial diversification in response to greater flexibility and segmentation of labour markets. Additionally, IRCA not only made traditional destinations less appealing, but exploration of new destinations possible. As Zúñiga and Hernández León (2005: xvi) point out:

> Once permanence and settlement became real possibilities, Mexicans were able to choose the destination best suited to their interests, leaving historic immigrant enclaves and settling out of itinerant migratory streams. Once they became residents in localities in Nevada, Idaho, Iowa, Nebraska, North Carolina, or Georgia, family reunifications gave rise to a second international migratory flow. Amnesty beneficiaries brought their wives and children directly from Mexico, something that had long been impossible or very dangerous. In little more than a decade, an array of new destinations had emerged, attracting fresh undocumented flows from Mexico.

The visibility of contemporary Mexican immigration also suggests the beginning of a new historical era. Most new destinations are smaller towns and cities: but it is not just the size of the receiving communities that makes invisibility more difficult. Increasingly, Mexican immigration is a family affair. The presence of wives, children, grandparents and nephews, among other relatives, has an immediate impact on the most important institutions and organizations of receiving towns and cities, churches, schools, clinics and business districts (Zúñiga and Hernández León 2005: xxvii).

The Southeast USA as a New Destination

Historically the Southern US was not an attractive region for Mexican immigrants: its industrial development was slow and 'the presence of a large number of poor blacks and whites who provided a steady pool of low-wage labor' was enough to meet the labour demand (Odem and Lacy 2009: xiv). This tendency drastically shifted during the mid- to late-1980s. During the last decade of the twentieth century the Latino[2] population of North and South Carolina, Georgia, Tennessee and Alabama grew by more than 200 per cent. Of these southeastern states, Georgia is the one where the Latino population represents the higher percentage of total population: 5.3 per cent. Many migrants moved to small towns and rural areas, with the greatest number (467,418 in 2006) in the sprawling Atlanta metro area (ibid.: xvii).

Georgia is now the eleventh state in the country in terms of Latino population. In Dalton County alone, Latinos represent over 20 per cent of the total population, while in five other counties (Echols, Colquitt, Atkinson, Hall and Gwinnett), their proportion ranges from 10 to 20 per cent. As Smith (2001: 1–2) observes:

> Here, the new immigrants who have arrived over the past decade enter a region where most people have no direct experience with immigration. There is little pre-existing infrastructure of Spanish-language institutions [...] Moreover, the distinctive history of the U.S. South means that new immigrants must find their way in a social landscape defined in many locations by the contentious racial divide between black and white.

The Triggering Factors of Immigration to the Southeast

The economic restructuring of this region since 1980 added to changes in immigration policies at the federal level to make it more attractive to immigrants. Labour demand grew exponentially, because of global neoliberal capitalist trends such as greater flexibility and informality, through subcontracting, in labour markets (Portes and Sassen 1987). At the same time local policies aimed at attracting capitals and investments were put in place, making this region very attractive for transnational corporations:

The need of an abundant and flexible workforce to undertake unpleasant and highly demanding jobs was the main tendency in industries such as construction, agriculture and meatpacking. Another magnet for immigrant workforce was the textile industry, including big carpet factories in Whitfield, Georgia. But on top of that Hirshman and Massey identify another fundamental although frequently invisible tendency that explains the fast growing demand for immigrant labor:

> The increasing availability of immigrant workers and their geographic dispersion throughout the country are not simply the product of large corporations trying to lower labor costs. Many individual American families, too, are purchasing more 'immigrant labor' to replace the traditional home-produced goods and services, including child care, lawn care, gardening, and food preparation (in restaurants, in grocery stores, or at home). (Hirshman and Massey 2008: 18)

At the same time, saturation of the labour markets in traditional immigrant receiving areas generated fierce competition for available, and frequently scarce, jobs, along with a notorious drop in wages, which 'pushed the immigrants (particularly those that had recently legalized their status under IRCA) to new destinations' (Zúñiga and Hernández León 2009: 36–7).

By 2010, the Latino population in Georgia numbered 853,689, 8.8 per cent of the total state population (US Census Bureau 2011), despite the fact that the 2008 economic crisis in the US was supposed to have drawn migrants away. Almost half are now American citizens either by birth or naturalization. The composition of the immigration population is particularly relevant for the analysis I present in the following sections: diversity is the norm. It combines immigrants with an ample migratory experience with the newly arrived, but also American-born children of Mexican origin, immigrants with legal status and undocumented immigrants.

Intangible Cultural Heritage as a Space of Conviviality

Culinary Traditions

Mexican culinary traditions (in the plural, since there are many different types of cuisines in the country) have worldwide recognition. My fieldwork in the Atlanta Metropolitan Area showed that food is one of the most valued elements of Mexican culture among Americans (along with music, diversity, festivities and dances, history and the sense of community). Statements such as '[about Mexican culture, I love] food. I'm a foodie and I love to experience cultures other than my own, through food' (EAL1, Afro-American woman, thirty-five years old), or '[I like] the variety and wonderful taste of Mexican food' (EAL18, white American woman, sixty-three years old), were a common thread among almost every conversation in which I was seeking information about positive and negative perceptions of Mexican culture.

When I first arrived in Norcross in 2004, I was surprised to see Mexico all over the public space of the Deep South, particularly through the colourful signs of businesses related to food: *panaderías* (bakeries), *carnicerías* (meat shops), small restaurants and chain restaurants were to be found everywhere. In Lawrenceville, the cyber presence of Mexican restaurants is quite extensive for a small town. A search in the website http://www.yelp.com/ shows twenty-two different places for having Mexican food: *Taco Depot*, *Taco Mac* and *Taquería Los Hermanos* have branches all over Georgia, but other places are unique family business such as *El Gallo Giro*, *Jalapeno Mexican Restaurant*, *Fridas Mexican Restaurant*, *GourMex*, *Don Pedro*, *La Cazuela*, *Cuernavaca Grill*, *The Real Mexican Grill*, *La Salsa Taquería*, *Mi Casa*, *Chona's Mexican Grill* or *La Enchilada*.

Although this variety shows a strong degree of penetration of Mexican food within relatively small communities, the stories behind these restaurants are varied. The owner of restaurant *Zapata* in Norcross was born and raised in Venezuela. He realized after opening his first restaurant that Mexican food was more marketable and profitable than Venezuelan cuisine, so he began incorporating Mexican dishes in his menu until his restaurant became a Mexican one with only a few Venezuelan dishes.

The story of *Willy's Mexicana Grill* is a very different one. With twenty-five branches, all of them located in Georgia, its founder was born in North Carolina. As a teenager he became a fan of what he thought was 'great Mexican food': *burritos*. He went to college in Chapel Hill and after graduating travelled to California where he 'unexpectedly discovered real and authentic Mexican food. Wow, I had no idea what spicy chilli peppers, roasted tomatoes and fresh cilantro could do for my taste buds. [...] Suddenly it all became clear. It hit me like a ton of pinto beans. I was being called to bring big, beautiful burritos to the masses ... or at least to Atlanta' (http://www.willys.com/willys-story). He opened his first restaurant at home with the help of his family; by 2012, he had opened eighteen branches and by 2015 was up to twenty-five.

This story is interesting for several reasons: first, because the owner is American and not Mexican, and, second, because although his chain claims to specialize in 'real and authentic Mexican food', *burritos* are practically unknown and rarely consumed in most of Mexico. Places like Guanajuato, Chihuahua and Sonora have the *burrito* as one of the elements of their local cuisines, but it was popularized as a Mexican dish in Texas and California. The story of *Willy's* thus mirrors the different Mexican migratory waves to the US, since it is based on the influence of Mexican food in the western states, a traditional receiving area for Mexican immigrants, and was consolidated as a successful business because of the more recent migrations (directly from Mexico but also from the traditional receiving areas) to the southeast. The success of *Willy's Mexicana Grill* is not only due to the exponential growth of Mexican population in this area but also to the great appeal that Mexican food has for the American population.

In general, Mexican restaurants in Lawrenceville and Norcross can be classified in three main categories. First, there are popular restaurants whose dishes and flavours are similar to those in Mexico. Frequently cheaper than other options, their settings are more homely (wooden chairs and tables, plastic tablecloths of vibrant colours, *norteño* or *banda* music or a blasting radio show in Spanish). Usually these types of restaurants are filled by Mexican immigrant families longing for familiar tastes and smells. Second, there are more elite (and overpriced) Mexican restaurants that offer more elaborate dishes with more complex presentations along the lines of '*nouvelle cuisine*', a more sophisticated ambiance and with colourful and elegant decorations. These cater to middle- to upper-class customers of both American and Mexican origin. Finally, there are restaurants that offer Tex-Mex or Cal-Mex cuisine, frequently either franchises (like Taco Bell) or fast-food-type restaurants with several branches. These attract a more diversified clientele (Americans and Mexicans of all social classes, incomes and legal status). Their prices are accommodating and the service offers all the advantages of fast and cheap food, along with some typical, standardized and frequently stereotyped flavours.

Day of the Dead

The ritual festivity known as the Day of the Dead is still a strongly held tradition all over Mexico but mainly in rural areas, where most immigrants to Georgia come from. This complex tradition presents a mixture of pre-Hispanic and Catholic-Spanish elements. In the last days of October and the first days of November families prepare to receive their dead relatives, who are thought to come back from the afterworld on those sacred days. Offerings are prepared consisting of the favourite food of the deceased, flowers, candles, incense, salt and water, among other elements. Practices vary from region to region, but generally there is a day devoted to welcoming children who passed away, another for those who did not die from natural causes and a day for honouring all other dead relatives. People expend a great deal of effort, money and emotion in preparing and staging this festivity. The constellation of rites includes cooking (both for the offerings and for the family and friends who visit on those days) and hard work at the cemetery to clean the graves in preparation for the last day (2 November) when a big part of the offerings are taken to the graves and people spend time, sometimes the whole night, accompanying their loved ones.

For many immigrant parents it is of the utmost importance that traditions are not lost, so they do everything possible to keep their children in contact with these and the associated belief systems. At the Day of the Dead celebration organized by the Mexican consulate in Atlanta, there is a yearly contest of offerings, along with a gastronomic and cultural festival. It is a family gathering in which not only Mexicans and Latinos of other nationalities participate, but also whites and African-Americans. During the 2009 celebration, a young father told me: 'I bring my kids so they can see, so they know even a little bit of what Mexico is, of what the nation of their parents is. I want them to feel proud of their roots' (EnM21, man, thirty-three years old). While observing the offerings prepared for this contest, he kept explaining to his children the meaning of each element: 'Look, this is a picture of the deceased ... there they put the clothes he used to wear ... they also put the food that he liked, that is why you see there the *molito*, the *piloncillo*,[3] the peanuts ... Hey kids, come and look (he said with a voice full of emotion), this little soda is called a *chaparrita*, your mother and I used to have it all the time when we were kids.'

Nevertheless, some of the people I interviewed, some with anger, others with worry, and others with shame or even indifference, explained that Mexican culture is being lost among immigrants in the US. While I was observing 'trick or treating' during Hallowe'en in 2010 at a shopping mall in Lawrenceville, where both Mexican and American kids wearing costumes ranging from pumpkins and witches to super heroes and current movie characters went from shop to shop trick or treating the employees, I approached one of the families and started a conversation. When I asked if they were from Mexico they reluctantly confirmed my assumption. After briefly explaining the purpose of my research, I asked them if they still made offerings to their dead relatives. The father answered quickly looking somewhat abashed: 'No, here we don't do it anymore …' (EnM26, man, Mexican), but his wife interrupted him to say 'Of course we do … I mean for some years we have done it. Not this one, because … really, we couldn't find the time, but other times we definitely do it' (EnM27, woman, Mexican). What I could perceive from the looks they exchanged is that they did not follow the tradition anymore, but were ashamed to admit it.

Although the Day of the Dead does remain an important and widespread tradition, not all Mexicans follow it. In urban areas a lot of people have ceased to celebrate the festivity altogether, while others only make a modest offering as a way of honouring the dead. The belief that their dead relatives come back to visit during that period of the year is mostly lost. Even in rural and indigenous areas the Day of the Dead tradition is maintained by younger generations of people who no longer believe that the dead come back, but feel it is an obligation towards their elders to continue with it. Older people really did use these days to feel in contact with their loved ones, to talk to them and update them on the latest successes within the family or the villages. In rural areas more and more people are celebrating Hallowe'en, with a local version of treat or tricking known as 'asking for the *calaverita*' (little skull) where kids go to houses in their neighbourhood to ask for candy, fruit or any other treat. In some villages Hallowe'en penetration, mostly due to media influence, is viewed very negatively and even banned in some places.

While documenting the Day of the Dead in the northeastern area of the state of Morelos, we asked people who had migrated to the US and come back if they reproduced the offerings while they were away. Most of them said no, but only one could explain why clearly. 'What's the point?' he said, 'When my [deceased] parents come back to visit us, they come here, where their home is. They won't be coming to the States, they don't know the way. So why make an offering there? It's absurd' (EnMRM42, man, Mexican, sixty-eight years old).

Yet, in spite of the changes in both form and meaning of the celebrations, the festivity is still alive, and even being admired and adopted by some American people. An elite private middle school in the Atlanta Metropolitan Area asked the parents of one of their Mexican students to organize a workshop for their eighth-graders (some Mexicans, some from other Latin American and Asian countries, and many from the United States) to learn about the history, significance and meaning of this tradition. They learned what elements should go into the offering and what they mean; they worked together at preparing a big offering that was set up in one of the school's hallways. The *Club Hispano La Voz* at Norcross High School organizes a collective offering sometimes accompanied by a gastronomic festival. Both students and teachers wait expectantly every year for this event, which has become emblematic of the Club. Finally, during my fieldwork I came across three American families that decided to make offerings to their own ancestors. One of them told me, that they think 'it is a beautiful way to remember our relatives, to keep their memory alive'.

The Virgin of Guadalupe

Regardless of social, economic, ethnic or educational backgrounds, millions of Mexicans have a great devotion for the Virgin of Guadalupe, and immigrants are no exception. The cult has been analysed from different perspectives by authors such as Giuriati and Masferrer (1998), Alberro (1999), Anderson and Chávez (2009), Gálvez (2009), Odem (2004), León-Portilla (2000) and Gruzinsky (1994), among many others who have addressed subjects such as its symbolism, its social function, its character as an acculturation mechanism or as a symbol of the foundational syncretism of the Mexican nation.

I found a wide array of festivities devoted to the Virgin all around the Archdioceses of Atlanta, whose November 2008 bulletin was entitled 'Events to honor our Lady of Guadalupe', and announced 'a list of the traditional celebrations of the feast of our Lady of Guadalupe around the Archdiocese of Atlanta'. Fifty-six Catholic Churches celebrated the Day of the Virgin (12 December) with a mass, but some organized more complex festivities, including 'bilingual rosary', 'Apparitions of our Lady of Guadalupe', and 'Procession around the Cathedral and ending at the parish hall'. In the Church *Divino Niño de Jesús Mission*, located in Duluth, the celebrations included 'rosaries at homes and apartments, celebration of the forty-seven stars of our Lady's robe'; and the Holy Family Church offered 'mass and dramatization of the apparitions'.

I attended festivities at the Sacred Heart Catholic Church, located in downtown Atlanta. The first part of the event was held at the church's basement where families were gathered around a human-size statue of the Virgin, decorated with dozens of red roses, white ribbons and candles. An eight-year-old girl holding the hand of her grandmother was wearing a traditional garment with an embroidered image of the Virgin. The grandmother proudly told me in Spanish: 'I made it for her myself, with my own hands. It's a lot of work but it's worth it. It's like a present to the Virgin. And my little girl loves to come […]. This is so important for us, because it helps us feel a little bit better, protected, it's like we were home' (EnM 12/12/08). One of the organizers was giving a candle to each of the nearly fifty participants asking us to get in line so the procession could begin.

We went out of the basement towards the church's car park. The statue of the Virgin shouldered by four young men dressed in baggy jeans and tennis shoes headed the procession, surrounded by a group of Aztec dancers playing their traditional instruments. We walked around the block and we went back in through the main entrance, so the Virgin could be respectfully placed in front of the chancel. In Mexico, on 12 December, millions of people from all around the country come to the basilica of the Virgin in Mexico City in huge processions, sometimes walking or doing relay races all the way from their places of origin. Entire streets are closed and one or two highway lanes are occupied by pilgrims. Members of the *Sacred Heart Catholic Church* reproduced their tradition on a smaller scale and within the authorized parameters of the host society, around the block and without interfering with vehicular circulation. According to Lourdes Arizpe: 'In Mexico, processions and parades are an essential component within the heap of practices creating social cohesion' (2009: 168). 'By walking the streets together, those who participate weave their social ties, thus creating or reaffirming a system of codes and communication constituted as intangible cultural heritage' (ibid.: 191–3).

After the procession, people took their seats in the church and more people, Latinos and Americans, begin filling it. One of the organizers explained, in both English and Spanish, the origin and history of the rosary and asked all those willing to participate to line up along the nave, alternating between English and Spanish speakers so that one mystery was recited in Spanish and the next one in English. The prayers (the Holy Fathers and the Hail Marys) were said in both languages. Once the rosary was over, the mariachi started singing *Las Mañanitas* as everyone sang along. They played for over an hour while more people kept coming in. The bilingual mass started with a full attendance, and the festivities continued well into the night with more music and the sharing of *tamales* and *atole*.

The Guadalupan worship in Atlanta is a symbolic and physical space where Mexicans in all their diversity encounter and recognize themselves from what they have in common. Ethnic, class and political differences fade way in a space of conviviality where immigrants can, at least temporarily, set aside the loneliness, vulnerability and fear with which most of them constantly live because for their undocumented status. Here, Mexicans find a safe place where they belong and with whose codes they are familiar.

In spite of it being a Mexican celebration, inclusion of American ways was accepted by all. In addition to the bilingualism of the celebration, accepted local cultural norms included the format of the procession mentioned above. In Mexico, particularly in rural areas and urban popular zones, we frequently find kids crying, screaming, playing and running around in church even during mass. This is not perceived as bad behaviour, but, in Atlanta, the Mexicans participating in the celebration were untroubled by having to abide by the local norm establishing that families with young children should follow the mass through loudspeakers installed in the narthex, which is separated from the nave by soundproofed glass doors, so as not to disturb other participants. The conviviality observed in this case does not, however, always happen so seamlessly. Some parishes build parallel communities to avoid conflicts between the Hispanic and the American ways. Sometimes parishioners actively avoid contact with their Hispanic peers, while others seek ways to promote encounters and better integration.

Conclusions

Migratory experiences and their diversity are crucial for understanding how immigrant lives and cultures are being reshaped and re-signified at the local level in constant interaction with the host societies. The experience of the first immigrants that came to Atlanta during the 1990s from traditional receiving areas in the US after having legalized their status was crucial in smoothing their settlement in this new receiving area.

Their knowledge of American ways of life, including the nuances of social organization, the implicit norms of conduct, and most effective channels for political or social negotiations, among others, constituted the social and cultural capital that they set in motion while exploring new areas. This accumulated social capital was extremely beneficial for new immigrants arriving directly from Mexico because it fostered the construction of social spaces where they could meet and integrate as they set foot into their new reality.

Through the spaces of conviviality, a migrant from Chiapas can encounter people from Veracruz, Morelos, Michoacán, Sonora, Zacatecas or Tabasco. A Zapotec can meet an Otomí or work shoulder-to-shoulder with a Maya. Ethnic and regional specificities mingle, with their characteristic cultural elements put into practice in a new context, generating transformations and new expressive forms whose dynamism and adaptability guarantee their survival. Little by little new cultural practices specific to 'Mexicans in the US' are formed that can be labelled the intangible cultural heritage of immigrants.

Although my research also shows that there are underlying and explicit tensions between 'old' and 'new' immigrants, the old immigrants function as mediators since they socialize the new immigrants into the 'ways things are done in this country'. Their combined presence has produced some familiarization of the local population with Mexican cultural and social practices. This process is not without conflicts and divergent stances. Just as Mexicans have had to learn how to live in the US, Americans have also been learning what being Mexican means. Both cultures are being transformed in the process.

Cultural practices constitute a symbolic space where differences clash and are negotiated, but they are also an arena of communication where people share with others what they are, and what makes them proud. The continuity of intangible cultural heritage as a mechanism for identification and construction of social ties is due to the adaptability that cultural practices show, particularly in contexts where diversity and not homogeneity are the norm.

Migration as a social phenomenon creates contact zones (Pratt 2005) that are diverse and dynamic; within these, immigrants' cultural practices generate the symbolic space needed to build a new community, to break isolation and to tame the vulnerability they live with, even encouraging spaces of political mobilization and organization. But intangible cultural heritage is above all a window through which people can show to others the most valuable and endearing part of what they are, their most deeply meaningful practices and expressions.

One of my reasons for deciding to focus on intangible cultural heritage is that social sciences frequently focus on social problems and conflicts, while setting aside positive and constructive sides of social life. I believe that a comprehensive outlook on social reality must consider not only its frictions, but also its negotiations and encounters.

Practically all the people I interviewed, immigrants and locals alike, were able to tell me stories of support, help, kindness and conviviality, stories of mutual learning that show that the more close, direct and daily is the contact between Mexicans and Americans, the more bridges are built between them. A greater comprehension of their respective life histories generates deeper solidarity and friendship ties. Although this does not always happen, conviviality spaces created in places such as churches, schools and restaurants can become spheres of mutual knowledge and recognition, where mores, traditions, and forms of being and understanding the world can be shared.

Notes

1. This instrument was not specifically designed for this project, but for a project called Intangible Cultural Heritage in Morelos on which I have been collaborating since 2004 under the direction of Lourdes Arizpe.
2. I use Latino or Hispanic interchangeably to refer to people of Latin American descent, bearing in mind that in the regions covered in my research this sector is mostly composed by people of Mexican descent (they represent 67.8 per cent of the Latino population).
3. *Mole* is a Mexican dish that could be compared to a thick sauce, made of chocolate, hot peppers of different kinds, milled grains and a wide variety of spices. *Piloncillo* is a compact mass of molasses used in Mexico as an ingredient in a plethora of traditional dishes, including beverages such a fruit water and *atoles* (sweetened maize drinks), but also as a candy.

References

Alberro, S. (1999) *El águila y la cruz, orígenes religiosos de la conciencia criolla*, Mexico City: Fondo de Cultura Económica and El Colegio de México.

Amescua, C. (2006) 'La Emergencia de Nuevas Formas de Transnacionalidad en la Nueva Era de las Migraciones entre México y Estados Unidos: el caso Amilcingo y Norcross', Master's Degree Thesis, Mexico: Facultad de Filosofía y Letras, Instituto de Investigaciones Antropológicas, UNAM.

Amescua, C. (2010) 'Cultura y migración. El patrimonio cultural inmaterial en las zonas de contacto: ¿una lucha por la autenticidad o una opción para la convivencia?', in *Cuadernos de Migración Internacional* 6, Mexico: Universidad Iberoamericana.

Amescua, C. (2013) 'Anthropology of Intangible Cultural Heritage and Migration: An Unchartered Field', in L. Arizpe and C. Amescua (eds) *Anthropological Perspectives on Intangible Cultural Heritage*, Heidelberg: Springer.

Anderson, C. and E. Chávez (2009) *Our Lady of Guadalupe – Mother of the Civilization of Love*, New York: Doubleday.

Arizpe, L. (2009) *El Patrimonio Cultural Inmaterial de México: Ritos y Festividades en Morelos*, Mexico City: CRIM UNAM, M.A. Porrúa, Cámara de Diputados.

Arizpe, L. (2011) 'Fusión y fricción en la creatividad cultural', in L. Arizpe (ed.) *Compartir el Patrimonio Cultural Inmaterial: Narrativas y Representaciones*, Mexico City: Centro Regional de Investigaciones Multidisciplinarias UNAM, Dirección General de Culturas Populares/CONACULTA.

Besserer, F. (2000) 'Política cuántica: el uso de la radio por comunidades transnacionales', in *Nueva Antropología*, vol. XVII, August, 11–21, México: INAH, CONACULTA, COLMEX, UAM.

Gálvez, A. (2009) *Guadalupe in New York: Devotion and Struggle for Citizenship Rights among Mexican Immigrants*, New York: New York University Press.

Giménez, G. (2007) *Estudios sobre la cultura y las identidades sociales*, Mexico City: Conaculta-ITESO Guadalajara.

Giuriati, P. and Masferrer, E. (eds) (1998) *No temas... Yo soy Tu Madre. Estudios socioantropológicos de los peregrinos a la Basílica*, Mexico City: Centro Ricerche Socio Religiose, Plaza y Valdés Editores.

Gößwald, U. (2007) 'Born in Europe: An International Programme on Representing Migrant Experiences in European Museums', *International Journal of Intangible Heritage* 2: 138–44.

Gruzinski, S. (1994) *La Guerra de las Imágenes: de Cristóbal Colón a Blade Runner*, Mexico City: Fondo de Cultura Económica.

Hafstein, V. (2009) 'Intangible Heritage as a List: From Masterpieces to Representation', in L. Smith and N. Akagawa (eds) *Intangible Heritage*, London: Routledge Taylor & Francis Group, 93–111.

Hafstein, V. (2011) 'Célébrer les différences, renforcer la conformité', in C. Bortolotto (ed.) *Le patrimoine culturel immatériel. Enjeux d'une nouvelle catégorie*, Paris: Maison des Sciences de l'Homme.

Hirshman, C. and Massey, D. S. (2008) 'Places and Peoples: The New American Mosaic', in D. S. Massey (ed.) *New Faces in New Places: The Changing Geography of American Immigration*, New York: Russell Sage Foundation.

Khaznadar, C. (2011) 'Desafíos en la implementación de la Convención de 2003', in L. Arizpe (ed.) *Compartir el Patrimonio Cultural Inmaterial: Narrativas y Representaciones*, Mexico City: Centro Regional de Investigaciones Multidisciplinarias UNAM, Dirección General de Culturas Populares/CONACULTA.

Kirshenblatt-Gimblett, B. (2004) 'Intangible Heritage as Metacultural Production', *Museum International* 56: 52–65.

Kurin, R. (2007) 'Key Factors in Implementing the 2003 Convention Safeguarding Intangible Cultural Heritage', *Journal of Intangible Heritage* 9: 9–22

Le Bot, Y. (2011) 'Migrantes transnacionales y reconstrucciones culturales', in L. Arizpe (ed.) *Compartir el Patrimonio Cultural Inmaterial: Narrativas y Representaciones*, Mexico City: CRIM-UNAM, CONACULTA-DGCP.

Lenzerini, F. (2011) 'Intangible Cultural Heritage: The Living Culture of Peoples', *European Journal of International Law* 22 (1): 101–20.

León-Portilla, M. (2000) *La California Mexicana. Ensayos acerca de su historia*, Mexico City: UNAM, IIH / UABC / IIH.

Levitt, P. (2005) 'Building Bridges: What Migration Scholarship and Cultural Sociology Have to Say to Each Other', *Poetics* 3: 49–62.

Littlefield Kasfir, S. and Olabiyi Babalola, J. Y. (2004) 'Tema de debate actual: autenticidad y diáspora', *Museum International* 221–2: 190–7.

Machuca, A. (2011) 'Transmisión y producción del sentido en el fenómeno migratorio: su incidencia en la conceptualización del Patrimonio Inmaterial', in L. Arizpe (ed.) *Compartir el Patrimonio Cultural Inmaterial: Narrativas y Representaciones*. Mexico City: CRIM-UNAM, CONACULTA-DGCP.

Margolies, D. S. (2011) 'Music in the 21st Century Transmission of Texas–Mexican Conjunto Music in the 21st Century', *International Journal of Intangible Heritage* 6: 26–33.

Nettleford, R. (2004) 'Migration, Transmission and Maintenance of the Intangible Heritage', *Museum International* 56: 78–83.

Odem, M. (2004) 'Our Lady of Guadalupe in the New South: Latin American Immigrants and the Politics of Integration in the Catholic Church', *Journal of American Ethnic History* 23 (Fall): 29–60

Odem, M. and Lacy, E. (2009) *Latino Immigrants and the Transformation of the US South*, Athens, GA and London: the University of Georgia Press.

Portes, A. and Sassen, S. (1987) 'Making it Underground', *American Journal of Sociology* 3: 30–61.

Pratt, M. L. (2005) 'Arts of the Contact Zone', in G. Stygall (ed.) *Reading Context*, Boston, MA: Thomson Wadsworth.

Rytina, N. (2002) 'IRCA Legalization Effects: Lawful Permanent Residence and Naturalization through 2001', Paper presented at *The Effects of Immigrant Legalization Programs on the United States: Scientific Evidence on Immigrant Adaptation and Impacts on US Economy and Society*, The Cloister, Mary Woodward Lasker Center, NIH Main Campus, 25 October.

Schmitt, T. M. (2008) 'The UNESCO Concept of Safeguarding Intangible Cultural Heritage: Its Background and Marrakchi Roots', *International Journal of Heritage Studies* 14 (2), 95–111, doi:10.1080/13527250701844019.

Smith, B. E. (2001) 'The New Latino South: An Introduction – A Product of the Joint Project Race and Nation: Building New Communities in the South', Memphis, TN: Center for Research on Women at the University of Memphis, the Highlander Research and Education Center, and the Southern Regional Council (December). Available online: http://www.intergroupresources.com/rc/The New Latino South An Introduction.pdf [accessed 16 June 2015].

Stefano, M., Peter, D. and Corsane, G. (2012) *Safeguarding Intangible Cultural Heritage*, Woodbridge: The Boydell Press.

Tsing, A. (2005) *Friction. An Ethnography of Global Connection*, Princeton, NJ: Princeton University Press.

UNESCO (1972) 'Convention Concerning the Protection of the World Cultural and Natural Heritage'. Available online: http://whc.unesco.org/en/conventiontext/ [accessed 12 June 2011].

UNESCO (2003) 'Convention for the Safeguarding of the Intangible Cultural Heritage'. Available online: http://www.unesco.org/culture/ich/index.php?lg= en&pg=00022 [accessed 12 June 2011].

US Census Bureau (2011) Available online: https://www.census.gov/prod/cen2010/ briefs/c2010br-04.pdf [accessed 18 December 2014].

Van Zanten, W. (2011) 'La cultura viva entre el amanecer y el crepúsculo. Reflexiones acerca del tiempo, la tecnología y el resgurado de la cultura viva', in L. Arizpe (ed.) *Compartir el Patrimonio Cultural Inmaterial: Narrativas y Representaciones*, México: Centro Regional de Investigaciones Multidisciplinarias UNAM, Dirección General de Culturas Populares/CONACULTA.

Villaseñor, I. and Zolla, E. (2012) 'Del Patrimonio Cultural Inmaterial o la Patrimonialización de la Cultura', in *Cultura y Representaciones Sociales* 6 (12): 75–101. Available online: http://www.revistas.unam.mx/index.php/crs/article/ view/30475 [accessed 15 February 2013].

Vlachaki, M. (2007) 'An Educational Programme about Migration in Crossing Cultures through the Intangible Heritage: An Educational Programme about Migration in Greece', *International Journal of Intangible Heritage* 2: 94–102.

Zúñiga, V. and Hernández-León, R. (2005) *New Destinations. Mexican Immigration in the United States*, New York: Russell Sage Foundation.

Zúñiga, V. and Hernández-León, R. (2009) 'The Dalton Story, Mexican Immigration and Social Transformation in the Carpet Capital of the World', in M. Odem and E. Lacy (eds) *Latino Immigrants and the Transformation of the US South*, Athens, GA and London: the University of Georgia Press.

Part Three

The Politics of Culture, Gender, Religion and Place

7

Local Histories and New Museological Approaches in China

Pan Shouyong

Introduction

This chapter investigates China's new museum movement through both diachronic and synchronic perspectives, offering a comprehensive interpretation of local history museums within the development of new museological approaches. Over the past twenty years, I have been involved in more than ten new village museum, ecomuseum, and county museum programmes, including Gong-mi-a Miao Village Museum, Xiaohuang Village Dong Chorus Museum, Anji Ecomuseum Cluster, Beichuan County Museum of Folklore (in the National Park created to remember the victims of the devastating earthquake of May 2008), the China National Museum of Ethnology, Taihang (Mountain Tai) Three Villages Museum, and Songyang Countryside Museum.

According to statistics published by the State Administration of Cultural Heritage, there are about 3,200 museums belonging to the regional and local history museum category among China's 4,510 museums, and more than 45 per cent of the National Exhibition Award winners from 2005 to 2015 are about local history. Many researchers are becoming increasingly aware of the local museum boom and new trends in the museum movement in China, yet a theoretically informed and methodologically systematic study designed to assess the meaning of this social and cultural development and the practices associated with it is still lacking.

A Brief History of Museum Development in China

The museum has been constructed as a symbol of civilization and a cultural instrument in China society since 1905, the year in which the first Chinese museum, Nantong Museum, was opened to the public (Wang 2001). Its founder, Dr Jian Zhang, built this new institution in his hometown himself, to declare both his new philosophy of Chinese-nationhood and his museological concerns. The symbolism of Nantong was complex and multi-layered, acting as a sign for Chinese modernity and national liberation. This museum and its followers mediated many of society's basic values, cultural, economic and political, through their collections, exhibitions and programmes.

Museum development in China can be succinctly divided into three phases (Su 1995). From 1905 to 1949 is the first period. In this period, the museum concept was brought into China from outside regions such as Japan, Europe and North America, and many big cities of eastern China began to set up their own museums. From 1905 to 1937, the China Museum was established, and during this period, the Palace Museum at Beijing and National Museum of History at Beijing opened to the public. The Central Museum at Nanjing, the capital city at that time, started its process of construction and preparation to house exhibits. These developments took place during the era of the (Nationalist) Republic of China. The main objective was to collect the national treasures and artefacts of aboriginal peoples, and to provide useful information for building the new Chinese *nation.* Unfortunately, when the Japanese colonial rulers intervened, Chinese museum development suffered a severe reverse. In fact, most museums were destroyed by the Japanese army: of the 140 museums that existed in 1937, only fourteen were left in 1949.

The second phase occurred from the establishment of the People's Republic of China in 1949 to the start of *National Opening and Reforms* in the 1980s. During the 1950s, five out of the ten 'Great New Buildings' in Beijing, the new capital, were museums, such as the China History Museum, Chinese Revolution Museum, China Military Museum, China Agriculture Museum and the Cultural Palace of Ethnic Minorities. The new central government attached great importance to museum undertaking, but China did not have museum theory of its own at that time. During the 1950s, China adopted the museum system of the former Soviet Union, changing the museum from an educational institution to a propaganda institution, an influence that we can still easily find today (Su 1995). To legitimate and consolidate Marxist Historical Materialism, every provincial museum was directed to collect archaeological finds and fine art works, while also offering a display of *general Chinese history* modelled on that of the China History Museum in Tian-an-men Square (Yu 1992). The kind representation of history offered by museums was made consistent with 'political correctness'. In Chinese, we refer to *cutting feet to fit new shoes*: archaeological findings, objects and exhibitions were *feet,* and the theory of the stages of development provided by Karl Marx were the *shoes.* When the *shoes* changed, the *feet* had to be cut to fit them.

We also say that the museum is 'the book on the wall', which means that in general the development of museums in relation to historical materialism, nationalism and cultural identity in China is inextricably linked to politics. During the *Cultural Revolutionary* period, i.e. from 1966 to 1976, every county government established a kind of museum known as a *Socialist Construction Achievement Museum.* Many of these *SCA* museums were the predecessors of county museums.

By the end of the 1980s there were more than 1,000 museums in the country, 300 of them county museums.

The third phase is from the 1990s to the present. The rapid economic growth and opening-up policy led to changes in the cultural, political and social-economic environment. During the new process of 'modernization' and identification with Chineseness, previously proscribed historical-political ideologies resurfaced and people in China experienced a period of history reconstruction and identity confusion. Experimentation with new ideas and new practices was encouraged. During this period, along with rapid social, cultural and political transformation, China also experienced a rapid growth of local history museums and regional museums. Many museums emphasize their 'regional roots' and the local history narratives that they provide (Nitzky 2012).

Moving into the twenty-first century, between 200 and 400 new museums were established each year in China, which brings the total number today to approximately 4,600 nationwide. More than three quarters of these museums are about local histories and *for local communities*. This is the new trend behind the museum boom, which will not slow down till the 2020s according to the National Report on Museum Planning and Strategy from 2010 to 2020 (Huang 2009).

Table 7.1 Chinese Museum Statistics, 1905–2015

1905	1937	1949	1980	1991	2005	2009	2010	2011	2012	2013	2014	2015
8	140	14	407	1215	2300	2970	3145	3489	3789	3866	4156	4510

The Museum Boom and New Museological Movement

With about 300 new museums being created each year, not simply in cities but also in small towns and villages, China has now become the country best known for the rapid growth in numbers and the steady improvement in quality of its museums, including those based on the collections of private individuals. We are accustomed to think of the twenty-first century as China's museum golden age.

As I noted earlier, more than 45 per cent of the National Exhibition Award winners from 2005 to 2015 are about local history. The approximately 3,000 museums dedicated to regional and local history represent a foundation upon which new interpretations and expressions of local histories are constructed and displayed, specifically rooted in oral history and collective memory. These local history museums, especially those village museums that offer unofficial representations of the history of local places and societies, are a new approach to museology in China, which marks an important departure from the *traditional* museums intended to promote national history narratives.

Based on the official list of museums published annually by China's State Administration of Cultural Heritage from 2002 to 2012 and the China Museum Society Annual Report from 2008 to 2012 we can highlight further important features of China's museum boom. First, all of the provincial museums rebuilt their main buildings between 2002 and 2012, and among them Shandong Provincial Museum, Liaoning Provincial Museum and Jilin Provincial Museum established a third new home. Second, of the 4,510 museums that now exist nationally, more than 75 per cent are middle-sized or small museums. Third, private museums are a totally new phenomenon in China. By the end of 2014, more than 745 private museums passed the national museum assessment. But in reality, there are around 1,700 private museums in China, which means that almost 1,000 of them are still not registered on the official list of museums.

The Entanglements of ICH (Intangible Cultural Heritage) Practices in China

China was one of the first countries to ratify the UNESCO 'Convention for the Safeguarding of the Intangible Cultural Heritage' in 2004. Subsequently, promotion and preservation of intangible cultural heritage in China has occurred through a number of policies and practices at the national, provincial and local levels. Along with national implementation of the Law on Intangible Cultural Heritage, a series of national surveys, and the Intangible Heritage Inheritor List, the government employs cultural traditions to enhance nation building, ethnic solidarity and social harmony.

Intangible heritage in China has therefore become another form of authorized discourse to organize and formulate local folklore, performing arts, rituals and social practices into a unified national body of knowledge. Many other actors besides the state participate in this national and regional campaign, including business operators, scholars, tourism investors and local community groups. Private collectors organize cultural museums to represent local living heritage. University scholars and academic institutes develop research projects to support local governments for the development and promotion of local culture. Various new terms relating to intangible heritage have emerged in the public media to fulfil the modern Chinese desire to search for 'authenticity' in conjunction with the influx of modernity and industrialization, such as 'yuan-sheng-tai–wen-hua' (the original and natural state of culture) or 'huo-tai-yi-chan' (living heritage). The growth of ethnic tourism – targeting domestic and international tourists – has also motivated a search for, and consumption of, living culture, especially in the ethnic minority areas. A range of understandings, interpretations and representation of intangible heritage has emerged in China. These practices are not isolated developments, but arose from different value systems that make specific claims to cultural heritage against the background of China's political, social and economic transitions. There is an interplay of multiple actor perspectives to examine in considering the different forms and values of intangible heritage.

China takes inventory-making as the core of its legal system for safeguarding ICH today. Its modes of classification, application and administration of inventories are very different from these of other countries. There are four different levels of inventory programmes: state-level, provincial-level, city-level and county-level. The State Council published in 2006 the first batch of state-level ICH items on a 518-item list that included the *Spring Festival, Beijing opera, Acupuncture,* the *Legend of Madame White Snake* and *Shaolin Kung Fu.* ICH items are classified into ten types: folk literature, traditional music, dancing, opera, arts and crafts, *quyi* (Chinese folk art forms, including ballad singing, story-telling, comic dialogues, clapper talks, cross talks, etc.), folk customs, acrobatic performances, traditional sports and traditional medicine. Obviously, this specifically Chinese classification cannot match UNESCO ICH domains. In 2006, 2008 and 2011, the thirty-one provincial governments (containing four Municipalities, five National Autonomous Regions and two Special Administrative Regions) published Provincial-level ICH Inventories on three occasions, which included 8,566 items. Almost every city or county government has also published a city-level or county-level ICH Inventory three or four times during the same period. According to what remain incomplete statistics, the total number of items listed at city-level and county-levels is more than 18,000. But only two kinds of inventories (state-level and provincial-level) are actually recognized by the Law on Protection of ICH in China.

The State Council has also announced on three occasions the names of 1,488 people who are designated to pass on China's intangible cultural heritage. These people are so-called ICH 'inheritors'. A fourth list of state-level ICH inheritors was made on the basis of 490 nominees from thirty-one provinces, regions and municipalities in October 2012, and this new inheritor list will be announced soon. The inheritor system is an important part of the inventory-making system. This system also has four different levels in practice, meaning that the provincial governments, city governments and county governments have named their own lists of inheritors.

Apart from inventory-making and the inheritors system, China has also established Cultural Ecological Protection Zones in order to build up a living culture area. This is a new creation that is a kind of ecomuseum. To date, fifteen Cultural Ecological Protection Zones have been established at the state-level. In 2012, China adjusted the process of inventory-making based on a one-year survey, self-assessment and reexamination. Six state-level ICH items have been cancelled, two items were scheduled for rectification with a definite time period, and ninety-seven items adjusted. The provincial-level items and local-level items are in the process of adjustment and rectification. Inventory-making will now be updated normally and regularly, and updates do not mean more items will be added to the lists.

Although China's national ICH policy making started in the mid-1990s, the concept and principles of ICH remained new to China before 2000. Nowadays, even a housewife knows the term *feiyi* (ICH in Chinese) and the benefits of *feiyi.* When I did my anthropological fieldwork in an ethnic minority village in Guizhou province ten years ago, the village leader showed me her grand plan to establish an ICH museum in the village. It was a little bit of a shock to me. I know that the local community takes the ICH Inventory at all levels as an important cultural resource from which they can themselves benefit sooner or later. The local people do not care much about the social and cultural changes in the wider world, increasing globalization and its perceived homogenizing effects on culture, but they do care about their lands, their way of life, history and tradition.

Local governors, such as town leaders and county leaders, take inventory-making as part of their regular administrative work, and care about the state-level and provincial-level inventory, but not about the local-level inventory. Most researchers, in contrast, have realized our rich and varied intangible cultural heritage is in danger of disappearing, not only in China but everywhere else. The ways to preserve or protect the heritage are to do a professional survey of it, to keep accurate records of it, and to make inventories of it at different levels in the whole country (and in the wider world). So we have realized that we do have the same aims as local people: to ensure the survival and vitality of the world's living local, regional and national cultural heritage. Heritage does not mean a good life always, but it never means a bad life. Another kind of heritage is traditional agricultural heritage, which is similar to ICH, and closely related to local history, community, land, agricultural technology and tradition, i.e. local-level heritage.

History Representation and New Museological Approaches

In 2003, the National Museum of China was established simply by merging two separate museums that had occupied the same building since 1959: the Museum of the Chinese Revolution in the northern wing, which originated in the Office of the National Museum of the Revolution, founded in 1950 to preserve the legacy of the 1949 revolution; and the National Museum of Chinese History in the southern wing, which originated in the Beijing National History Museum, founded in 1949, and the Preliminary Office of the National History Museum, founded in 1912. In 2011, the museum reopened after four years of renovation. This vast comprehensive museum, tasked to safeguard and to display China's larger historical legacy, has a total floor space of nearly 2.2 million square feet and twenty-eight exhibition galleries. But the permanent exhibition (*General Chinese History*) was replaced by *Ancient Chinese Civilization*, meaning that you cannot find Chinese national history in this museum. Indeed, the new National Museum of China has changed its mission from safeguarding national history to focusing on both history and arts. Some professionals in fact criticized the National Museum of China for taking over the material of the China National Museum of Art (Song 2011).

At the same time, most provincial museums turned to pay more attention to representation of local history, emphasizing both ancient history and contemporary history. Their historical narratives, representations and interpretation systems have changed from displaying a macro history to focusing on local stories and memories that provide a living history.

Local or community museums, such as village museums, ecomuseums and community museums, emerged from the late-1990s onwards. From these museums on ethnic minorities or local history, we can learn about the multiple histories and forms of life of local villages and villagers that were previously unrepresented in Chinese museums. Ethnic minority museums are very different from the Ethnic or Folk Cultural Park in eastern China that emerged during the 1990s. Critics have pointed out that this Chinese tourism-style theme park only represents 'the way of being ethnic minorities' in a park context and not in real life. Looking into the different museum narratives, we can find the common values that they share with each other, that is, preserving tangible and intangible heritages for future generations, trying to know the past, make sure of the present and foresee the future. History is a kind of resource. But this is only a fraction of the whole story, which only skims the surface of this influential phase in the Chinese living heritage industry.

Up to 2015, forty ecomuseums, twenty community museums and more than 500 county museums made a wide contribution over the whole country. Ecomuseums such as Suo-jia Miao Ethnic Ecomuseum and Tang-an Dong Ethnic Ecomuseum in Guizhou province took the whole community as a museum, including settlements, the landscape, living cultural heritage and the local people. Looking at specific practices among these new museums, we notice big changes in museological approaches in China. I will specifically review the shift in museological philosophy in the evaluation of objects, technological practices and curatorial methods recently introduced for the protection of intangible cultural heritage.

My team and I were involved in constructing more than ten local museums, but I will focus here on two specific museum programmes and give an account of the impact of these museums on village life. These two museums are located in Guizhou province, southwestern China. One is the Gong-mi-a Village Museum in Leishan county and the other is the Xiao-huang Village Dong Chorus Museum in Congjiang county.

Gong-mi-a Village Museum opened in the spring of 2008, the Chinese Olympic Year, which was supported by the Chinese National Museum of Ethnology, Beijing. *Gong-mi-a* in the Miao language means 'a beautiful place to live', but the Miao name is too difficult for outsiders to spell and memorize, even including members of Han Chinese and Shui-zu ethnic groups living in neighbouring villages. They only knew its Chinese name 'shang-ma-lu', meaning 'going to highway or the upper highway'. The name is a strange one, given that for centuries the villagers hadn't even known a highway. If 'ma-lu' does mean 'highway', or any kind of modern road, such things became known to the villagers only very recently. It has been suggested that this word might be a link with the transport and trading of tea by horse in history, meaning the 'horse way'. Yet since the museum opened, villagers tried to let their neighbours and visitors know they are *gong-mi-a* and it really worked. The Miao people have preserved a legend of history of migration from far eastern China, and the story they tell is solemn and stirring.

'No more than three sunny days in a row, and no more than three square feet of flat ground' – so the saying goes. Communication in Guizhou province is extremely difficult. Gong-mi-a is about 117 km from the county town, and about 300km from the capital. Beyond this point, there is no public transport, and it is a bumpy and circuitous drive along country roads that wind up into the mountains, dusty on sunny days and muddy when it rains. The villages on either side of the road are built on the hillside, and are hidden deep in the mountains. They are all very similar in appearance, and it is hard to tell the difference between Gong-mi-a and the Han Chinese or Shui-zu villages around it, meaning that they share the same landscape or place with other ethnic groups. The villagers didn't even know the correct date for when their ancestors first settled in this beautiful land. The Shui-zu had the historical record of their own writing system, whereas the Miao made cloth decoration and oral legends their history book.

With a population of only 130 (this number dropped to 100 in 2015), this small branch of the Miao ethnic group decided to build a museum of their own in the village in 2008. They would like to let the younger generation and their neighbours know their history, title and culture. At that moment, Mrs Wei Ronghui, a deputy director of the China National Museum of Ethnology, had just visited the village during one of her research surveys. Wei's grandmother was born in the village, her father had been a teacher in the community, so she stopped by to see some relatives. They talked about the village museum plan, and they wanted her to give them some help, because the village itself did not have sufficient funds or experience to set up a museum. We discussed with the villagers why they wanted a museum, what kind of museum it would be and how they could get it built. We tried to let them know what other museums were like, and they quickly grasped the idea of the ecomuseum, asking questions like 'isn't that kind of making the whole village into a museum?' But they didn't want to hear all about the first Chinese ecomuseum Suo-ga, and they didn't want just to copy it. They wanted to focus on their own history and stories.

To represent their history in a museum is a big challenge for this Miao group. They have only oral history and legends. It is said that their ancestors settled in this place a long time ago, but no historical records shed light on the matter. It is also said that this branch belonged to the Ba-zhai Miao, who came from the far east of China thousands of years ago. Even the local elite and local governors had no idea about the history of Gong-mi-a and its legends. The only exceptions to this focus on oral culture would be the King Frog Festival (Wa-gong-jie) and traditional costume, both of which are important elements in their history. During the discussion, the Wei family offered to lend their house for use as a temporary museum until the new building was completed. During this interim period, everyone talked enthusiastically about the museum, which they knew was 'good for the village', and which they believed would bring constructive change and hope. Just three months later, with our team's help, the museum was built, villagers re-established a legendary and traditional festival and even set up a small cultural heritage foundation. In the early autumn of 2008, the small village museum opened to the public. Because it contains their history and traditions, the villagers see the museum itself as a part of their history, and do their best to improve it, even if it is still small. At the same time, the museum became one of the UNESCO-sponsored culture and development projects linked to the United Nations Millennium Development Goals. From that point on there was a lot of support for the Gong-mi-a group, and village life changed considerably. For example, more than thirty villagers visited Beijing and more than twenty villagers visited the USA in 2010. By May 2011, the new museum building was complete, and the previously dusty and muddy road connecting the village to the outside world had been completely rebuilt. The new museum is a two-storey timber building, covering 300 square metres. As one villager put it, 'We were late for the Industrial Revolution. We will not be late for this new revolution. Our people only began to know about the outside world, we would like our young generations to know ourselves better too.'

Xiaohuang Village Dong Chorus Museum is a village museum too. Xiaohuang village is famous for the Grand Songs of the Dong Ethnic Group inscribed on the UNESCO Intangible Cultural Heritage List. The county town is about 70km from Xiaohuang village, but it will take three hours to get there. The inhabitants of Gong-mi-a and Xiaohuang did not even know of each other's existence until September 2009, when our programme team took Gong-mi-a villagers to visit Xiaohuang. Now the villagers frequently visit each other, for the museum programme led them to make friends. The Dong Chorus, which is called Dong Ka Lau in the Dong language, is not only on UNESCO's World Oral and Intangible Heritage List, but also on China's National Intangible Heritage List. Since 2005, when the Dong Chorus was added to the national list, the local government has supported the idea of building a performance and exhibition hall (rather than a museum) in the village. Xiaohuang's situation was similar to that of Gong-mi-a before it became known as the home of the Dong Chorus a few years ago. Of course, the intangible heritage protection programme in China, and indeed in the world, only began at the beginning of the twenty-first century. The Dong ethnic group established their villages along rivers, not hidden away in the mountains as the Miao ethnic group did, so their lands are richer than those of the Miao and their villages bigger. At the end of 2008, we decided to choose the Dong museum as one of cultural outputs 2.1 project sites of the United Nations Millennium Development Plan in September 2009. The subsequent story of the museum was similar to that of the Gong-mi-a Village Museum in many other ways as well. Villagers discussed every practical detail with us, such as the museum's focus, its name and its management structure.

In April 2010, our team helped villagers carry out a detailed survey in Xiaohuang village, including a careful study of the space, scale and the exhibition environment of two buildings that could be used for museum display, drawing up floor-plans and analyzing the strengths and weaknesses of the two buildings. Also, some villagers visited Gong-mi-a village and the Beijing Capital Museum. The residents came up with the specific proposal to enhance the Xiaohuang Village Dong Chorus Museum, as it was finally called, by making the whole village a museum. The main means of exhibition follows a multipoint interactive model. Alongside the main, relatively unchanging, museum, which includes objects collected from local families, there are items on display everywhere in the village, and every family provides an exhibit site. There are to be display areas throughout the village, showing the history and culture of the Dong people, the history and legends of Dong Ka Lau and the achievements of the 2.1 Programme, all stemming from the decision to turn the village into an ecomuseum.

A little later, construction work began on the new museum building, with financial support from the State Ethnic Affairs Commission. It cost about 400,000RMB, including the museum building, and software and hardware for displays. The museum is a three-storey timber building with wooden walls and a wooden floor, extending over 432 square metres, each side twelve metres long. The County Bureau of Culture, Radio and TV and Tourism was in charge of the museum display, which took Dong Ka Lau as its main theme. On the ground floor is a display of Xiaohuang's natural ecology and farming culture; the theme of the first floor is the Dong Chorus, focusing on introducing 'zuo-ge-xing-yue' or 'song and moon' singing,[1] by means of scene recreation; on the second floor is the exhibition of folk customs and costume. There are ninety-six objects in the museum, all of them modern and contemporary items. In addition, there are some examples of embroidery, a collection of which is in the process of being built up. What impact has the museum had on Xiaohuang village? Has it been positive or negative?

The chief representative of the UNESCO office in Beijing once asked: 'What is it that we find? What is it that we do? What do we leave to the villagers?' Perhaps it is not yet possible to answer this question, but the answers might be as follows: 'What we do is try hard to answer these three questions, which means that what we find is the legend and power of the Dong Chorus; what we do is respect the villagers' thoughts and choices, and meet their demands about the songs; and what we leave the villagers is a sense of their own cultural identity and an awareness of cultural protection'. The villagers also tried to give their answers to these questions: 'we found our special feathers different from our neighbours, and we found a good opportunity to develop our community in the future; we had a museum of our own, and we received a lot of support from outside, so that we no longer fear for our future. We like our songs, which are a part of our life, something we get from our ancestors and our land; we need to keep them and pass them on to our descendants'.

Davis (1999) has pointed out that the 'ecomuseum is a sense of place'. Ashworth and Graham (2005: 3) suggested that 'senses of places are ... the products of the creative imagination of the individual and of society, while identities are not passively received but are ascribed to places by people'. They are thus 'user deter-mined, polysemic and unstable through time'. Ashworth, Graham and Tunbridge (2007) have emphasized how heritage and museums are used to encourage people to identify with particular places and 'traditions', but Tilley (2006) pointed out that landscapes are 'actively re-worked, interpreted and understood in relation to differing social and political agendas, forms of social memory'.

We insist that the 'ecomuseum is a sense of history and place', and that 'senses of places and histories are … the products of the creative imagination of the individual and of society, while identities are not passively received but are ascribed to places and histories by people'. 'History identity' has the same importance as 'place identity', and these two cases challenge any way of thinking about history, culture and environment as discrete social facts rather than as a whole.

History cannot be separated from the whole context. For example, the Gong-mi-a people said they came from the far east of China and used to be prosperous. This could be seen as just a statement about the past by a historian, but for the Gong-mi-a it represents their whole identity, their origins, migration story, land, rice, festivals, traditions and so on. This is why they made their whole village into a museum. As for Xiaohuang, they thought a museum of their traditional song was good enough, and that they only needed to focus on one thing not everything. Some anthropologists have defined the past as a negotiable good (Herzfeld 1991; Nitzky 2012). According to this argument, historical narratives of events, people and sites are historically legitimated authenticities, and repositories of objects, architecture or landscapes from the past. But a museum is not just a container to hold them all, but an interacting medium for communication. Did Herzfeld imply that history is a handmaiden of politics, economics and culture? If so, history means everything but itself, and I would not agree with that.

Many other examples of new approaches in China could be reviewed in more depth here, such as the Anji Ecomuseum cluster, the Beichuan County Museum of Folklore and the memorialization of the May 2008 earthquake, and the private museums movement, but my space is limited. Graburn (2015: 4) described Anji Ecomuseum cluster as the 'grown up ecomuseum'. It is certainly not a 'traditional' ecomuseum in the sense of those originating in 1970s' France, and transferred to China (via Norway) in Guizhou and later in Guangxi. Graburn argued that 'The overall plan of showing how the county consists of industries and people who are in turn dependent on traditions of agriculture and forestry which are in turn dependent on the soils, land forms and climate of the area is a logical enlargement on the original Ecomuseum premise' (ibid.). In fact, Anji Ecomuseum might be closer to the roots of Eco- which is derived from the Ancient Greek οἶκος (OIKOS) meaning 'family household business' like a farm, referring as much to human management (as in Eco-nomics) as 'nature', as in Eco-logy. Only five years after Anji Ecomuseum opened in 2009, we find that there is an increasing polarization among the twelve ecomuseums in the cluster. The White Tea Ecomuseum,[2] which is run by a local (public) corporation and the White Tea Society, and the Bamboo Ecomuseum, which is run by the Bamboo Botanical Garden, a completely private corporation, have received more investment and are proving very successful, attracting a growing number of visitors, whereas village museums are not enjoying the same kind of success. Yet history needs to be taken particularly seriously in this region if the local museums are to provide the maximum social benefits for local people as well as an educational experience for visitors. Ninety-two per cent of the residents of Anji county are descended from immigrant families that settled there after the original population was decimated during the Taiping Heavenly Kingdom rebellion of 1851–64 against the Qing imperial government, increasingly weakened by the encroachment of the Western European powers.[3]

Conclusion

Museums play an important role in shaping and defining both history identity and place identity. A museum is a place not only for storing old things such as objects, memories and histories, but also for communicating and sharing cultural values. This place makes it possible for a local community to look through its history and foresee the future better. Every local person forms personal and collective level links to the past, thus developing his/her history and place identity, and experiencing it in an emotionally laden way.

Many social theorists and historians have suggested that we are currently living in a period in which the identities of the past are becoming increasingly irrelevant and in which new identities, and new identity formations, are being created. The major identity colossus forged in the nineteenth century, and subsequently spread over much of the globe – nation-state identity – has been the subject of particular debate; and theorists have attempted to identify alternative, post-national (in the sense of post-nation-statist) identity constructions. The proliferation of museums in the nineteenth century was undoubtedly closely bound up with the formation and solidification of nation-states in, and subsequently beyond, Western Europe. A crucial question for museums today concerns their role in a world in which nation-state identities are being challenged. Are they too inextricably entangled in 'old' forms of identity to be able to express 'new' ones?

Understanding how and why museums are able to act as manifestations of identity or sites for the contestation of identities requires a 'de-naturalizing' of the concept of 'identity'. That is, we need to be able to see our notions of particular identities, including 'national identity', not as universal but as historically and culturally specific. What is entailed in 'thinking' and 'doing', 'the nation' or 'the public'? And what role have museums played in such 'thinking' and 'doing'? What is it about museums that makes them suitable – and sometimes not so suitable – for certain kinds of identity 'work'?

This exploration of the new museum movement and new museological approaches in China has resulted in a range of findings that suggests that the local museums such as local history museums, ecomuseums, county museums or community museums are the significant sites and landscapes through which local people construct a sense of locality and knowledge of themselves through their history, memories, traditional song or legends. The research also illustrates the new trend of the museum movement towards the awakening of consciousness of local history all over China, paralleled by the retreat of national museums like the China National Museum and the provincial museums from making history-centred exhibitions and their replacement by art history exhibitions or exhibitions of national treasures. Perhaps the influence of the former Soviet Union on the Chinese museum enterprise is finally going with the wind.

Notes

1. '*zuo-ge-xing-yue*', can be translated as 'song and moon'. It means singing songs the whole night. By tradition, Dong people encourage their teenagers to court boyfriends or girlfriends through singing these love-songs. It is said that 'rice nourishes the body and songs nourish the soul', so song is the only way to date a girl.
2. White tea is a kind of green tea.
3. Before the Taiping Heavenly Kingdom period there were two counties, Anji and Xiaofeng county, with a total population of 540,000, settled during the Han Dynasty (206 BC to AD 220). As a result of the drastic reduction of population provoked by the violence, the Qing governor decided to merge them into a single county, Anji. Even today, Anji county's population of 520,000 remains below its mid-nineteenth century level.

References

Ashworth, G. J. and Graham, B. (eds) (2005) *Senses of Place: Senses of Time*, Aldershot: Ashgate.

Ashworth, G. J., Graham B., and Tunbridge, J. E. (eds) (2007) *Pluralising Pasts: Heritage, Identity and Place in Multicultural Societies*, Ann Arbor: Pluto Press.

Davis P. (1999 *Ecomuseums: A Sense of Place*, London: Leicester University Press.

Graburn, N. (2015) 'Anji County – The Ecomuseum Grows Up!', in Anji Ecomuseum (ed.) *Papers on Chinese Ecomuseum Forum: Anji, China*. Hangzhou Anji Ecomuseum.

Herzfeld, M. (1991) *A Place in History: Social and Monumental Time in a Cretan Town*, Princeton: Princeton University Press.

Huang, C. Y. (2009) *The National Report on Chinese Museum Planning and Strategy from 2010 to 2020*, Beijing: China State Administration of Cultural Heritage.

Nitzky, W. (2012) 'Community Empowerment at the Periphery? Participatory Approaches to Heritage Protection in Guizhou, China', in T. Blumenfield and H. Silverman (eds) *Cultural Heritage Politics in China,* New York: Springer.

Su, D. H. (1995) 'Museums and Museum Philosophy in China', *Nordisk Museologi* 2: 61–80.

Tilley, C. (2006 [1997]) *A Phenomenology of Landscape: Places, Paths and Monument,*. Oxford: Berg.

Varutti, M. (2008) *Which Museum for What China? Museums, Objects and the Politics of Representation in the Post-Maoist Transition (1976–2007)*, PhD thesis, Graduate Institute of International and Development Studies, University of Geneva.

Wang, H. J., ed. (2001) *Chinese Museum Basics*, Shanghai: Guji Press.

Yu, W. C. (ed.) (1992) *Eighty Years of China National Museum of History*, Beijing: Wenwu Press.

8

Muslim Women: The Gendered Universality of Legal Rights and Cultural Pluralism

Shalina Mehta

The subject of control over women's bodies as an expression of political power (Katrak 2006; Furseth 2009) has been debated for decades now, and the status of Muslim women in parts of Asia has invited particular controversy (Robinson 2009; Sultana 2014). Several Asian countries have witnessed political and social turmoil on the question of universality of women's rights, attacked as a Western-derived subjectivity. This has been questioned both by women in these countries and by scholars working on gender studies from different parts of the world. Opinions in Asia have assumed varying positions, ranging from liberal right to conservative left, with many opting for the middle path deliberating on slow and steady shift from conservative left to liberal right. Left and right in this construct do not represent 'capitalism' or 'communism'. Left stands for orthodox, fundamentalist constructs, placing deliberate emphasis on the fact that it does not exclusively refer to religion but also to a sociological construction of masculinity and patriarchy, camouflaged under the disguise of religious and cultural sanctions. This paper examines positions articulated by Muslim women in a comparative perspective, drawing data from primary studies and comparing it with commentaries that appear in the popular media and official UN documents. Primary data was acquired from India and Iran. Secondary data was drawn from the UN websites, social media, and debates on gender forums, newspapers and women's studies journals. I attempt to comprehend the complexities of the debates by juxtaposing data from different cultural locations. We now live in the era of multi-sited ethnographies in which empirical or secondary data is generated from several locations and compared based on a common theme that defines the context (Melhuus 2002).

Preamble

My first impression of a 'Muslim girl/woman' in 1973 was that she lived the enclosed and circumscribed life of 'frogs in a well' (Jeffery 2000). My mandate was to do an empirical study of 'Hindu-Muslim relations' in a ghettoized slum of Delhi that was inhabited by Muslims prior to the partition of India. After partition a large number of Hindu refugees had moved in as they were allotted properties in this area as part compensation for their immovable assets left behind in Pakistan. My family were refugees from Pakistan and were allotted a house in Delhi in return for our parental property in Lahore. We had the privilege of living in a *haveli* (a huge house with a central open courtyard and large number of rooms built around it) that was originally owned by a Muslim family that had moved to Pakistan. We had a number of Muslim families living in our neighbourhood. But this proximity did not necessitate a better understanding of the young Muslim women in my neighbourhood, as I never had occasion to study with a single Muslim girl either in school or in Delhi University. For me they were women in black or coloured *Nakabs* (veils) and 'peculiar'. The 'peculiar' in my understanding at that point of time was not 'particular' but probably meant being different. I was trained in a colonial tradition of anthropology with an overdose of positivism and objectivity and had not yet learnt the terminology of 'reflexivity', 'deconstruction', 'pluralism', 'context', and 'cultural flows' that guided my future research.

The caricature of a Muslim woman in my mind was that of an overburdened, perpetually pregnant housewife who had to share her restricted home-space with her husband's other co-wives and was constantly beaten by her husband and harassed by her mother-in-law. The image of a Muslim male that I partly inherited in my early socialization was that of a man whom I should fear. Imagine my anxiety before going to the field. But my subjective constructs fell apart and I realized how distant and remote I had been from the empirical reality. Muslim girls of my age were going to schools and colleges, albeit *Madrasa* or exclusive Muslim girls schools. Those going into higher education were studying in Aligarh Muslim University or in Zamia Milia (now a university) in Delhi. Contrary to common perception not all of them got married between the ages of nine and twelve; young Muslim men and women occasionally managed to marry by choice and say no to preferential parallel cousin marriages. Most of my male respondents had only one wife and many were romantic, like the famous Urdu poet Galib. They were like the other boys and girls, and men and women, that I had known in the other communities with which I had interacted previously.

My anthropological vision changed radically as I realized that I was not meeting with a homogenous bounded community but with a diverse Muslim population comprised of Punjabi Muslims, Shia and Sunni, Boharas and many recent converts living with their caste identities and previous cultural peculiarities. My engagement with the population that I selected for my study of Hindu-Muslim relations was very different from what I had imagined. The caricature that got dented the most was that of the 'frogs in the well'. There is no denying that a large number of the women I met on an almost daily basis for nearly three years often felt 'restrained' and 'cloistered', but they did not necessarily feel 'caged'. There was a substantial section of Muslim women who had access to Western education, came from elite Muslim families and were liberal in their perspective, trying to weave threads of a 'modern agenda' based on the dominant discourse of Western civilization into their lives.

The first phase of my fieldwork for doctoral research was conducted in what is often described as the 'dark period' of Indian democratic politics, in the year 1975. Press freedom was curtailed, our mobility was under perpetual surveillance, and the dominant political discourse was openly propagating 'decongestion' of Muslim ghettoes by demolishing some slums in Delhi that had large Muslim populations.[1] I worked under tremendous political pressure because the localities in which I had been generating my data had witnessed violent communal clashes in 1974. India had a Muslim president then, and his wife, a proactive 'liberal right' activist, gave public speeches in ghettoized localities, urging Muslim women to come out of Purdah and opt for secular education. The average Muslim woman in those days believed that this was against their religious and cultural traditions. Voices of dissent were loud and clear and fear of the clergy and rejection by male-centric households absolute.

Forty years on in the profession and my methodologies have changed, my theoretical vision is more fractured but also more honest, and my ability to detail contestations more focused. Discourse on Muslim women has changed too. When I returned to the same field sites in 2008, there was a different 'reality' to what I had experienced earlier. In 2012, when I went to Iran to generate some first-hand information about the status of women there, I was better prepared to deal with the challenges of deconstructing the images with which the media in all its forms (social, virtual and print) has bombarded us over the last decade. I was also better prepared to incorporate these deconstructed stereotypical images into my text later in this chapter as another side of 'reality', in the sense often discussed in post-modernist discourse. There were several rejections and some affirmations of theoretical debates in these empirical trajectories, which invited me to re-visit dominant discourse on feminist debates and the United Nations-sponsored Universal Declaration on Human Rights and subsequent legal frameworks that all nation states, whether or not they were signatories to the charter, were expected to respect. After talking to several women respondents representing different localities, my conviction about the universality and commonality of hegemonic discourse on what is 'correct' and what is 'wrong' was being challenged.

The Grand Narrative of Universal Human Rights

Human rights are not among the 'trusted ideas' on a global scale
Kirsten Hastrup (2002)

The clamour for the implementation of the UN Charter on Universal Human Rights is believed by many to be the modern day mantra to bring gender equity to all women across the world. Yet from the start of the declaration of a 'Universal Human Rights' mandate, anthropologists have not been comfortable with the idea of its being a game changer (Donnelly 1984, 2007; Zivi 2010). They were never convinced that it could actually replace cultural particularity with a Western-centric charter of equality and assumed universality of fundamental principles. I want to develop my arguments by first reviewing some of the recommendations of the Vienna Declaration of Human Rights of 1993. A re-reading of these recommendations and the inherent contradictions in their formulation will facilitate a focused discussion on the subject. Put together Articles One and Two of this declaration read:

> Human rights and fundamental freedoms are the birthright of all human beings; their protection and promotion is the first responsibility of Governments.

> All peoples have the right of self-determination. By virtue of that right they freely determine their political status, and freely pursue their economic, social and cultural development.

The first and second articles when read together become problematic. Article One talks about 'fundamental freedoms and birthright of all human beings' but by 'whom' and for 'whom' is left in the domain of ambiguity. It exhorts the governments to take ownership of that responsibility and while doing so takes away the individual's right to 'self-development' that the charter proposes in the second article by imposing a common charter of what are 'good human rights'. Indirectly it takes upon itself the right to decide what 'good human rights should be', and then asks its member states and its signatories to ensure the implementation of the endorsed discourse of 'good human rights'. This is further augmented in Article Five, which states:

> All human rights are universal, indivisible and interdependent and interrelated. The international community must treat human rights globally in a fair and equal manner, on the same footing, and with the same emphasis. While the significance of national and regional particularities and various historical, cultural and religious backgrounds must be borne in mind, it is the duty of States, regardless of their political, economic and cultural systems, to promote and protect all human rights and fundamental freedoms.

On the one hand, the article recognizes 'cultural particularities', but on the other hand, by endorsing a collective notion of 'universal human rights' seems to negate such recognition. In an article focused on the constructive character of language Kirsten Hastrup argues that 'the language of rights probably remains more suited to classify the world than to change it' (2002: 35).

To this I want to add another caveat: that we are not using one language but several languages that are cultural languages, a language of re-construction guided by our readings and experiences and a language of writing in which we crystalize all the different forms of our translations. The UN charter seems to be doing that with the assumption that all translations can be explained through a common paraphrase. The actors are not adequately defined and thus roles and responsibilities remain diffuse. Ownership gets constructed in the controversial domains of 'us' versus 'them' commonly conveyed in constructs of 'we'. Nigel Rapport (1997: 45, cited in Hastrup 2002: 35) calls writing a 'meta-experience' that constitutes an 'ordering of experience in symbolic form and a conscious production of meaning'. If the Vienna declaration is reviewed in this perspective then the policy document conveys the experiences of those responsible for drafting it and is not taking multiple languages and their meanings into consideration. For instance, consider Article Eighteen, which states:

> The human rights of women and of the girl-child are an inalienable, integral and indivisible part of universal human rights. The full and equal participation of women in political, civil, economic, social and cultural life, at the national, regional and international levels, and the eradication of all forms of discrimination on grounds of sex are priority objectives of the international community.

> The human rights of women should form an integral part of the United Nations human rights activities, including the promotion of all human rights instruments relating to women.

> The World Conference on Human Rights urges Governments, institutions, intergovernmental and non-governmental organizations to intensify their efforts for the protection and promotion of human rights of women and the girl-child.

Urging the government and non-government sectors to promote a universal language of rights is utopian. Many representative of the state have conditioned mind-sets that simply regard any imposition of universality as a demonizing of their tradition. Plural and multi-cultural societies find it even more difficult to communicate in a language that would be equally acceptable to all its cultural cohorts.

In terms of implementation, Article Nineteen seems extremely problematic:

> Considering the importance of the promotion and protection of the rights of persons belonging to minorities and the contribution of such promotion and protection to the political and social stability of the States in which such persons live ... The World Conference on Human Rights reaffirms the obligation of States to ensure that persons belonging to minorities may exercise fully and effectively all human rights and fundamental freedoms without any discrimination and in full equality before the law in accordance with the Declaration on the Rights of Persons Belonging to National or Ethnic, Religious and Linguistic Minorities.

The assumptions in the above declarations are paradoxical in content. To comprehend the intricacies of a complex reality, one has to go beyond rhetoric and intent. I will now illustrate these contradictions with a focused discussion of gender in Islam.

Gender Debates in Islam

A discussion on gender in Islam – I deliberately use the neutral expression instead of feminist terminology – evokes a highly divisive debate. Four models are often cited as representative of scholarship on the subject: *Euro-centric*, *Orientalist*, *Developmentalist* and *exegetical or Islamist* (Baden 1992). To this I would add the categories of political activists and cultural protagonists.

I lack the space here to go into the details of the plural nature of interpretations of Islamic teachings in order to arrive at some consensus on the position of women in original Islamic texts. Many of these details are as contentious as the charter of human rights is for many anthropologists. Islamic theology and its diverse social and cultural practices recognize four distinct sources that the followers of Islam fervently feel are responsible for the contemporary foundations of Islamic law. These are the *Quran*, the *Sunna*, *Qiyas* and *ijma*.[2] In Sunni interpretations of Islamic law itself there are more than four versions. These are the *Hanafi*, the *Shafi'i*, the *Hanbali* and the *Maliki*.[3] To this one should add the diversity contained in the texts of various other sects, particularly among the *Shia*s, *Boharas*, *Ahmediaya* and various other movements that claim to have incorporated teachings of their respective prophets into their religious charters.

Existence of multiple sources for promulgating codes of conduct suggests that there was more fluidity in the practice of early Islam than what is now found in practice in several Islamic societies and in their respective cultural discourses. Ahmed (1991) argues that the differences in these multiple texts of different sects may be marginal but that they can dramatically alter the kind of rights attributed to women living in the diverse communities commonly called 'Muslim societies'. Each of these communities has equally varied issues to deal with, and arenas of conflict, determined by external and internal political and social agencies. One of the most contentious issues being debated in India in the context of Muslim women is Muslim personal law (Shahida 1990; Patel 2009; Sultana 2014) and demand for a uniform civil code (Parashar 1992; Gosh 2007). There have been different political dispensations for and against accepting any legal discourses that do not conform to Sharia law, with the Muslim *Ulema* (clergy) prominent in the latter camp. There are civil society groups, predominantly groups of Muslim women, on both the sides of the spectrum. The political establishment, irrespective of party ideology and proclaimed agenda, have dithered on the issue as will be argued later. Yet the fact is that it has been an issue since India's independence and continues to be an issue today (Rajan 2000). It also reflects the state's weakness with regard to implementing the universal declaration on gender equity despite being a signatory to the charter.

Muslim Personal Law and the Demand for a Uniform Civil Code in India

In India, Muslim Personal Law (1937) operates in accordance with the precepts of *Shariat*. The law regulates all matters relating to the Muslim women, including affairs of marriage, succession, guardianship, divorce, the property rights of women and rules for conduct. It is un-codified and the All India Muslim Personal Law Board (AIMPLB) takes all legal decisions (Mahmood 1997; Gosh 2007; Menski 2008; Nichols 2012). They have the authority to define those principles of *Hadith* and Quran that in their opinion have issued commandments for Muslim women. The AIMPLB along with *Jamiat Ulemma-e-Hind* (JUH) claims to be representative of the Muslim population in the country. These two organizations regard themselves as legitimate representatives of the voice of Muslims in India. India is one of the few countries that continue to subscribe to varied interpretations of Islam.

The rights of men and women with regard to divorce are one area of controversy. Muslim marriages are normally not registered in any civil court, and only the clergy maintains the record. Another debated issue relates to restrictions on women being allowed to pray in the mosques even today in India. It is paradoxical that most Islamic countries in the world have done away with some of these discriminatory practices but that with a view to protecting the rights of the minorities, many Muslim women remain at the margins of Indian society, although this certainly does not imply that non-Muslim woman in India necessarily enjoy a better position.

The UN charter on fundamental human rights states:

> Gender-based violence and all forms of sexual harassment and exploitation, including those resulting from cultural prejudice and international trafficking, are incompatible with the dignity and worth of the human person, and must be eliminated. This can be achieved by legal measures and through national action and international cooperation in such fields as economic and social development, education, safe maternity and health care, and social support.

The UN declaration makes no specific mention of marriage and divorce. Structural violence against women finds its most fertile grounds in domestic violence and the Indian state has persistently refused to admit any plea to make even marital rape a criminal offence. Signatories to the UN declarations on protection of the individual rights of women belonging to different religious and ethnic communities that are citizens of a nation state are the governments of the day.

According to colloquial perception a married Muslim woman is not endowed with the right to divorce and a Muslim male is entitled to marry four women at the same time (polygyny) and to divorce any of his wives irrevocably by merely saying '*Talak*' (I divorce you) three times. He is at liberty to support or deny sustenance to his children from his divorced wife. There is no legal provision for alimony in Muslim Personal Law nor is that right assured to them by the Indian legal system. The Venice Declaration states:

The persons belonging to minorities have the right to enjoy their own culture, to profess and practise their own religion and to use their own language in private and in public, freely and without interference or any form of discrimination.

Ambiguity and conflicting interpretations of the declaration give the fundamentalists the freedom to interpret it to their advantage. The international or the external support that the state agencies may need to reform these laws would not be forthcoming because the declaration defends the right of the minority to protect their religious freedoms and practise their sanctions. The Shah Bano case serves as one of the most appropriate illustrations of this paradigmatic situation and for developing our discussion of Muslim women, the gendered universality of legal rights, and cultural pluralism.

In April 1978, sixty-two year old Shah Bano went to court and filed an application for maintenance under section 125 of the code of Criminal Procedure against her husband. In November 1978 her husband, a practising lawyer, divorced her in accordance with the provisions of Muslim personal law through an irrevocable *Talaq*. He paid her a nominal sum of 3,000 rupees for her maintenance during the period of separation as ordained by the procedures of *Talaq*. Shah Bano appealed for a compensation of 500 rupees per month in the Indore judicial court against which her husband petitioned in the Supreme Court through a special leave petition making the plea that section 125 of the code of Criminal Procedure was not applicable to Muslims.[4]

Discussions that followed the Supreme Court judgement upholding the validity of High Court judgement that awarded her maintenance have on occasion taken exception to the language of the judgement, which in their opinion violated the right of the minority community to practise the dictates of its own religious sanctions and laws. The judgement upheld the validity of section 125 of the Criminal Procedures Act that provides for maintenance for all those persons who are not able to support themselves by relatives with affordable means.[5] The ambit of relatives includes even a divorced wife not capable of providing for herself. Judges in their wisdom did not take it as a case of a Muslim woman but treated it as a general appeal in which a person not able to maintain herself was seeking monetary compensation from her estranged and affluent spouse. To every rational reader of this judgement this comes as a logical conclusion given the fact that it was being reviewed under the provisions of the uniform Criminal code and not a civil code, and all Indian citizens fall within its purview. But as Das (1995: 98) points out, 'the judgement went beyond this issue. It considered questions relating to interpretations of the Quran and Islamic law on the issue of maintenance of divorced wives. The judges also made several comments on the desirability of evolving a common civil code as a means of achieving national integration and gender justice.'

One may assume a position and suggest that the judges' perspective was in consonance with the expectation of the Vienna Declaration but this indeed became problematic. Any argument about the universal validity of human rights as individual rights of each Muslim woman irrespective of geographical or cultural connotations evokes similar contestations. In the judgement reference was made to gender justice saying '… it raises a straightforward issue which is of common interest not only to Muslim women, not only to women generally, but to all those who, aspiring to create an equal society of men and women lure themselves into the belief that mankind has achieved a remarkable degree of progress in that direction' (Das 1995: 98). Similar assumptions were made in the preamble to the Universal Declaration of Human Rights, which states that 'recognition of the inherent dignity and of the equal and inalienable rights of all members of the human family is the foundation of freedom, justice and peace in the world' One has to make a fine distinction between the rhetoric, even when made with good intentions, and the 'unintended consequences' of these 'well-intentioned' statements.

What followed after the Shah Bano verdict is representative of these unintended consequences and symptomatic of the tensions that imposition of any notion of universality provokes. The Supreme Court's judgement in this case in the opinion of many observers breached its jurisdiction, when it wrote 'Article 44 of our consti-tution has remained a dead letter … . A common Civil Code will help the cause of national integration by removing disparate loyalties to laws, which have conflicting ideologies.' Critics regard this as an infringement of the rights of individuals in multi-cultural, multi-religious and multi-ethnic pluralities. It also defies the spirit of Legal Pluralism and raises the question of 'whether powers of the state should be extended to encroach into the sphere of the family' (Das 1995: 104). Cultural and Legal Pluralism discourse contends that the opposition to the judgement was meant to 'reinstate the *Shariat*' (Baxi 1986). A common perception among the *Ulemma* was that this judgement was in violation of the prescribed norms of *Sharia'h* (the Muslim Personal Law) and subversive of Muslims' minority rights in a Hindu majority state.

These are challenging issues that have no simple answers. The Muslim Women Protection of Rights on Divorce Bill that was debated in the Indian Parliament after the Shah Bano judgement resulted in the promulgation of The Muslim Women (Protection of Rights on Divorce) Act of 1986, which was enforced retrospectively to deny any monetary compensation to the victim. The promulgation of the Act gave legal sanctity to the provisions of the *Shariat* and ordained its judiciary to deal with the divorce cases of Muslim women not as per the general law of the land but in accordance with the provisos defined in this act. Some of the salient features of the Act stipulate:

3. *Mahar* or other properties of Muslim woman to be given to her at the time of divorce-
(1) Notwithstanding anything contained in any other law for the time being in force, a Muslim divorced woman shall be entitled to –
   a) a reasonable and fair provision and maintenance to be made and paid to her within the *iddat* period by her former husband;
   b) where she herself maintains the children born to her before or after divorce, a reasonable and fair provision and maintenance to be made and paid by her former

husband for a period of two years from the respective dates of birth of such children;

c) an amount equal to the sum of *mahr* or dower agreed to be paid to her at the time of her marriage or at any time thereafter according to Muslim law; and

d) all properties given to her before or at the time of marriage or after the marriage by her relatives or friends of the husband or his friends.

(2) Where a reasonable and fair provision and maintenance or the amount of *mahr* or dower due has not been made or paid or the properties referred to in clause (d) of sub-section (1) have not been delivered to a divorced woman on her divorce, she or any one duly authorised by her may, on her behalf, make an application to a Magistrate for an order for payment of such provision and maintenance, *mahr* or dower or the delivery of properties as the case may be.

Before looking at reactions to provisions that bring rules defined in *Shariat* within the legal framework of the state, it is important to say more about the period of *Iddat*. *Iddat* is the period of separation before the divorce is finalized, defined in the Act following prescribed norms in the *Shariat* as:

i.   Three menstrual courses after the date of divorce, if she is subject to menstruation; and

ii. Three Lunar months after her divorce, if she is not subject to menstruation; and

iii. If she is enceinte at the time of her divorce, the period between the divorce and the delivery of her child or the termination of her pregnancy, whichever is earlier.

Some of these stipulations may result in denial of fundamental rights to Muslim women in a country in which women from other religious, ethnic and linguistic affiliations may get better security from the same legal institutions. A divorced Muslim woman is entitled to maintenance only for a period of three months and has claims to a dowry that was promised to her at the time of marriage.[6] What troubles most is that these sanctions have now moved from the domain of religion and its practice to the secular domain of state law. State legal institutions vow to protect the dignity of the individual, but with these provisions, Muslim women have become particularly vulnerable. It is also known that some men from other religions have taken advantage of these provisions and have sanctified either bigamy or divorce without giving alimony to their estranged wife simply by converting from their previous religion for entirely pragmatic reasons.

There are a number of active women's organizations in the country protesting against these interpretations of the Quran. One of these organizations, *Bhartiya Muslim Mahila Andolan*, with nearly 20,000 members coming from fifteen states in the country, is actively organizing protests against this form of oppression. The following excerpt from an interview given by one of the leaders of this organization to The *New York Times* provides a glimpse into some of the voices of dissent:

The clerics are ignorant about what the Koran has to say on the subject of women's lives. The Muslim Personal Law Board is not representative of all Muslims. Nobody elected them, and they have very few women in their organization. They don't consider women equal, which is extremely un-Islamic. God does not distinguish between men and women.

Zeenat Shakut Ali, professor of Islamic studies at St. Xavier's College Mumbai told the reporter of the newspaper that:

> We shouldn't forget that the prophet himself was one of the first feminists. We need to settle the legal reform debate. Let the clerics and male scholars come and discuss this, with the women activists on the other side. (Mukherji 2012)

Partial success of this organized protest movement was registered in a meeting of *Jamiat-ulemma-i-Hind* in a resolution passed in May 2012 agreeing that the Islamic mandate for women in accordance with the norms of the Quran is not being given to Indian Muslim Women. The rights endorsed included the right to inheritance of agriculture land, the right to any inheritance, and the right to education. However, veiling and educating girls only in exclusively female educational institutions is endorsed and if veils are not allowed in public or private school, the organization deems it a denial of their fundamental rights as enshrined in the Hadith.

The judicial system in India has on occasion taken a different view of the modified 1986 law. In a recent court judgement Mumbai Court did not allow a Muslim male to marry for the second time before settling the claims of his first wife (Sequeira 2015). The petitioner's advocate argued in the court that perception of four marriages as the legitimate right of Muslim men is an 'end product of misrepresentation of the holy Quran'. The plural, secular and democratic systems that define the Indian polity provide freedom for debate and diverse opinions although in certain ways they also restrict the state from taking progressive decisions, as happened at the time of Shah Bano case. But to understand what happens to gendered universality of legal rights in religious authoritarian regimes, I turn to Iran through the lens of an outsider.

Gender and the Law in Iran

The Islamic Law that is followed in Iran is known as *Ithna'ashari* (also called the 'Twelver branch') (Campo 2009).[7] It was accepted as the 'official religion' in the fifteenth century by the *Safavid* dynasty and incorporated into the Persian constitution in the year 1905/6. The *Ulma,* commonly referred to as *mujtahids* in Iran, kept the religious translations and their dictates alive. In contemporary Iran Allamah Tabataba'I, Allaman Nuri and Ayatullah Mutahhiri are maintaining interpretations with regard to women in the *Ithna'ashari*. Their interpretation of the status of women in the Islamic tradition maintains that in the pre-Islamic World, women were not even treated as humans and it is Islam that has given women dignity and status in society. This contention supports *Bhartiya Muslim Mahila Andolan*'s reasoning that Prophet Mohammad was the 'first feminist'. They also argue that Islam did not invent the veil but that women were wearing the veil in several societies prior to the foundation of Islamic civilization. Many scholars contend that Islam came to the Middle East in the seventh century as a social revolution and provided for women's security and fundamental rights. But the interpretations by the *Ulma* have restricted the role of constitutional provisions (Mahdavi 1985: 257–8). It is often assumed that Islam is a monolithic religious, social and cultural system. However, various belief systems within Islam constitute a plurality in itself. *Ulema* defending *Shariat* in Shah Bano's case followed the *Sunni* tradition but most Muslims in Iran follow the *Shia* tradition.

In Iran's Islamic tradition, family law provides for a 50 per cent share in the husband's property on divorce and the practice of polygamy is restricted. Divorced men and estranged husbands are allowed to get into temporary marital alliances locally, called *muta'h*. This form of temporary marriage is not permitted in the Sunni tradition. Kazemi (2000) analyzes the reform trajectory for women in Iran and places it in three chronological stages starting with the

> establishment of the Islamic Republic after the national plebiscite of 1979 that ended in early 1980, soon after the Iranian forces expelled the Iraqis from occupied land. Phase two lasted for the duration of the war until its termination in 1988. The final and continuing phase began with the death of Ayatollah Khomeini and the important constitutional revisions of 1989 … which converted Iran into a presidential system.

I visited Iran in 2012, when the country was preparing for another election and hoping for more liberal reforms. In 2013, moderate cleric Hassan Rohani became the president of Iran after defeating a hardliner conservative. Women from all walks of life whom I met during my twelve-day stay were hopeful that his election would usher in a new phase of liberal Islam and provide greater freedom and basic rights to women. Islam is followed by nearly 98 per cent of Iran's population: Shias comprise 89 per cent of the total religious population and Sunnis make up the other 9 per cent. But before I dwell any further on what I may term a fourth phase of reform, I mention how my short field trip once again shattered the stereotyped images that I had in my subconscious of Iranian women, partly the product of representations that emanated from the media.

Media creates images and excels in transforming the isolated impressions captured into static stereotypes that misrepresent a complex and diverse everyday reality. Fareed Zakaria, comparing women in Iran and Saudi Arabia after having visited these countries in 2011, wrote that in the 'Islamic Republic of Iran – a regime that is, by most accounts retrograde, particularly with regard to women's rights – you are struck by how defiantly women try to lead normal and productive lives' (Zakaria 2011). He then went on to show how women in Iran were better placed than those in Saudi Arabia. I had a similar experience and will reach similar conclusions by comparing Iran with my own home country, India.

I visited various Iranian provinces, starting with the province of Mazandaran in the north and moving on to one of the oldest cities, Isfahan in central Iran. The many women with whom I had casual to extended conversations were from both rural and urban areas. Most of them came across as confident and self-reliant, though restrained in public spaces. Although fearful of being seen without their head covered, they were gregarious in exclusively female gatherings. It was a common sight seeing families sitting out in sprawling green spaces, in particular on Friday evenings, roasting Kababs and enjoying time together with family and friends. Pitched tents for nights out were a common sight. Contrary to the impression I had carried with me to Iran, women were not left locked inside the house but roamed about freely with friends and family.

My host in Isfahan was a fifty-plus woman who drove alone after midnight to guide us to our guesthouse. She was an entrepreneur running two independent schools and had previously worked as a schoolteacher for nearly twenty-five years. One of her schools is a crèche-cum-playschool that opens at six in the morning: working mothers drop off their children in the age group of one to four years before going to work. My host informed me that on average she has 100 children on the rolls in her playschool and about 300 in the nursery school. She has three daughters, all pursuing PhD programmes in science at prestigious institutions in the USA and Germany. She was open to the idea of any of her daughters marrying according to their own choice but was hopeful that they would choose their husbands from the *Shia* Muslim community, preferably Iranian.

She was not an exception. Other women were training to be lawyers, doctors, engineers or specializing in humanities, social sciences and languages, confident of having independent careers. Men in the sample were supportive of their daughters studying, though wanting them to conform to the norms of their society. Married and unmarried men were open to the idea of being married to working women and many were willing to help their spouses in taking care of children. I had the opportunity to visit a few university campuses in the country and the girls were moving freely in large numbers.

On my return, I examined the demographic and literacy profile of the country, particularly after reading that the UN has rated Iranian women on its Gender Empowerment Measure (GEM) at 103 out of 108 countries. Statistics and my empirical experiences tell a different story. Female literacy was 70.4 per cent, according to the 2002 census, jumping to 80 per cent in 2011; enrolment for primary school students according to the UNICEF (United Nations Children's Fund) report is 99.9 per cent. The sex ratio was 1.05 males to females and maternal mortality was reported to be only 24.6 deaths per 100,000 live births in 2008–12. The birth rate was only 16.89 births per 1,000 population and average household size was 3.6. There were reports suggesting that women's employment outside the house was significantly low, with only about 14.7 per cent working outside the agricultural sector. But my friends and various other people with whom I had extended conversations told me that between 35 and 40 per cent of women are working outside the house.

According to a United Nations Population Fund report fertility rates have dropped significantly, from 'seven lifetime births in 1986' to only 1.78 children born to each woman today. Infant mortality rate has dropped considerably, and according to UNICEF data for 2012 had come down to fifteen per 1000 live births for children below the age of one year and eighteen for children below the age of five years. I learnt from my respondents that even though polygamy was permitted by law, there were strict social norms in place that discourage a man from having more than one wife without the consent of his first wife. I came across several cases of serial monogamy but elders in the family discouraged even that. Yet that did not necessarily empower women. In most cases after divorce fathers had exclusive rights over the children, even where family courts had granted visiting rights to the divorced mother. Patriarchy and male dominance in the affairs of the family was rampant even for highly educated and financially independent women.

Nevertheless, I am provoked to compare some of the Iranian statistics with those from India. In India the female literacy rate was only 47.8 per cent in 2001 in comparison to Iran's at 70.4 per cent in 2002; the maternal mortality rate was 230 deaths per 100,000 as compared to only 30 in Iran. In the Human Development Index report of the UN Iran is ranked 94 and India 128.

Iranians love Hindustan and India has remained their favoured destination for higher education. I must admit that travelling in Iran with my head covered was an experience that I certainly would not want to live with forever. Not all women in Iran enjoy wearing a *hijab* or *chaddar* either, but the point is that they do not want to give up their religious or cultural right to do so. Women resisted Reza Shah's attempt to enforce unveiling as early as January 1936. I have met highly educated Muslim young women in several international conferences on gender, including women born in the UK, France or USA, who opt to wear the *hijab* as a symbolic gesture of religious independence, when their mothers rejected the same on moving to Western destinations. To assume that this symbolizes women's complete subjugation is erroneous, especially when we examine the state of fear in which women in most cities in India live. I feel obligated to make further comparisons.

The recent decision of a *khap panchayat* (caste council) in Uttar Pradesh to ban women below the age of fifty from carrying a mobile phone or wearing jeans, and the political leadership of the state's almost endorsing it, is as shocking as the public reprimand of women in Iran. Most women that I spoke to in Iran were confident that in the coming election to the *Majlis*, they would be able make significant inroads in regaining their fundamental rights. The fact that a moderate won the election in Iran reinforced these women's belief in democratic traditions as a way of achieving their fundamental rights. In democratic India, even during the 2014 elections, political leaders across the political parties were not willing to condemn *khap panchayats* despite episodes such as these councils ordering the public rape of young women for acts committed by male members of their families, and, in January 2014, gang-rape of a twenty-year-old tribal girl in Bengal by twelve men acting on the orders of the caste *panchayat* for marrying a man from a higher caste and for failing to pay a fine of 50,000 rupees.[8] The media continue to report similar incidents from other states in India.

Democratic India has failed to secure significant representation for women in our assemblies and parliament. Activist groups have been demanding a 33 per cent quota for women in the Indian parliament: the bill has been pending since 1996. The present prime minister of India had to take a proactive stance to ensure that the sex ratio does not decline further in a country where son preference is known to be a norm. The Indian maternal mortality rate remains high: 190 per 100,000 births in comparison with Iran's present 21 per 100,000.

Indian roads and cities have become increasingly unsafe for women and I would not dream of driving alone at midnight in any part of the country. In Tehran, women drive taxis at midnight outside the Milad tower, the new symbol of national resurgence. Democracy and the assurance of equal rights in constitutional provisions alone is not necessarily the path for granting equality to women in society. If Iran needs to change its political culture to ensure equal rights for women, India has a long way to go to ensure equality and security for its women.

Conclusion: Converging Contours

Gender theories have consistently held the view that oppression of women in some form or the other is prevalent in almost all societies across the world. What varies are its manifestations and the intensity of this violence and discrimination. They also agree that this discrimination is deeply rooted in social structure and cultural practices and has nothing to do with the theory of binary oppositions that would like to explain away these differences in nature–culture oppositions or in principles of sociobiology. What we are trying to discern in this paper is the reason for commonality in public discourse reflected in universal definitions of human rights by the UN and widely different interpretations of both the universal discourse on gendered equality of rights and differing cultural variations of the same religious normative control. When, in our capacity as practicing anthropologists, we contest the universality of the charter of human rights, we are equally puzzled by strikingly different interpretations of the same religious discourse. If the human rights approach is riddled with Euro-centric ideas, the cultural rights debate is not able to come to terms with multiplicities or peculiarities of practices within the same cultural traditions. One common point of tension relates to contestations over ownership, in particular of property and other economic assets. The other commonality can be read in historical terms as a deliberate denial of power and knowledge to women. The *Ulemma*, as we recently witnessed in the attack on the schoolgirl Malalla by the Pakistani Taliban, can treat denial of education as a preventive measure to maintain exclusive social and political control. At the same time the inability of the women's bill to get the backing of all political players in

India can be located in the threats to political control and the challenges to be posed by these new entrants to the decision making process when they achieve parity with the 'other' – the men.

Notes

1. One example was the infamous demolition of Turkman Gate in Delhi during the Emergency, graphically described by Salman Rushdie in *Freedom at Midnight*.

2. The Quran literally meaning 'the recitation' is the central religious text of Islam, which Muslims believe to be a revelation from God (Allah). The *Sunna* also spelled Sunnah, literally means the 'path'. It is the traditional social and legal custom and practice of the Prophet Muhammad. *Qiyas* in Islamic law is analogical reasoning as applied to the deduction of juridical principles from the Quran and the Sunna. With the Quran, the Sunna and *Ijma*, it constitutes the four sources of Islamic jurisprudence. *Ijma* refers to the consensus or agreement of the Muslim community basically on religious issues.

3. *Hanafi* is one of the four schools of thought of religious jurisprudence (*fiqh*) within Sunni Islam. Named after its founder Imam Abu Hanifa, it is considered the oldest and most liberal school of law. *Shafi'i* is one of the four schools of Islamic law in Sunni Islam and was founded by the Arab scholar Al-Shafi'i. The Shafi school predominantly relies on the Quran and the *Hadiths* of Sharia. *Hanbali* is one of the four orthodox Sunni Islamic schools of jurisprudence (*fiqh*). It is named after the Iraqi scholar Ahmad ibn Hanbal and is the smallest of four major Sunni schools, the others being the Hanafi, Shafi'i and *maliki*. *Maliki* is named after Malik ibn Anas, a leading jurist from Medina. This school recorded the Medina consensus of opinion and uses Hadith as a guide. Following the tradition of Imam Malik, this school appeals to 'common utility – the idea of the common good'.

4. For details see Engineer (1987).

5. Persons not in a position to support themselves include aged parents, children and physically and mentally vulnerable adults. In support of their arguments the judges cited Sir James Fitzjames Stephen, who was responsible for drafting this particular clause with the intent of 'preventing vagrancy or at least of preventing its consequences', see http://indiankanoon.org [accessed 16 June 2015].

6. My field notes collected over a period of more than thirty years reveal that at the time of marriage a sizable section of my woman Muslim respondents had surrendered their right to these claims by simply saying *Mehr maaf kiya*, implying that the individual forsakes her right to marital security right on the day of her marriage.

7. The Twelver branch or *Ithna*, the largest branch of Shia Islam, regard twelve descendants of Mohammad as Imams having religious and political authority.
8. '12 Gang-Rape Tribal Woman on Kangaroo Court order in Bengal's Birbhum District', *Hindustan Times*, 24 June 2014. See http://www.hindustantimes.com/india-news/12-gang-rape-tribal-woman-on-kangaroo-court-order-in-bengal-s-birbhum-district-/article1-1175776.aspx [accessed 25 May 2015].

References

Ahmed, L. (1991) 'Early Islam and the position of women: the problem of interpretation', in N. Keddie and B. Baron (eds) *Women in Middle Eastern History: Shifting Boundaries in Sex and Gender*, New Haven: Yale University Press.

Baden, S. (1992) *The Position of Women in Islamic Countries: Possibilities, Constraints and Strategies for Change*, BRIDGE Development Report, Falmer: University of Sussex, Institute of Development Studies.

Baxi, U. (1986) 'Discipline, Repression and Legal Pluralism', in P. Sack and E. Minchin (eds) *Pluralism, Proceedings of the Canberra Law Workshop VII*, Canberra: Australian National University.

Campo, J. (2009) *Encyclopedia of Islam*, New York: Facts on File.

Das, V. (1995) *Critical Events: An Anthropological Perspective on Contemporary India*, New Delhi: Oxford University Press.

Donnelly, J. (1984) 'Cultural Relativism and Universal Human Rights', *Human Rights Quarterly* 6 (4): 400–19.

Donnelly, J. (2007) 'The Relative Universality of Human Rights', *Human Rights Quarterly* 29: 281–306.

Engineer, A. A. (1987) *'Status of Women in Islam'*, Delhi: Ajanta Publications.

Furseth, I. (2009) 'Religion in the Works of Habermas, Bourdieu, and Focault', in P. B. Clarke (ed.) *The Oxford Handbook of the Sociology of Religion*, New York: Oxford University Press.

Gosh, P. S. (2007) *The Politics of Personal Law in South Asia: Identity, Nationalism and the Uniform Civil Code*, New Delhi: Routledge.

Hastrup, K. (2002) 'Anthropology's Comparative Consciousness: The Case of Human Rights', in A. Gingrich and R. G. Fox (eds) *Anthropology, by Comparison*, London: Routledge.

Jeffery, P. (2000) *Frogs in a Well: Indian Women in Purdah*, 2nd edn, New Delhi: Manohar Publications.

Kazemi, F. (2000) 'Gender, Islam, and Politics', *Social Research* : An International Quarterly 67 (2): 455–47.

Katrak, K. H. (2006) *Politics of the Female Body: Postcolonial Women Writers of the Third World*, New York: Rutgers University Press.

Mahdavi, S. (1985) 'The position of Women in Shia'a Iran: Views of the Ulma', in E. W. Fernea (ed.) *Women and the Family in the Middle East: New Voices of Change*, Austin: University of Texas Press.

Mahmood, T. (1997) *Islamic Law in the Indian Courts Since Independence: Fifty Years of Judicial Interpretation,* New Delhi: Institute of Objective Studies.

Melhuus, M. (2002) 'Issues of Relevance: Anthropology and the Challenges of Cross-Cultural Comparison', in A. Gingrich and R. G. Fox (eds) *Anthropology, by Comparison*. London: Routledge.

Menski, W. (2008) 'The Uniform Civil Code Debates in Indian Law: New Developments and Changing Agenda', *German Law Journal* 9 (3): 211–50.

Mukherji, N. (2012) 'Muslim Women in India seek equal rights under personal law', posted 12 June 2012. Available online: http://insideislam.wisc.edu [accessed 5 July 2013].

Nichols, J. A. (2012) 'Multi-Tiered Marriage: Reconsidering the Boundaries of Civil Law and Religion', in J. A. Nichols (ed.) *Marriage and Divorce in a Multicultural Context: Reconsidering the Boundaries of Civil Law and Religion*, New York: Cambridge University Press.

Parashar, A. (1992) *Women and Family Law Reforms in India,* New Delhi: Sage Publication.

Patel, R. (2009) 'Indian Muslim Women, Politics of Muslim Personal Law and Struggle for Life with Dignity and Justice', *Economic and Political Weekly* 44 (44): 44–9.

Rajan, R. S. (2000) 'Women between Community and State: Some Implication of the Uniform Civil Code Debates in India, *Social Text* 18 (4): 55–82.

Rapport, N. (1997) *Transcendent Individual: Towards a Literary and Liberal Anthropology*, London: Routledge.

Robinson, K. (2009) *Gender, Islam and Democracy in Indonesia,* London: Routledge.

Sequeira, R. (2015) 'Family Court stops Muslim Man from Marrying Second Time', *Times of India*, 6 June, 11.

Shahida, L. (1990) *Muslim Women in India: Political and Private Realities*, New Delhi: Kali for Women.

Sultana, P. (2014) 'Muslim Personal Law and the Status of Women in India: A Case for Reforms' *The Chronicle* 2 (1): 27–32.

Zakaria, F. (2011) 'Zakaria: Comparing the Status of Women in Iran and Saudi Arabia', *Global Public Square*, 27 October. Available online: http://globalpublicsquare.blogs.cnn.com/2011/10/27/zakaria-comparing-the-status-of-women-in-iran-and-saudi-arabia%E2%80%A8/ [accessed 25 May 2015].

Zivi, K. (2010) 'Human Rights', in R. Couto (ed.) *Political and Civic Leadership: A Reference Handbook*, California: Sage Publications.

Websites

Vienna Declaration and Program of Action (1993) Available online: http://www.
unhchr.ch/huridocda/huridoca.nsf/(symbol)/a.conf.157.23.en [accessed 7 July
2013].

Charter of the United Nations (1945) Available online: http://www.un.org/en/
documents/charter/intro.shtml [accessed 7 July 2013].

UNICEF (2013) *Iran Statistics*. Available online: http://www.unicef.org/
infobycountry/iran_statistics.html [accessed 19 June 2015].

9

The Politics of Reincarnation, Time and Sovereignty: A Comparative Anthropological Exploration of the Syrian Druze and the Australian Anangu

Maria Kastrinou
Robert Layton

Equality is believing that you are not stuck with yourself forever.

Druze poet cited in Khuri 2004: 116

That's a rock, but that's got to have something else,
because that's got all those old men's memories inside.

Young Anangu man speaking of Uluru ('Ayers Rock')

Introduction

Much of the anthropology of ethnic groups, boundaries and nation states is concerned with the ethnographic description and analytical exploration of 'blood' and/or boundaries as core metaphors in the politics of contemporary sovereignty (Alonso 1994; Banks 1996; Eriksen 2002). However, in the cases of Druze and Anangu, instead of the lifeforce and materiality of substances, we encounter transient forms of eternal souls; instead of descent or segmentation we encounter kinship in the earth and embodiment of the landscape (Layton 1995; Morphy 1995; Strang 1997). On the basis of probing this comparison, we argue for an anthropological approach to reincarnation as a *politics of time*: an alternative contemporary discourse of *autochthony* that lays an eternal geographical claim over time, directly confounding state-bound forms of sovereignty and belonging.

This article examines how the Druze, a religious minority in the Middle East, and the Anangu, traditional owners of Uluru and the surrounding region of central Australia, appear to have in common a distinctive belief in reincarnation, in which the living re-embody an ancestral community that existed at the beginning of time.

This belief is distinctive because it sets both of these communities apart from their historically related neighbours. Such differences, not by themselves but in among others, constitute both the Druze and the Aṉangu as *minorities*, the first religious, the second indigenous, in the context of the nation states in whose geographically-bounded sovereignty they currently find themselves in.

We explore reincarnation in Druze beliefs and practices through death rituals, recollected stories of past lives, and the role of reincarnation in reproducing but also in subverting endogamy. These ethnographic instances underline the social and political spectrum in which reincarnation is a religious metaphysical belief but also a discourse in and through which social, economic and political claims are articulated and contested. The association of land, birth, and kinship provides a powerful framework for claims to land, band membership, and for the definition of the Aṉangu vis-à-vis their neighbours and the Australian state, acknowledged through a successful land claim and the repatriation of ownership of Uluṟu. The Aṉangu case further evidences that reincarnation is best understood as a flexible and adaptable discourse through which not only social, political and economic claims are negotiated, but also potential connections and relations are forged.

This comparative approach allows us to go beyond geographically state-bound sovereignties, in order to probe the role of reincarnation as a powerful contemporary political discourse, and second to explore how two otherwise dissimilar communities embed reincarnation in formulating powerful claims of autochthony, sovereignty and belonging. Through our comparative lenses it becomes apparent that reincarnation discourses in both Aṉangu and Druze bypass the current geography of their respective states, in a way that allows them to slip through the net of state-bound geography, only to reappear as those people, of the land, that have always been here and shall always return.

Our comparative exploration builds upon existing and emerging insights in the anthropology of religion. Ideas of reincarnation/rebirth as a continuous journey between the world of the living and that of the ancestors – as transformative processes unrelated to concepts of religious salvation or ethical compensation – have been documented across a large geographic terrain in different forms and in (mainly) small-scale as well as large-scale societies, such as in North America, Africa, Australia (for a summary of anthropological engagement with reincarnation across these locations, see Mills and Slobodin 1994: 16–18), and worldwide; (Stevenson 1980; Gupta 2002; Playfair 2006). Filling a significant void and decentering reincarnation from the theological paradigm of South Asia, Mills and Slobodin's edited volume (1994) compiles a rich record of practices and cosmologies from the American continent. This work threads together a variety of papers that engage provocatively with Amerindian rebirth concepts and practices exploring, among others, cosmology and eschatology (Turner 1994), personhood, identity and identifi-cation (Turner 1994; Mills 1994), kinship, terminology and social structure (Nuttall 1994; Matlock 1994; Slobodin 1994), and also discussing how to study the actuality of reincarnation ethnographically.

We follow their path by further decentering the regional specificity of reincarnation through comparing reincarnation among the Druze and the Anangu. Their principle of reincarnation differs from that of Hinduism or Buddhism in that it is not a forward-looking quest to escape from an endless cycle into a higher plane of existence rather than be drawn downwards into hell (*Tibetan Book of Dead*, Coleman 2008: 239, and see Samuel 1993: 210; Obeyesekere 1994: xii–xiii, xx). On the contrary, it is a quest to ensure that ancestral prototypes are renewed in each generation, in order to revivify the original community (also see Geertz 1973; Lévi-Strauss 1966: 231). Moreover, our cases are similar to how Kutchin concepts of reincarnation have been affected through a process of secularization, and yet secularization of reincarnation beliefs did not challenge, but reinforced community cohesion and continuity (Slobodin 1994: 136–55).

Obeyesekere (1994: xiv–xix) outlines nine propositions for studying reincarnation. The first three are (1) death is a temporary stage; (2) there must be a cultural impetus to bring back the dead; and (3) ancestral beings should have power to influence life. These propositions hold for the Druze and the Anangu, although the latter does not strictly conform to Druze concepts (among whom reincarnation takes place instantly). Next, Obeyesekere notes the importance of (4) kinship and prevalence of endogamy in contexts where reincarnation is not connected to ethical compensation, through two subsequent mechanisms; (5) by not crossing between other species; and (6) because reincarnation of ancestors does not take place among strangers but within the same group, clan or lineage. This cosmologically rendered form of endogamy is one of the greatest similarities between the Anangu and the Druze. Nor does Anangu or Druze reincarnation entail reward or punishment for past deeds – there is no ethical compensation for good or bad deeds. For Obeyesekere, these kinship-reproducing patterns evident in concepts of reincarnation are therefore related to another characteristic: (7) a fixed, finite number of spirits or souls. This characteristic is usually accompanied by the existence of culturally specific ways to identify one's relative after reincarnation has taken place (for example through revelatory dreams, marks or memories of past lives). This characteristic exists within the rebirth of both Druze and Anangu, albeit in different cosmological perspectives. Finally, the last two propositions identify some of the key problems with these renditions of reincarnation: (8) if the other world is a replica, then why come back; and (9) the problem of sexual intercourse vis-à-vis spirit conception (i.e. as in Malinowski's description of virgin birth, 1916).

In this paper, we investigate the possibility not so much of a completely different ontological cosmos inhabited by the Anangu and Druze, but rather how reincarnation discourses in these two particular peoples, first, affect *time* in a general way, and, second, how the temporal ripples of reincarnation are articulated socially and politically as claims of minorities to *autochthony*. It is through this transformation that both communities come to relate to both state issues of citizenship and belonging, and other segments of the population.

The Social Context of Druze and A<u>n</u>angu Religious Philosophy

The Druze of Jaramana

Four kilometres from the Syrian capital, in the suburb of Jaramana, its Druze inhabitants do not wake up in the morning to the sound of *adhts*, the Muslim call for prayer, as neither mosques nor a commandment for the public expression of religiosity exist (Khuri 2004). Relation to God is perceived as a personal matter. They frequently wake up to the sound of Abu George's voice coming out of a megaphone on a car: 'With contentment and submission, we declare the death of …' (Khuri 2004: 226).[1] Then Abu George gives the name and the family of the deceased person, and the time the funeral will take place in the *mawqaf* (Druze mourning space). Based on Druze belief in reincarnation (*taqamuṣ*), the death of someone not only affects those who knew them while alive, but also those who might have known them in a past life, and those to whom they might be a relative or a friend in the future (Hood 2007: 148; Bennett 2006; Oppenheimer 1980). In this way, death is not the abrupt cessation of relationships, but their corporeal and on-going transformation.

This section introduces Druze religion and contemporary society, showing how beliefs in reincarnation interact with contemporary political discourses and social practices. Writing on Druze religion is problematic because, among other reasons: historiographies of all religious minorities in the Levant are political; the canon of Druze religion is considered sacred and only initiates have access to it, this means that theological interpretations of reincarnation are based on second-hand sources; while a distinct religious community in Syria, the Druze are not homogeneous (Kastrinou 2014); and the ethnographic material in this paper rests on fieldwork conducted during the period immediately before the start of the on-going war in 2011.

'Druze' is the popular name given to the religious community that emerged during the Fatimid Dynasty in eleventh-century Cairo. Speculations on the origins of the name 'Druze' are diverse and contested while 'Druze' is considered derogatory by most of the followers of the doctrine, who, although using it, prefer to be referred as *muwah'id* (pl. *muwah'iddun*), meaning followers of the *Tawh'īd* doctrine, *ahl al-tawh'aw* ('people of *tawh'e* ', Khuri 2004: 18), or *Bani Ma'raa* ('the sons of benevolence', see Betts 1988: 16; Khuri 2004: 19).[2] The Druze are estimated to number one million worldwide, of which 420,000 reside in Syria (Makarem 2007). In Syria, the majority of the Druze population lived, until the current war, in Jaramana and in the district of Suwayda. In recognition of their status as a distinct religious community in Syria, Lebanon and Palestine, the Druze have their own courts that arbitrate over issues of family and personal status (Alamuddin and Starr 1980; Layish 1982; Khuri 2004).

Historical Beginnings of the Druze: Time and Eternity

Druze religion was founded by the Fatimid ruler al-Hakim bi-Amr Allah (996–1021), who proclaimed himself to be the last manifestation of divinity through a public declaration in 1017 that a new era had dawned: after *al-shar'ia* and *al-tariqa*, the final cycle of *al-haqhaq* (truth, self-realization and unity). Re-appropriating Sufi terminology, Isma'ili doctrine, and neo-Platonic philosophy, the new religion, *Tawh'ri*, holds that God manifests himself to humans according to their capabilities and perceptiveness through periodic manifestations, of which tawh'īd, personified in al-Hakim, signalled the final manifestation. Based on this eclectic perception that divine knowledge cannot be acquired by everybody, the Druze Canon, the *Book of Wisdom* (*Rasahl al-Hikmah,* written between 1017 and 1042), is consequently viewed as an intimate divine manifestation not to be shared with those incapable of grasping it or prone to corrupt it. This esoteric distinction differentiates the community internally, by distinguishing between those enlightened and initiated into the secret and sacred knowledge, the *'uqqāl,* and those uninitiated and ignorant, the vast majority of the followers, the *juhhal* (Betts 1988: 16). This distinction provides a structural power-balancing mechanism whereby religious authority rests with the *uqqāl* and political authority with the *juhhal* (Khuri 2004). This distinction allows uninitiated Druzes to occupy themselves with profane politics, while *shaykhs* are bound to sacred law: *shaykhs* in Jaramana often publicly defied state policies.

Although the social structure of Druze communities varies historically and geographically, attachment to the land and prescription for endogamous marriage have been significant factors in maintaining cohesion, exclusivity and avoiding persecution. Attachment to land has historically formed the basis of Druze autonomy from the time of dynastic Islam. Khuri notes that 'the saying that land (*ard*), honour (*'ird*) and religion (*din*), in this order of significance, constitute a sacred trinity among the Druze carries considerable weight … the Muwahhidun believe that he who has no land cannot protect his honour and he who has no honour has no religion' (2004: 55). Kastrinou's Druze 'mother' once remarked that *'al-alaqat al-Druzie kabire, yahtazu ard kabir'* (the [social] relationships of the Druze are big, and they need land that is large), while a young Druze emphatically noted that *'ard majal al-hurrieh'* (land is the place of freedom). In this way, land becomes a basis and a fixture upon which Druze cosmology and contemporary identity is anchored, an originary *topos* where the autochthonous Druze were always already born.

Reincarnation in Druze Theology

> O you who are distracted, how can he who is devoid of his corporeal means obtain knowledge? […] And O you who are perplexed, how can the souls exist by themselves?
>
> (al-Muqtana Baha'uddin, Druze Epistle 75, cited in Makarem 1974: 54–5)

Druze informants portrayed the body as the garment or shirt (*qamis*) of the soul: a temporal body dresses an eternal soul, and as the corporeal body withers, the soul passes to another body, because the soul cannot be manifested or expressed except through its corporeal means. The 'strict and uncompromising' (Abu-Izzeddin 1984: 111) unity of God forms the basis of *Tawh'īd* doctrine. The interlocking of spirituality and corporeality within an on-going process of the soul's actualization in corporeal embodiment is the basis of the Druze belief in reincarnation, or human-to-human transmigration of the soul (*taqamuṣ*).[3] These theological views on reincarnation underpin the importance of the body in ritual and everyday practices in the Druze community: 'Just as a meaning makes sense only when expressed through its word, so must the human soul be expressed in a human body' (Makarem 2005: 5).

The Druze doctrine of the *tawh'īd* may fruitfully be considered as a different religion to Islam, albeit one with a historical relation to it (cf. Betts 1988: 17–18). One of its main differences is its non-proselytizing character. With al-Hakim bi-Amr Allah, the third and last cycle (*dawar*) of divine manifestation began and, after twenty-five years, ended in 1046. During this period of the Druze *da'wa* (divine call) new adherents would sign their names and profess their faith by taking a binding oath. The finite period of proselytism ended in part due to the historical circumstance (in 1021 al-Hakim bi-Amr Allah disappeared and his successors persecuted adherents of *tawh'īd*). In *tawh'īd* cosmology, Druze souls were created once and their number stays constant throughout time because Druze souls reincarnate only in Druze bodies. Divine justice (*'adl*), operates not on the basis of punishments and rewards or as ethical compensation for actions carried out over one lifespan and exacted in the next, as is often the case for reincarnation within the South Asian context (cf. Obeyesekere 1994: xii, xx–xxii). Instead, the *Muwahiddun* are granted equality and the vindication of divine justice through the continuous transmigration of the *Muwah'id* soul only to a *Muwah'id* body (Firro 1992: 12). Through the actualization of every possible state, gender and status, reincarnation becomes the eternal equalizer without referent to morality.[4]

One of the social ramifications of this form of reincarnation is a strong impetus to *egalitarianism* – in fact this seems to be a characteristic shared between groups for whom reincarnation does not depend on ideas of karma or morality. The impetus for egalitarianism among the Druze has historical roots. During the rule of al-Hakim egalitarian religious and social reforms took place, such as the revocation of the *imāma* hereditary system (Firro 1992: 10), abolition of slavery and redistribution of state property (Abu-Izzedin 1984: 79), while under the new doctrine, for the first time, *Muwah'id* men and women were granted equal rights in marriage, divorce and property, and polygamy was denounced. Even the divine became more immediate as ritual and symbolism were deemed unnecessary: 'A spiritual doctrine without any ritualistic impositions' was born (Taqiyyuddin, in Makarem 1974: 23; Khuri 2004, 2006: 61–78).

The Foundation of Social Order Among the Anangu

The Anangu (Pitjantjatjara and Yankunytjatjara) live in Australia's Western Desert.

Their northern neighbours, within the better-watered MacDonnell Ranges, are the Arrernte (Strehlow 1947; Morton 1987), while further north, the Warlpiri (Meggitt 1962; Munn 1973) occupy the Australian Central Desert. The following ethnography was collected by Layton between September 1977 and April 1979, and in July 1994. The ethnography summarized here provided supporting evidence for the successful 1979 land claim to the area surrounding the Uluru National Park, the 1985 return of the Park's title to its traditional owners, and the Park's 1995 inscription on the UNESCO World Heritage List as an indigenous landscape of universal value (Layton 2004).

In Anangu oral tradition, the social order was established during the Tjukurpa, the Creation Period or Time of the Law. During this foundational time, ancestral beings who were simultaneously human and animal frequently travelled long distances through the central Australian desert, crossing the land of many local bands. Their adventures established the rules of social behaviour: the need to honour social obligations such as sharing meat, to accept invitations to ceremonies, and so forth. Sometimes they encountered localized, non-travelling ancestral beings such as the Willy Wagtail Woman. As they travelled, the ancestors created 'sacred sites' where they left their animating power. Sacred sites can be construed as disturbances in the space-time continuum, where energy is transformed into matter, and can be released again as energy. 'Becoming' (-ringanyi) is a key concept in Anangu thought. Sacred sites are physically dangerous and major sacred sites can only be approached in the company of a custodian.

The cultural landscape created during the Creation Period provides a structure against which the contingencies of people energy is transformed into matter, and can be released again as ancestor energy. Sacred sites can be construed as disturbances in the space-time continuum, where energy is transformed into matter and can be released again as energy. 'Becoming' (-ringanyi) is a key concept in Anangu thought.

Apu-ringanyi = become a rock

Walytja-ringanyi = become kin

Sacred sites are physically *dangerous*. Major sacred sites can only be approached in the company of a custodian.

The cultural landscape created during the Creation Period provides a structure against which the contingencies of people's lifetimes are played out. Each person is an incarnation of a named ancestor and each generation tends to reproduce the founding generation of the Creation Period. The fundamental ontology on which Anangu religion is built is that described by Munn's (1970) insightful paper 'The Transformation of Subjects into Objects ...'. Her discussion (1970: 146) of the ways in which living Pitjantjatjara identify themselves as the ancestor who formed their birthplace or father's country is particularly relevant to this paper. While Munn worked with Pitjantjatjara who had moved to the MacDonnell Ranges,

Layton was fortunate to work with men who had later returned to their own country.

Anangu reincarnation is not about physical reproduction (which is achieved by sexual intercourse), but spiritual reproduction (cf. Warner 1937: 24). A person acquires their *kurunpa* (self or will) from the ancestral site at which, when they were newborn, the stub of their umbilical cord fell off. The *kurunpa* of the ancestor who became a rock at that site enters through their 'belly button' as if through an animal burrow (*pulyi*) that closes behind it.

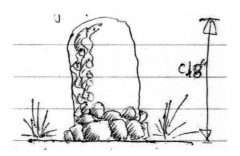

Figure 9.1: Extract from Layton's fieldnotes, 21 May 1978 – sketch of representative stone at the site elucidated by Mintjantji and Tjinguna

Although ancestors who did wrong in the Creation Period are reincarnated in the same way as any other, people have sufficient agency/*kurunpa* to alter their destiny (Layton 1995: 219–20). Figure 9.1 was sketched at a site where the speakers' ancestors are embodied in standing stones. Leslie Mintjantji, a middle-aged man, and Tjinguna, an elder, explained the significance of the stones in relation to members of the local group who 'sat down' here, that is, chose to make this place the focus of their life movements. They include Wintjin – another living elder, Mintjantji's deceased father Pingkari and Tjinguna's deceased father Wanpiti. '*Mama ngayuku palatja* – that's my father right there,' says Leslie, pointing to one of the stones, 'and here is Tjinguna's father, next to him.' Nearby, a double, perforated stone is lying on its side. Another of the men present explains that his ancestral prototype killed the two men embodied in the perforated stone during an argument. The reincarnated aggressor points out the stones and comments, with some pride, 'I'm a proper cheeky bugger.' Before we left, however, Leslie stood up the fallen stone, propping it with smaller pieces of rock. Re-embodiment might be described as cyclic, but it is more accurately represented as a form of repeated realization by living agents.

The Social Background to Reincarnation Among the Anangu

Until European settlement (cattle ranches, church missions) reached the area in the 1930s the Anangu were full-time hunter-gatherers. From 1977 to 1979 Layton was able to work with people who were adults when colonial settlement took place, and who could therefore describe the traditional way of life from personal experience. The following paragraphs are written in the 'ethnographic present'.

The fundamental problem for social life in Australia's Western Desert is to survive and adapt to the low and irregular rainfall in a sandy desert where surface water only persists in sheltered rock holes, or in 'soaks' where water is protected from evaporation in shallow sand deposits over rock, or in the beds of normally dry creeks. Rainfall is unpredictable, both in time and space. Fortunate bands will welcome visitors from drought-stricken areas, because next year the situation might be reversed. Since local resources will have been exhausted during dry months, people leave their own base camp after rain, forage more widely and visit relatives in other bands. Survival demands, on the one hand, cultivating long-term commitment to a band whose foraging activities centre on a particular reliable source of water and, on the other hand, developing a widespread network of kin who will provide hospitality when one's own area is afflicted by drought.

Each more-or-less permanent water source is surrounded by a foraging territory or *ngura*. Anyone who wants to join the band holding pre-eminent rights to that water source must get permission from the core of long term, local residents. Genealogies collected during fieldwork indicated that a band (*utulu* = a band or 'mob') numbered about thirty people, a figure supported by explorers' and travellers' records (Layton 1986).

A person holds a country (*ngura witini*) by making it their base camp (*nguranka nyinanyi* = camp+at sitting). To hold a country one must both know its law (legends and sites), and make it the base for your life movements (see Layton 1983). At birth a person has potential rights in the area around the site at which they were born, and to their mother's and father's *ngura*, but they must choose (*ngura kanankuku* = selecting a country).

The responsibilities of being a member of a band are two-fold. One must look after subsistence resources by keeping water sources clear of debris, and by firing the bush after rain to make walking easier. At the same time this allows new grass providing feed for kangaroos to grow, and germinates the seeds of plants that produce edible berries. One must also look after sacred sites in the *ngura*. Only members of the local group can go to sacred sites and perform rituals there. Newcomers to the district must forage with members of the local band in case they accidentally trespass on a sacred site. Sacred sites are always near water, itself a creative medium. The defence of access to sacred sites may implicitly have been defence of access to water (cf. Gould 1980: 141ff.).

The Cultural Construction of Anangu Kinship

In the course of carrying out their responsibilities within a *ngura* a person becomes kin to, or a carer of, the land: *ngura walytja ringanyi. Walytja* denotes synonymously a kinsperson and someone you care for (Goddard 1987: 170). People of the same generation who live in the same band address each other as siblings, even if there is no specifiable genealogical relationship between them. In societies where children consistently join their father's group and women marry out, these women's children (cross cousins) will always belong to another group. However, a consequence of the principle of ambilineal descent (Layton 1983), by which people can choose whether to join their mother's or father's band, is that the distinction between parallel and cross cousin has no systematic social significance among the Anangu. Cross cousins call each other 'brother' or 'sister' if they and their parents foraged together: 'We were like brother and sister, always travelling together,' said Paddy Uluru of his grandfather's sister's grandchildren. The following table gives the figures I collected for the band affiliation of middle-aged and elderly people born before intensive colonization.

Table 9.1: Transmission of band membership among the Anangu

Transmission	number	%
Join father's band	79	69
Join mother's band	23	20
Join band of parent's sibling where different to parent's	9	8
Join grandparent's band where different to parent's	3	3
Total	**114**	**100**

Fathers prefer their children to be born in their own country, but where one is born is an 'opening gambit' in establishing rights to the land (Layton 1995: 221–2). Parents try to return to the mother's or father's country when birth is imminent but drought or attendance at a ceremony may render that impossible, and the place of birth may be dismissed as *unytju* (trivial) if a person chooses to make another place the focus of their responsibilities and rights.

The marriage rule states that one must marry someone from a distant group, and kinship defines all one's adjacent groups as 'brothers' and 'sisters'. This system is almost certainly a response to the harsh and unpredictable environment of the Western Desert, where flexibility of movement and an open network of social relationships is essential. There is no tendency for alliances between specific groups. People in distant bands are classed as 'in-laws' (*marutju* = cousin or brother in law). Dousset (2005) translates the term for marriageable members of one's own gener-ation in distant groups (*watjirra*) as 'cross cousin', but 'distant cousin' is spatially, not genealogically, defined.

Time, Memory and Sedimentation

Time, memory and al-nutq among the Druze

It is a well-noted paradox that, while the Druze are secretive about their religion with outsiders, they are open about their beliefs in reincarnation. Talking about Druze *'asabiyya*, translated as 'unity, solidarity and internal cohesion', Khuri (2004: 102) states that religion, and specifically *taqamuṣ*, is at the heart of Druze solidarity: 'solidarity is based upon unity of belief, standard rituals, the sense of equality, the lack of formally-graded hierarchy – and exclusivity, in the sense that a member has to be born into the group. [...] Once a *Muwahhid*, always a *Muwahhid*' (Khuri 2004: 103).

Past lives, however, do not always come in strict succession, one after another, but sometimes past or future permeate or protrude into the present. An instance of this porosity, perhaps more accurately described as the sedimentation of past into the present, is *al-nutq*. Literally meaning 'the speech', *al-nutq* refers to occasions when a person recalls things, memories, and actions from her previous life in her current one (Playfair 2006: 54; Khuri 2004: 105). This occurrence most often takes places among Druze children between the ages of four and twelve, and there is a popular belief that *al-nutq* usually happens in cases of violence and tragic death. Kastrinou heard of some such examples during fieldwork, although she never met anyone who had personally experienced *al-nutq*. The anthropologist Fuad Khuri collected two such case studies, which he presents in his book *Being a Druze* (2004: 109–14). Playfair discusses many Druze reincarnation stories (2006: 54, 111), and includes three in-depth case studies from the material of Erlendur Haraldsson (Playfair 2006: 133–57), which is based on further study of some fifty-five cases collected by Ian Stevenson, who was the first to make a systematic study of reincarnation among the Druze, between 1964 and 1981.

In these stories children recognize a village, house or family, and these claims are then carefully examined and cross-checked (Bennett 2006). When these claims are proven and believed a relationship is forged between the reincarnated child and its past family. Salim Kheireddine, the founder of the Druze Heritage Foundation in London, has written about his own experiences of past memories, and the relationships that he continued with his past-life family (in Playfair 2006: xi–xii). Indeed, in most of the case studies explored in the literature, when *al-nutq* is proven, then old relationships are reborn and new relationships are created between the two families. This establishes new kinship connections in a material sense across boundaries such as villages and often countries.

Reincarnation establishes a passage to different networks that connects a geographically dispersed community. Because instances of *al-nutq* emerge as traumatic memories of violence or crisis, they embody the Druze ideal of *'asabiyya*, in connecting life and death through a form of eternal relatedness. This is all encapsulated in the expression often heard in the field: '*kulna qarra q hounn*' (we are all relatives here), or 'we are all born in each others' houses' (Oppenheimer 1980).

Yet 'we are all relatives' can be understood in different manners. As the strict rule on endogamous marriage, this has to do both with maintaining exclusivity as well as the social status of offspring (Khuri 2004; Oppenheimer 1980). Occasionally, exogamous marriages are also justified by the discourse of reincarnation, on the grounds that the out-marrying person had reincarnated, almost by divine mistake, a non-Druze soul. Kastrinou (2014) was given the following explanation regarding an 'accepted' interfaith marriage: 'In our community there are some people who accept this [marrying out]. Maybe they are a bit sad, but what can be done, they love the person and must accept that some are born here but are not Druze. It is natural for the soul to return where it belongs.' This use of reincarnation serves to underline its flexibility and plasticity since it is not the specific rules (the prohibition for marrying outside) that make a 'community' or a 'society' or even 'kinship' but the very fact that for these to exist there must be social relations. Reincarnation makes mistakes too (Kastrinou 2012: 288–9). The idea that the soul seeks to return to its original place is relevant because autochthony – 'originating where found' – explains both the constant return of Druze souls into Druze bodies but also, the occasional mistake in reincarnation becomes a geographic miscalculation.

Time and Memory Among the Anangu

Key to understanding native Australian cosmology is the short time separating the Creation Period from the present (Layton 2004: 145). The founding ancestors lived at a time not far beyond living memory. The limited generational span of Anangu genealogies can be seen from the following table, listing the number of individuals recalled by name during collection of genealogies for the Uluru land claim (speakers were from the two generations comprising elders and adults of child-bearing age):

Table 9.2: Names of individuals recalled in deceased and living generations of Anangu

Generation level	Number	%
Deceased +2	6	2
Deceased +1	51	18
Elders	80	29
Child-bearing adults	80	29
(Grand) Children	63	22
Total	**280**	**100%**

Anangu kin terms demonstrate both the strong element of bilaterality in their system and the tendency to associate grandparents with grandchildren. The greatest differentiation of kinship positions occurs in *ego's* own generation and the one above, where the distinction between the close kin whom one meets regularly, and distant marriageable kin, is crucial. At two generations above or below *ego* relatives are merged rather than distinguished. At +2 generations they are addressed as *tjamu* (grandfather) or *kami* (grandmother), at -2 generations as 'little' *tjamu* and 'little' *kami*. This tendency is made more concrete through the recognition of two generational levels, referred to as 'shade side' and 'sun side' (Wiltjaluru and Tjintaluru). Ego belongs to the same generational moiety as his/her grandparents and grandchildren. All these factors are consistent with the pattern of reincarnation characteristic of Anungu, with the merging of living people and their ancestral prototype in each generation.

One interesting case concerned the local affiliation of Paddy Uluru, the senior custodian of sacred sites at Uluru during Layton's fieldwork. Paddy had been born while his parents were attending a ceremony in the Musgrave Ranges, 100 kilometres to the south of Uluru. His birthplace was associated with the *Minyma Mingkiri* (Mice Women). During the Tjukur, a man was making a spear there, at his campsite. He had softened the wood by warming it in his campfire and stood up to straighten the stick, holding it under his bent leg as he forced it straight. The effort made him fart, causing the Mice Women, who were watching from a rock shelter in a nearby ridge, to giggle. Later, the Mice Women went into the ground at a nearby 'soak' or temporary water source that forms after rain. Pompy Douglas justified Paddy's right to be custodian of Uluru on the grounds that all his older brothers had been born at Uluru and, now that they had passed away, Paddy had taken their place. After Paddy Uluru's death near the end of Layton's 1979 fieldwork, he was re-identified with one of the ancestors at Uluru. Men's and women's rituals are strictly segregated; neither may watch the other's ceremonies. During the Creation Period, Men found the Willy Wagtail Woman 'dancing like a man' at Uluru, for which she was speared by a left-handed Mala Wallaby man. Paddy Uluru told Layton that the left-handed man was his deceased *kuta* 'elder brother' (but genealogically, his father's brother's son) Muraku. After Paddy's death, younger men told Layton that Paddy himself was the left-handed Wallaby Man. This raises the possibility that the memory of each ancestor may be built from a palimpsest of his or her successive embodiments.

Performance and Embodiment of Reincarnation in Druze Mortuary Rituals

Birthing and dying in Jaramana are ceremonials through which the ritual and the everyday interpenetrate, temporal and spatial occasions that negotiate religious, political and socio-economic orders, instances where the cosmological and the ordinary, life and death, become intertwined. In the mortuary rituals, there are three occasions in which we note the strong correlation between reincarnation and social practice, namely, condolences, attendance and the ritual of *al-'usbū'*.

Death is a communal affair (Khuri 2004; Hood 2007) and communicating news of death is shared between family members and neighbours. As a communal affair, death is not an individual loss but affects the whole of Druze community; hence, condolences are not given only to the deceased's immediate family but are exchanged between all members of the community, regardless of personally knowing the deceased person or not. There is a tacit expectation for most people to attend funerals; when a funeral is not well attended it is *harām*. Khuri (2004: 227) explains attendance at funerals as a religious duty and as a marker of social status, while Hood adds that the obligation to attend is a fulfilment of the Druze commandment ' *ḥifz al-ikhwik'* (protecting or safeguarding the brethren) in addition to the performance of the religious duty of mercy (*al-raḥma*) (Hood 2007: 147). Indeed, when guests salute each other at funerals they do so by exchanging condolences without necessarily being a member of the deceased person's family. Both death and loss here are communal, shared and equalized.

The actual burial takes place quickly, either eight hours after death or on the next day. The body travels from the house first to the female mourning space, *mawqaf*, then to the male. The *mawqaf* is the main space where ritual mourning takes place, and hence it is viewed as more important than the cemetery. In fact, during my initial fieldwork in Jaramana, the male and female *mawqaf*s were the most elaborate and well-kept religious buildings of the neighbourhood. The coffin is carried to the Druze cemetery, where only male mourners are permitted. The body is taken out of the coffin and sand is placed on the eyes of the dead, so that, informants explained, s/he leaves '*sabaan*' (fulfilled, as in not hungry), because 'we come from the earth and return to the earth,' and also because '*khalās* [finish, as in 'done'], now the soul has left it is just the body.' Although Hood (2007: 152) mentions that the cemetery is visited by relatives for forty days after death, Kastrinou's Druze 'mother' insisted that they do not visit the cemetery: 'In our religion we believe that the body is not important – the soul is. In death only the body is lost. The soul will come back.'

After bereavement, the deceased's family is seldom left alone: relatives, neighbours and eventually most of the region's household representatives visit them, spending long hours in the company of the family. Pain is a communal affair and taking part in sharing the pain is socially more important than celebrating happy occasions (Hood 2007: 147). 'All things are born small and grow up. Only pain is born large and then gets smaller. Like the soap,' Umm Samir explained to Kastrinou, pointing out that pain gets smaller only through communal bonds and sharing. The reconciliation between personal pain and communal solidarity comes from the communal embodiment and sharing of pain that combines individual and social loss into a designated spatio-temporal ceremonial ritual: *Al-'usbū'*.

Al-'usbū' (lit. week) is a week-long ritually structured pattern of visitations following the funeral. While there are important ethnomusicological accounts of mortuary lamentations among the Druze (Racy 1986; Hood 2007: 153–8), not much attention has been paid to these on-going mortuary visitations. Solidarity in the face of loss is embodied by the constant presence of other people in the deceased's house.

Neighbours take care of the eating arrangements for family and guests, sharing food and stories. Emphasis on the deceased *per se* becomes slowly transformed into a social emphasis on the living, realigning the cosmological perspective of the eternal soul within the existential realm of living social bodies. Death is not a *telos*, and reincarnation and restraint means that a social shift takes place from the dead to the *'asabiyya* of the community.

Traditional Anangu burials were, in contrast, extremely simple. The body of the deceased was quickly buried in a shallow grave covered with rocks, sticks or branches, enabling the *kurunpa* to escape from the body; after some weeks or months, depending on what was practicable, relatives would return and cover the grave with soil (Edwards 2013). Edwards notes that Anangu burial practices began to change, to make them compatible with life on permanent settlements, during the early 1970s.

Conclusion

In this paper, we explored reincarnation cosmologies and practices among the Druze and Anangu. Our ethnographic descriptions and comparisons, our puzzle – now set out – necessitates our own 'cyclical return' to the heart of this comparative exercise: what can reincarnation tell us about contemporary religion and politics?

Complicating the scholarship on ethnic groups, nationalism and boundaries, in the cases of the Druze and the Anangu we encountered sedimentation: transient forms of eternal soul and embodiment of the landscape. Specifically, we explored reincarnation in relation to the Druze in terms of their history, theology, and their contemporary practices. Practices of death, recollected stories of past lives and the role of reincarnation in reproducing but also in subverting endogamy were explored. These ethnographic instances underlined the social and political spectrum in which reincarnation is not only a religious metaphysical belief, outside of social action and political realities, but is also an active discourse in and through which social, economic and political claims are articulated, negotiated and contested.

Similarly, for the Anangu of the Western Desert, reincarnation is a complex platform onto which metaphysical ideas about the cosmos are mapped and connections between the past and the future embodied. The association of land, birth, and kinship provides a powerful framework for claims to land, band membership, and for the definition of the Anangu vis-à-vis their neighbours and the Australian state, acknowledged through a successful land claim and the repatriation of ownership of Uluru (Layton 1986, 2004). The Anangu case further evidences that reincarnation is best understood as a flexible and adaptable discourse through which not only social, political and economic claims are negotiated, but also potential connections and relations are forged.

Second, what might an anthropological approach to reincarnation be? In view of our comparative examples, reincarnation can be considered as a discourse (as in Foucault's use of enunciation, cf. Layton 1995) that articulates the changing social, economic and political demands. This discourse is not determined by its context but, rather, its political relevance provides occasions in which the discourse is publicly presented. In this way the discourse of reincarnation serves, in both cases, a political and social purpose in reinforcing claims of autochthony for minorities. This discourse establishes the Anangu and the Druze within their respective locales, as the necessary parts of a larger landscape. Although reincarnation as discourse firmly grounds the two 'minority' populations within complex physical and social landscapes, it is perhaps the cyclical or sedimentary attributes associated with reincarnation that most importantly serve to eternalize the Anangu and the Druze as *permanent fixtures* in their respective historical landscapes. Thus, the most prominent similarity between the Druze and the Anangu is their use of the discourse of reincarnation as a political claim to time: they have always existed, here and elsewhere; and they shall always return. Natural decay, social entropy and even the brutal institutionalization of modern states and violence are but transient phases in their cycles of rebirth and struggles of unity. Their quality of *timeliness* transcends and actually negates time, flying not beyond but before history. Now, emanations and struggles go in and out of the earth, and beyond the earth. Reincarnation is a discourse that lays a political and a geographic claim to time, in a similar fashion that nationhood implies, in the sense defined by the Treaty of Westphalia, 1648, a claim over sovereign boundaries and frontiers.

For the Anangu and the Druze, material boundaries are, of course, important metaphysically as well as practically. Yet, their legitimacy collapses geography, while their time is place. Empires rise and fall. Nations wax and wane. Frontiers change hands. But, and here is the powerful potential of the discourse of reincarnation as a political claim to eternity, theirs is an autochthonous reckoning, a sovereignty of time.

Notes

1. All names from the Syrian material are pseudonyms.
2. *Tahwīd* is translated as 'unity in being', as well as Unitarianism or Monism.
3. Druze reincarnation takes place from human to human only, and the Arabic word used by Druze is *taqamuṣ*. Other groups, such as the Alawis, believe that reincarnation may take place between human and any other living form; this is called *tanashoukh*.
4. Accounts are not clear on this: in the Druze case, literature suggests that the soul most probably returns with the same gender, but informants hold diverse opinions (cf. Khuri 2004; Playfair 2006).

References

Abu-Izzeddin, N. (1984) *The Druzes: A New Study of their History, Faith and Society,* Leiden: E. J. Brill.

Alamuddin, N. S. and Starr, P. D. (1980) *Crucial Bonds: Marriage among the Lebanese Druze.* New York: Caravan Books.

Alonso, A. M. (1994) 'The Politics of Space, Time and Substance: State Formation, Nationalism and Ethnicity', *Annual Review of Anthropology* 23: 379–405.

Banks, M. (1996) *Ethnicity: Anthropological constructions,* London: Routledge.

Bennett, A. (2006) 'Reincarnation, Sect Unity, and Identity Among the Druze', *Ethnology* 45 (2): 87–104.

Betts, B. R. (1988) *The Druze,* London: Yale University Press.

Coleman, G., ed. (2008) *Tibetan Book of the Dead,* Harmondsworth: Penguin Classics.

Dousset, L. (2005) 'Structure and Substance: Combining "Classic" and "Modern" Kinship Studies in the Australian Western Desert', *Australian Journal of Anthropology* 16: 18–30.

Edwards, W. (2013) 'Changes in Pitjantjatjara Mourning and Burial Practices', *Australian Aboriginal Studies* 2013 (1): 31–44.

Eriksen, T. H. (2002 [1993]) *Ethnicity and Nationalism: Anthropological Perspectives* (2nd edn) London: Pluto Press.

Firro, K. M. (1992) *A History of the Druzes,* Leiden: E. J. Brill.

Foucault, M. (2007) *Security, Territory, Population: Lectures at the Collège de France, 1977–78,* M. Senellart (ed.) translated by G. Burchell, Basingstoke: Palgrave Macmillan.

Geertz, C. (1973) *The Interpretation of Cultures,* New York: Basic.

Goddard, C. (1987) *A Basic Pitjantjatara/Yankunytjara to English Dictionary,* Alice Springs: Institute for Aboriginal Development.

Gould, R. (1980) *Living Archaeology,* Cambridge: Cambridge University Press.

Gupta, A. (2002) 'Reliving Childhood? The Temporality of Childhood and Narratives of Reincarnation', *Ethos* 67 (1): 33–56.

Hood, K. (2007) *Music in Druze Life: Ritual, Values and Performance Practice,* London: Druze Heritage Foundation.

Kastrinou, A. M. A. (2012) *Intimate Bodies, Violent Struggles: The Poetics and Politics of Nuptiality in Syria.* Doctoral thesis, Durham University 2012. Available online: http://etheses.dur.ac.uk/4923/ [accessed 1 December 2014].

Kastrinou, A. M. A. (2014) 'Sect and House in Syria: History, Architecture, and *Bayt* Amongst the Druze in Jaramana', *History and Anthropology* 25 (3): 313–35.

Khuri, F. I. (2004) *Being a Druze,* London: Druze Heritage Foundation.

Khuri, F. I. (2006) 'Aspects of Druze Social Structure: "There are no Free-floating Druze"', in K. Salibi (ed.) *The Druze: Realities and Perceptions,* London: Druze Heritage Foundation.

Layish, A. (1982) *Marriage, Divorce and Succession in the Druze Family: A Study Based on Decisions of Druze Arbitrators and Religious Courts in Israel and the Golan Heights*, Leiden: E. J. Brill.

Layton, R. (1983) 'Ambilineal Descent and Pitjantjatjara Rights to Land', in N. Peterson and M. Langton (eds) *Aborigines, Land and Land Rights*, Canberra: Australian Institute of Aboriginal Studies Press.

Layton, R. (1986) *Uluru, an Aboriginal History of Ayers Rock*, Canberra: Aboriginal Studies Press.

Layton, R. (1995) 'Relating to the Country in the Western Desert', in E. Hirsch and M. O'Hanlon (eds) *The Anthropology of the Landscape: Perspectives on Place and Space*, Oxford: Clarendon Press.

Layton, R. (2004) 'The Politics of Indigenous "Creationism" in Australia', in S. Coleman and L. Carlin (eds) *The Cultures of Creationism. Anti-evolutionism in English-speaking Countries*, Aldershot: Ashgate.

Lévi-Strauss, C. (1966) *The Savage Mind* [anonymous translation of *La Pensée Sauvage*, 1962], London: Weidenfeld and Nicolson.

Makarem, J. M. (2007) 'Druze Population', *American Druze Heritage*. Available online: http://americandruze.com/Druze%20Population.html [accessed August 2011].

Makarem, S. (1974) *The Druze Faith*, New York: Caravan Books.

Makarem, S. (2005) 'The Druze Faith', in K. Salibi (ed.) *The Druze: Realities and Perceptions,* London: Druze Heritage Foundation.

Malinowski, B. (1916) 'Baloma; The Spirits of the Dead in the Trobriand Islands,' *The Journal of the Royal Anthropological Institute* 46 (July–December): 353–430.

Matlock, J. G. (1994) 'Alternate-Generation Equivalence and the Recycling of Souls: Amerindian Rebirth in Global Perspective'. In A. Mills and R. Slobodin (eds) *Amerindian Rebirth: Reincarnation Belief Among North American Indians and Inuit*, pp. 263–83. Toronto: University of Toronto Press.

Meggitt, M. (1962) *Desert People: A Study of the Walbiri Aborigines of Central Australia,* Sydney: Angus and Robertson.

Mills, A. (1994) 'Reincarnation Belief Among North American Indians and Inuit: Context, Distribution, and Variation', in A. Mills and R. Slobodin (eds) *Amerindian Rebirth: Reincarnation Belief among North American Indians and Inuit*, Toronto: University of Toronto Press, 15–37.

Mills, A. and Slobodin, R. (eds) (1994) *Amerindian Rebirth: Reincarnation Belief among North American Indians and Inuit,* Toronto: University of Toronto Press.

Morphy, H. (1995) 'Landscape and the Reproduction of the Ancestral Past', in E. Hirsch and M. O'Hanlon (eds) *The Anthropology of the Landscape: Perspectives on Place and Space*, Oxford: Clarendon Press.

Morton, J. (1987) 'Singing Subjects and Sacred Objects: More on Munn's "Transformation of Subjects into Objects" in Central Australian Myth', *Oceania* 58 (2): 100–18.

Munn, N. D. (1970) 'The Transformation of Subjects into Objects in Walbin and Pitjantjatjara Myth', in R. M. Berndt (ed.) *Australian Aboriginal Anthropology: Modern Studies in the Social Anthropology of the Australian Aborigines*, Nedlands, Western Australia: The University of Western Australia Press.

Munn, N. D. (1973) *Walbiri Iconography*, Ithaca: Cornell University Press.

Nuttall, M. (1994) 'The Name Never Dies: Greenland Inuit Ideas of the Person', in A. Mills and R. Slobodin (eds) *Amerindian Rebirth: Reincarnation Belief among North American Indians and Inuit*, Toronto: University of Toronto Press, 123–35.

Obeyesekere, G. (1994) 'Foreword', in A. Mills and R. Slobodin (eds) *Amerindian Rebirth: Reincarnation Belief among North American Indians and Inuit*, Toronto: University of Toronto Press.

Oppenheimer, J. W. S. (1980) '"We are Born in Each Other's Houses": Communal and Patrilineal Ideologies in Druze Village Religion and Structure', *American Ethnologist* 7 (4): 621–36.

Playfair, G. L. (2006) *New Clothes for Old Souls: Worldwide Evidence for Reincarnation*, London: Druze Heritage Foundation.

Peterson, N. (1972) 'Totemism Yesterday', *Man (N.S.)* 7: 12–32.

Provence, M. (2005) 'Druze Shaykhs, Arab Nationalists and Grain Merchants', in K. Salibi (ed.) *The Druze: Realities and Perceptions*, London: Druze Heritage Foundation.

Racy, A. J. (1986) 'Lebanese Laments: Grief, Music, and Cultural Values', *World of Music* 28 (2): 27–40.

Samuel, G. (1993) *Civilised Shamans: Buddhism in Tibetan Societies*, Washington: Smithsonian.

Slobodin, R. (1994) 'Kutchin Concepts of Reincarnation', in A. Mills and R. Slobodin (eds) *Amerindian Rebirth: Reincarnation Belief among North American Indians and Inuit*, Toronto: University of Toronto Press, 136–55.

Stevenson, I. (1980) *Cases of the Reincarnation Type, 3: Lebanon and Turkey*. New York: Alloh.

Strang, V. (1997) *Uncommon Ground: Cultural Landscapes and Environmental Values*, Oxford: Berg.

Strehlow, T. G. H. (1947) *Aranda Traditions*, Melbourne: Melbourne University Press.

Turner, E. (1994). 'Behind Inupiaq Reincarnation: Cosmological Cycling', in A. Mills and R. Slobodin (eds) *Amerindian Rebirth: Reincarnation Belief among North American Indians and Inuit*, Toronto: University of Toronto Press, 67–81.

Warner, W. L. (1937) *A Black Civilisation*, New York: Harper.

Part Four

Navigating Engagement with Public Issues

–10–

Toilets for Africa: Humanitarian Design Meets Sanitation Activism in Khayelitsha, Cape Town

Peter Redfield
Steven Robins

Our chapter introduces an underappreciated artefact of global connection – the humble toilet – and examines a convergence between two different human imaginaries around it. The first of these visions is an earnest amalgam of humanitarian sentiment and ecological sensibility, emanating primarily from what is currently glossed as the 'global north'. The second animates an unexpected social justice movement in a highly specific part of the 'global south', post-Apartheid South Africa, particularly the Western Cape. Both agree that current sanitation arrangements are a problem and seek a different future. However, they disagree on what that future should include, and the contrast between them reveals significant tensions related to the material politics of infrastructure. In the pages that follow we outline both of these two perspectives in turn. We then consider their stakes, including differing conceptions of the good at planetary, national and personal levels as well as the elusive matter of human dignity, which in this case adheres conspicuously to the toilet. Throughout, we seek to forward a critical examination that remains sympathetic to both conceptions of the problem. Although the topic does not lend itself to antiseptic writing, the issues it raises remain stubbornly complex and not easily resolved. In addressing them we hope to highlight expectations and aspirations linking states to service delivery, and raise the ever-political question of who defines the future, and with what terms.

Toilets and Global Design

As anthropologists we first note that a problem of sanitation grew alongside human settlements and increasing population density. Whatever stories we might tell about a longer, species-level genealogy, it is clear that as people lived in greater numbers and closer together the disposal of waste became an increasing issue. However thoroughly 'natural' waste may be in the sense of representing a species-level concern, the issue of what to do with its accumulation as a byproduct of living together is an inherently social and political matter. For people living in cities the satisfaction of daily physical needs necessarily implicates others, whether or not those relations are directly visible to neighbours or seamlessly whisked away through a complex of well-functioning infrastructure. Human excretions, especially faeces, evoke a range of visceral reactions and also constitute a physical substance with particular properties. From the perspective of both contemporary urban sensibilities in places like Cape Town and expert knowledge in fields such as ecology and public health, it goes without saying that human byproducts pollute, and it makes a significant difference what happens to them. This is where toilets come in: and different visions of related to their past, present and future.

By framing the matter in this relatively distanced and dispassionate way, we have already begun to hint at the first of our two imaginaries. We identify this perspective with a loose group we will designate as 'global humanitarians' – people who seek to improve the human condition and reduce suffering on a planetary scale. We begin with them because they too tell a general story, centred in this case around technology and thus can introduce some history for us. In the best tradition of ethnography we will step out of the way, and allow a prominent native speaker to represent this perspective. What follows is an extended excerpt from a speech delivered by Sylvia Mathews Burwell, the President of the Gates Foundation's Global Development Program, on 19 July 2011:

> Let me begin today not in the present, but in the past. I'd like to bring you back more than 200 years to 1775 … In London, a talented Scottish mathematician and watchmaker named Alexander Cummings was turning his energies to solving a major crisis of his time: improving sanitation. He believed there was a better way to handle waste than the chamber pot and open trenches of his day. In 1775, thanks to his ingenuity, Cummings became the first person to patent a 'water closet' or what we know as the flush toilet. His invention helped spark a sanitary revolution of waterborne sewage systems that have saved hundreds of millions of lives by keeping communities safe from diseases. More than 200 years have passed since Cummings's invention. And a lot has changed. Innovation has touched nearly every part of our lives. What was once seemingly impossible is now possible. Automobiles and airplanes. Electric lights and television. Smart phones and smarter computers. We've developed life-saving vaccines. Looked inside the smallest molecules. Glimpsed at the farthest stars. But more 200 years later, one thing hasn't really changed: The toilet … The sanitation solution that Cummings helped invent – water closets connected to sewer systems – is effectively what we still have today. And we've paid the price for this neglect. More than 2.6 billion people – 40 percent of the world's population – don't have access to these basic sanitation services that many of us take for granted. This includes more than 1 billion people who still defecate out in the open … The second largest killer of children under five is diarrheal disease, which is responsible for the deaths of more than 1 million children every year, more than AIDS and malaria combined. Most of these deaths could be prevented with proper sanitation, combined with safe drinking water and better hygiene. Let me repeat that. More than 1 million children die each year for lack of a basic technology which is now more than

200 years old … No innovation in the past 200 years has done more to save lives and improve health than the sanitation revolution triggered by invention of the toilet. But it did not go far enough. It only reached one-third of the world … At the Bill & Melinda Gates Foundation, asking tough questions like these are at the heart of our work. We are guided by the values of the Gates family, who believe that every life has equal worth. We believe that a child's birthplace shouldn't pre-determine whether they will have access to health and opportunity. To that end, the foundation is involved in a range of health efforts in Africa, from vaccines, AIDS, and malaria to mother and child health … What's clear to us is that existing sanitation solutions – ones based on 200-year-old ideas – are not meeting the challenges we face. Not only is using the world's precious water resources to flush and transport human waste not a smart or sustainable solution, it has simply proven to be too expensive for much of the world. What we need are new approaches. New ideas. In short, *we need to 'Reinvent the Toilet'*. It should be a toilet for the 21st century – a toilet for the billions whose needs are not being met. It should be a toilet that is pleasant to use and makes safe sanitation available simply and cheaply to people everywhere. It should save children's lives by controlling disease. It should eradicate the worst job in the world, that of the latrine emptier. It should bring safety and dignity to all people, especially to women and children. And most importantly, it must be a toilet created in partnership with the people who will use it. This will not be easy. It will demand innovation. Not just new technologies, but new ways of thinking. In this case, it will require turning an age-old problem on its head. We all view human waste as, well, 'waste' and nothing more – something to be flushed away, kept in the dark, not talked about – a taboo. But human waste actually contains valuable and recyclable materials such as water, energy, urea, salts, and minerals. What if we viewed waste as a valuable resource to be tapped? What if human waste powered lights and homes? What if it helped farmers grow more crops? What if it generated potable water?

Mathews Burwell clearly outlines one version of why toilets constitute a problem. To underscore some central themes: a once-brilliant invention has grown into an anachronism. Not only has the flush toilet failed to reach many in the world's population, but it also wastes water; at a moment of heightened ecological awareness this is clearly not a sustainable solution on a global scale. At the same time lack of sanitation remains a threat to human health, and thus a central humanitarian concern. From this perspective the answer is clear: innovate! Bringing the vigour and initiative of expert knowledge to bear promises not only new solutions, but also a way of reconceiving waste itself. Rather than a threatening substance, we might reconceive of it as a resource, rising above taboos to recognize a potential asset for recycling.

For the Gates Foundation this is not simply idle speculation, or even a policy study, but an active call for product development. Mathews Burwell continued her speech to note that the project of reinvention was already underway, announcing the first set of winners from the many teams that had responded to their funding challenge. Rather than bolstering states or municipal governments, or exploring the history of human traditions and attitudes related to waste, the Gates focus here, as in global health, rests on technical innovation and scientific enlightenment (see

Rees 2014). Their competition seeks to mobilize the resources of university-based expertise and private sector technology companies to redesign a 200-year-old invention and thereby address sanitation problems and waterborne diseases experienced by the 2.6 billion who lack adequate toilet facilities, some 40 per cent of the world's population. This '40 per cent' figure derives from estimates of material conditions; it is conceived as a uniform, standardized target population passively waiting for global solutions to their localized sanitation problems. The Gates Foundation's innovation-driven vision is surely the most prominent and explicit expression of a technical model of humanitarianism. However, it is far from unique; as we shall see there are many earnest and clever efforts to create new sanitation technologies. Before we do, however, let us introduce our second imaginary swirling around toilets.

Toilet wars in South Africa

In the spring of 2011, shortly before Mathews Burwell delivered her speech, an episode known as the 'toilet wars' erupted in South African politics. During the run-up to the local government elections, images circulated in the press of exposed flush toilets in poor township settings. These pictures struck a raw nerve; the sight of modern porcelain fixtures without walls offered a mini-spectacle of unrealized infrastructure. Their appearance in the press was not accidental, but part of a larger struggle between the nationally dominant party, the African National Congress (ANC) and its rival the Democratic Alliance (DA), which had managed to come to power in the Western Cape Province. ANC Youth League activists came across unenclosed toilets in Makhaza informal settlement in Khayelitsha, outside Cape Town, in 2010. The activists realized that they had stumbled across a political goldmine and began mobilizing around the issue of open toilets, protesting that people had to cover themselves in blankets while using them in public. Meanwhile the Democratic Alliance-controlled City of Cape Town claimed that it had told Makhaza residents during consultation processes that its limited budget allowed for either communal toilet blocks or household toilets, as long as residents themselves provided the enclosure. The majority of residents did so, but fifty-one were unable to do this for various reasons. The activists tore down hasty enclosures made of timber and corrugated iron that the city government tried to erect, as part of larger and longer protest against what they perceived as ineffectual and unequal local government. They also went about destroying the fixtures and demanding their replacement with properly enclosed toilets. When the City brought charges for the destruction of property, the activists took the matter to the South African Human Rights Commission, framing it as a racist violation of the rights and dignity of black South Africans, and, with the support of the activists, a seventy-six-year-old woman who been attacked while using an unenclosed toilet filed a claim in the Western Cape High Court. The Commission agreed with them, and the Court found that the

City had indeed violated the residents' constitutional rights to dignity and privacy (Robins 2014).

When images of these open toilets went viral, the DA leadership in the Western Cape denounced the ANC's campaign as political opportunism. Then journalists reported on more unenclosed toilets in an ANC controlled municipality elsewhere in the country. The result was general embarrassment on all sides. As a news analysis report from the era recounted:

> The municipal election campaign is in the toilet, literally – the delivery of the most basic service of all has come to dominate what may be the first democratic poll in South Africa fought principally on issues of government performance. A Cape High Court judgment a fortnight ago slamming the Democratic Alliance-controlled City of Cape Town for erecting 50 unenclosed lavatories gave the ANC an opportunity to attack the twin planks of the DA's campaign—effective governance and the shedding of racial baggage under the slogan 'we deliver for all'. It was a chance once again to portray the party as a voice of privilege in particular and to fight on the familiar ground of race. But this strategy backfired just ten days before voting when 10 month old media reports of about 1,600 open toilets in the ANC-controlled municipality of Moqhaka in the Free State were reprised in the Sunday press. ... ANC spokesperson Keith Khosa said the leaders who went [to Moqhaka] were 'received warmly' and within two days 300 enclosures were built. The ANC also emphasizes that, in contrast to the DA, which went to court, it has acknowledged its error and has started to build proper toilets. ... All this took place against the backdrop of simmering discontent over service delivery in poor areas across the country. (Rossouw and Dawes 2011)

Although the issue went dormant following the elections, it would soon experience a fertile afterlife, as we describe below.

First, however, we should underscore some elements of the South African perspective forwarded by ANC Youth League activists. As they wrote in an open letter to the Human Settlements Minister in 2010: 'Our complaint is based on the reality that African people residing in Makhaza, Khayelitsha, are forced to shit in full view of the public ... This satanic action by the [Democratic Alliance] city council is tantamount to gross human rights violations and undermines the people's right for their dignity to be protected as stipulated in Section 10 of the Constitution' (*Mail & Guardian* 2010). The problem with toilets was the indignity and inequality they materialized. The Apartheid system of government in South Africa had not only emphasized racial purity and separation between different racial groups: it had also constructed separate and unequal forms of infrastructure to serve them. For Africans living in township areas sanitation primarily took the form of the notorious bucket system of removal where those living in poor neighbourhoods without flush toilets had to rely on plastic buckets. In response, the post-Apartheid Constitution promised equality as a citizenship right, even as the government struggled to fulfil this mandate in material terms. The High Court judge acknowledged this in his formal finding, when he noted both that 'most of the self-enclosed toilets were unsatisfactory to satisfy dignity and privacy' and that 'the Constitution asserts dignity to contradict our past in which human dignity for black South Africans was routinely and cruelly denied' (High Court of South Africa 2011: 14, 21). In this context, sanitation was a national concern, and a direct measure of citizenship. Any sign of inequality could appear as a regressive return to the racialized indignities of the past.

The Grid of Modern Life

Here then we have two distinct concerns intersecting in toilets. In the first, the disposal of human waste is a global ecological and humanitarian issue, a problem to be solved through private initiative and technological innovation. In the second it is a fundamentally political matter, understood in local and national terms, and ultimately a state responsibility. The specificity of South Africa is revealing in this regard. Rather than a floating space of 'Africa' void of infrastructure, it is something of a frontier zone between norms of the global North and South. The Western Cape in particular displays a wealth of impressive buildings, roads, sewers and electrical lines. The dispute over toilets described above is less one of absolute absence, than one of uneven distribution. In South Africa middle-class households – in keeping with middle-class norms worldwide – enjoy properly enclosed flush toilets. The absence of such facilities in poorer informal settlements thus reflects a visible contrast between those who live on and off a larger grid of services.

For this discussion we will use the term 'grid' to gloss a wider complex of state-administered infrastructures, the material goods they provide and the norms they enable. Toilets are a particular charged register of this grid, a vital site in the formation of a distinctly modern subjectivity (Dutton et al. 2002; Morgan 2002). Put in these terms, a key difference between the global humanitarian view and that of the South African activists lies in their different historical relation to the infrastructural grid and their perception of it. For the Gates Foundation reworking the sanitation grid to extend the reach of its health norms and increase its ecological sustainability constitutes a technical challenge. Their formulation of the problem floats free of any legacy of the past, aside from the design of the talented Alexander Cummings. It focuses on health metrics and norms projected into life expectations at a global scale (Redfield 2012). For activists of the ANC Youth League, the partial appearance of the grid in settings like the Makhaza informal settlement in Khayelitsha only serves to highlight an outrage of continuing inequality. The indignity of open toilets evokes a history of racial injustice in intimate terms. In the language referenced above, they are not 'proper' in the sense of fulfilling a middle-class standard. At the same time, the thought of going 'off-grid' recalls the bucket system of the past. In contrast to the Gates perspective, the activists' formulation of the problem remains saturated with history and political sensitivity. To live adjacent to a grid, and yet not enjoy its benefits, vividly renders continuing inequity in material terms. In this sense, for South Africans the relative 'modernity' of service delivery is less an abstract conceptual dispute than a continuing political issue.

It is important to recall that the history of sanitation involves as much in the way of political will as engineering ingenuity. To cite a famous example, the City of London came to a standstill in 1858 due to the stench oozing from the Thames River. For centuries, the Thames had functioned as a dumping ground for human and industrial waste, as well as dead animals. An extended heat-wave that summer boiled centuries of accumulated waste, and produced a ghastly and all-pervading odour in what became known as London's 'Great Stink'. Overwhelmed by the stench wafting into the English Parliament, and fearful of its miasmic health threats, politicians fled committee rooms shielding their noses (Allen 2007: 56). Dousing Parliament's curtains with a mixture of chloride and lime had no effect. It was only when Parliament could no longer function because of the stench that legislators agreed to a systemic overhaul of the entire infrastructure of the Thames, acting with record speed.

In political terms then, a landmark sanitation decision at the heart of the British Empire derived less from dispassionate debate about the merits of a collective good, or an engineering competition such as that sponsored by the Gates Foundation, than an immediate concern over pollution. Richard Fardon traces Mary Douglas's famous phrase 'dirt is matter out of place' to a comment by Lord Palmerston during the long build-up to the Great Stink (Fardon 2013: 2). As Palmerston pointed out, surplus human waste produced in towns belonged in country fields, where it might productively substitute for imported guano fertilizer. Taken up during the sewerage debate, the witticism accurately reflected the essential dynamic at play. Penetrating to the symbolic seat of power and threatening the city's public image, the unbearable smell compelled MPs to cough up the financial resources needed to establish a comprehensive, modern sewage system (Allen 2007: 91).

The Matter of Dignity

The Gates Foundation initiative was not the first humanitarian effort to foster interest in redesigning the toilet. In 2007, the Humanitarian International Design Organization (HIDO) sponsored a competition to reimagine 'Sanitary Facilities for Africa'.[1] A nonprofit entity established under French law and sporting the motto 'design for people in need', the group highlighted three designs out of those submitted to the competition, including an Italian 'WWC' (Without Water Closet) based on a principle of composting, and a Romanian proposal for a modular cabin and bin 'based on African native architecture'. The winning entry came from a Canadian company called Cooler Solutions (now known as Bridgeable), under the impressively ambitious name 'Dignity Toilet'.[2] A clever update on the chamber pot rendered in stylish green and grey, the design encouraged the user not only to carry its contents to an appropriate discard location, but also then to auger the contents into the ground for decomposition. Cooler Solutions saw its invention as addressing 'sanitation compliance, health and personal dignity'.[3] In a blog post four years after this conceptual triumph, a member of the team suggested an even more ambitious aim worth quoting in full:

> Beyond its functional benefits the Dignity toilet takes an empathetic approach to its design. The Dignity toilet is a system that relies on community instead of a government built infrastructure, empowering the individuals within the community. Aesthetically, instead of a disposable bag or box, the Dignity toilet is an attractive product that inspires pride and dignity within its users. It provides a possession for a family and community that they can be proud of, not simply hide or throw away. (Loveless 2011)

Although this design remains conceptual, its name underscores a central thread running through all the cases we have mentioned. Toilets, it seems, have a great deal to do with dignity. Both humanitarian designers and South African activists agree on that, even if they may understand its terms differently.

For the designers, dignity is a question of technology and the aesthetics of its individual experience; improvement and empowerment might be found through innovation. For the activists it remains a matter for political relations, and they look to the state to demand justice. Before returning to those differences, however, we will spend a moment to unravel the connection between dignity and privacy in defecation. As several anthropologists have noted, this is neither a timeless nor a universal assumption. Public toilets take many forms, and the experience of human waste is not always a matter of embarrassment (e.g. Chalfin 2014; van der Geest 2002). European history recalls the same, where royal bowel movements could be the concern of high courtiers, including the English 'Groom of the Stool'. In his aptly titled book, *The History of Shit*, Dominique Laporte recalls that prior to the sixteenth century, in Europe, human waste was usually dumped in the streets, fields or rivers. A French ordinance introduced in 1539, however, required that human waste be stored in the basement of houses and that 'every individual or individual family hold on to personal waste before carrying it out of the city' (Laporte 2000: 29). Laporte then connects this legal watershed to what he terms the 'archaeology of the private' and the literal invention of the privy (Laporte 2000: 44). At a critical juncture, privacy in performing bodily functions became powerfully associated with dignity, and coded into architecture. Chris Otter observes that even Jeremy Bentham included screens in his plans for the Panopticon, to preserve the dignity of defecating inmates, and that by 1844 the Metropolitan Building Act in London directed all privies to have a door (Otter 2008: 5, 124). The water closet patented by the celebrated Alexander Cummings only added another degree of distinction, as well as hygiene. Now that excrement could be effortlessly flushed away, the toilet entered the home, first of the privileged and then the middle classes. The consequence of this privatization and domestication of human waste is still with us today. In the lineage of Rousseau then, not to mention Sigmund Freud and Norbert Elias, we might suggest that shit provides a ready index of civilization, understood as both a technical term and a legacy of colonial history.

It is against this background that the open toilets of South Africa become a highly charged point of political reference and a polar opposite to the dream object of humanitarian designers – the 'anti-dignity toilet' if you will. Whereas the Dignity Toilet imagines an Africa of rural landscapes and fields ready for fertilizing, the bare installations of Makhaza, Khayelitsha and Moqhaka in the Free State Province expose the harsh inequality of urban slum life. One promises pride and self-empowerment while bypassing state infrastructure; the other evokes outrage over continuing injustice and demands government action.

More Matter Out of Place

The South African toilet wars have not ended. In the winter of 2013, Cape Town had its own 'Great Stink' with the flinging of faeces at Western Cape Premier Helen Zille's vehicle convoy, on the N2 highway, on the steps of the Western Cape legislature, in the Cape Town International Airport departures terminal, and the Bellville Civic Centre. These 'poo protests' targeted the Western Cape government's sanitation policies. The developments in Cape Town, however, are in many respects quite different to what happened in London. Whereas the Thames River was the lead actor in the odorous drama it exuded into London's Parliament in 1858, in Cape Town in 2013 the stench at the airport required the active intervention of a small group of renegade ANC activists. Because of the spatial legacies of Apartheid urban planning, these activists had to make their point about poor sanitation in informal settlements by transporting the smell of the slums on the urban periphery to the sanitized city centre and seat of state power. Travelling by taxis, trains and cars, they literally hauled bags of shit from the margins to the city centre. For their trouble, those who dumped faeces at the airport were arrested and charged under the Civil Aviation Act. Meanwhile, their detractors accused them of political opportunism, ill-discipline and hooliganism. The Health Minister Aaron Motsoaledi denounced them for creating a potentially lethal health hazard in their 'direct attack against the whole population'.

Concerns over health can unite or divide, depending on social geography. MPs in the London Parliament perceived their own lives and interests at risk from the awful stench of the Thames, which brought the problem to their doorstep. Sanitation activists in Cape Town, however, have faced a more difficult challenge in trying to convince the political elite and middle classes that the smells and e-coli levels in some of the informal settlements in Cape Town constitute a dangerous and urgent health crisis. The problem of waste and its effects remains unequally distributed rather than shared. Separated by the historical layout of urban planning as well as access to the grid of the existing sewer system, some in the city flush effortlessly and privately, even as others struggle daily to process their waste and that of their neighbours. Under activist pressure to create some sort of sanitation system in informal settlements, the city had introduced a form of portable flush toilet. Yet these 'portaloos' offer little privacy and pose their own issues of storage and cleaning. In a warehouse not far from the airport, workers struggle to empty and clean portable toilets for a contractor serving Khayelitsha's Site C every Monday, Wednesday and Friday, fresh from collection runs on Tuesdays and Thursdays. The smell is overwhelming, and workers receive inoculation against disease every three months (Swana 2015). It is this world of improvised housing, contested land and inadequate services that the protesters sought to connect to the centre of power by directly transporting its effluent.

Not all toilet politics have taken such dramatic form. While the poo protesters, led by ANC militants, have resorted to these spectacular tactics, members of the Khayelitsha-based Social Justice Coalition (SJC) have organized over a number of years around what they regard as an ongoing and systemic sanitation crisis. The SJC has developed forms of 'slow activism', involving protests, petitions and threats of litigation, in order to lobby, pressure, blame and shame the state into improving sanitation conditions in informal settlements. While the SJC may not be getting the same media profile as the faeces flingers, their daily struggles to transform supposedly private concerns such as toilets and defecation into matters of public debate and politics has made significant strides. They have also taken to deploying the bureaucratic language of facts and figures, as well as novel forms of 'data driven activism' to make their case (Robins 2014). Along with broad resentment over the continuing inequality and slow pace of infrastructural development, the recent poo protests have been driven by a number of grievances, including a labour dispute with contractors responsible for sanitation service delivery in informal settlements, the infamous 'bucket system', and the DA government's distribution of portable rather than permanent flush toilets.

Here the two imaginaries we have outlined come into direct confrontation. The alternative systems of waste management designed to engage sanitation as a purely technical matter fail to factor in human sentiment about comparative experience. A common – and eminently reasonable – approach to reinventing the standard form is the urine diversion toilet (UDDT or UD) promoted by organizations such as EcoSan and AfricaSan. UDDTs are dry and self-contained sanitation systems that are meant to divert urine into a separate compartment from faeces, thereby ensuring that the latter dries out quickly and can be more easily disposed of on-site. This not only addresses concerns about water scarcity, but it also has the advantage of allowing human waste to be recycled as compost (see Penner 2010). However, evaluation studies have found that these innovations routinely encounter 'local opposition' and users tend to reject these eco-friendly appropriate technologies on 'cultural grounds'. Whereas the middle classes in most parts of the world can simply flush away human waste, which instantly becomes the problem of state sanitation infra-structure systems, the recipients of these alternative technologies are called upon to engage more intimately with human waste.

As we have been suggesting above, the political edge to such 'cultural' obstacles to the adoption of toilet alternatives becomes graphically evident in South Africa. South Africa's long histories of racial and class inequalities have created a situation whereby people living in chronic poverty in shacks often refuse to accept anything but standard middle-class conventional solutions to their problems. So when poor communities are living in close proximity to those with flush toilets, it becomes difficult for them to accept UD toilets or portable loos. Studies suggest that the South African poor tend to demand the same toilet technologies that are available in middle-class homes. This observation is confirmed by studies of the low acceptance of UDDTs in Durban's informal settlements. There a study spells out the implications of a project introduced by eThekwini Municipality as part of Durban's large-scale, peri-urban and rural sanitation programme (SuSanA 2011). The programme provided households with free basic water supply and sustainable sanitation in the form of UDDTs, serving some 450,000 beneficiaries. The findings of evaluation studies of the programme indicate that the flush toilet is considered to be a 'symbol of social emancipation' and such aspirations contribute to the low uptake of the UDDTs:

> The HSRC study showed that while acceptance of water supply tanks was generally high, *user satisfaction with the UDDTs was lower (Kvalsvig et al., 2003). Particularly people living in peri-urban areas close to the sewer system aspire to get flush toilets, considered a symbol of social emancipation. Conversely, rural communities showed better acceptance of the UDDTs, as no households with flush toilets were nearby and thus no direct comparisons were made.* The greatest challenge in terms of acceptance was the emptying of the vaults. The establishment of local faecal vault clearing services by micro-enterprises in the respective communities was a method of mitigating this … . (SuSanA 2011: 9)

Barbara Penner (2010) has insightfully analyzed low acceptance of new toilet technologies in her study of the ambitious rollout of 90,000 units in Durban. Penner found that members of poor communities generally desired the 'proper', modern, flush toilets associated with middle-class homes and lifestyles, rather than ecologically friendly dry alternatives like the UD toilets promoted by the Swedish-based Ecosan, an organization that has inspired many dry toilet projects in Africa. Penner exposes the limits of the market-driven framework of Gates Foundation-funded programmes that rebrand users as 'consumers' and toilets as 'products': 'In highly polarized societies like South Africa, toilets convey more than one's status as a consumer; they convey one's status as a citizen. And a central reason why improvement projects stumble is not indifference to sanitation, but rather the perception and, crucially, the reality of asymmetrical provision and resource allocation.' Penner emphasizes how poor residents exposed to UD toilets in Durban expressed a 'strong preference for flush toilets' and found it 'culturally unacceptable' to engage with faeces and urine, an attitude only heightened by health education following a cholera outbreak in 2002. As she puts it:

South African society is notably fecal-phobic, an attitude encouraged by educational initiatives that seek to end open defecation by stressing the link between feces and disease. … If the main aim of the government is to improve public health, then is it wise to make householders responsible for moving potentially infectious matter? Rather than making public health paramount, this closed system, which puts users in charge of maintaining their own infrastructure and disposing of their own feces, transfers labor and risk from public bodies to individual householders, who tend to be blamed for incorrectly using their toilets if problems arise. (Penner 2010)

Given the low uptake of these eco-friendly 'appropriate' toilet technologies Penner calls for reworking the entire sanitation system to address its structural inequities, and starting at the top, however daunting that task might be: 'Persuading rich people, along with poor ones, to give up waterborne sanitation might prove the hardest—but most essential—sell of all' (Penner 2010).

How to treat sanitation as a collective, rather than individual problem (see Mehta and Movik 2011)? Any return to an expansion of conventional sewers depends on the capacity of a centralized authority to roll out the necessary infrastructure and administer it. This approach has failed to materialize in contexts where weak or dysfunctional states cannot connect citizens to 'the grid' of infrastructure systems. Durban does offer one final, potentially intriguing example on this score. The 'faecal sludge pelletizing machine' is a device also aimed at improving sanitation in Durban's informal settlements by processing the contents of pit latrines. Although designed and developed by a private company, LaDePa Technology, it has been piloted by a government agency, namely the eThekwini Municipality Department of Water and Sanitation. The citation for an IWA (International Water Association) Kuala Lumpur Development Congress Award won by the technology outlines the potential magic of its sanitation alchemy:

[The machine] converts this waste into a product that is pathogen free and environmentally safe, making it potentially marketable to the agricultural sector, and thereby reducing the overall sludge disposal costs. The plant is small … self-contained [in a shipping container] and therefore mobile. Capital and operational costs are low and the mechanics are simple and robust which suits low skilled operation and maintenance, and allows access to this technology by cash-strapped Municipalities and/or small entrepreneurs alike.[4]

Like the urine diversion toilet, the 'fecal sludge' machine seeks to transmute waste into a culturally neutral substance potentially marketed as fertilizer. However, by operating at a remove and being integrated into existing state sanitation system, it does not rely on individual users' physical interaction with the waste conversion process. If lacking the symbolic prestige of the flush toilet, this approach has the potential to offer incremental systemic improvement in a politically acceptable way.

The Gates Foundation dream of recasting waste 'as a valuable resource to be tapped' is an old one. Indeed a desire not just to neutralize human waste – to sanitize shit – but also to turn it into natural fertilizer, runs through much of the reformist literature of the last two centuries. The dry toilet was a viable alternative to flush technology in the nineteenth– century, and the outcome was by no means assured. Figures as different as Baron Haussmann and Karl Marx bemoaned the waste-fulness of dumping excrement into sewers, and the French political philosopher Pierre Leroux envisaged a world in which every worker 'could live off his own manure' (Laporte 2000: 131; Penner 2010). Even the minimal, plastic bag known in urban slums as the 'flying toilet' can be reimagined this way, as the Peepoople of Sweden have demonstrated (Redfield 2012).[5] Yet public perception remains key to the success of any such effort, and behind it the wider cultural politics of perceived modernity that coalesce around toilets (Dutton et al. 2002; Morgan 2002). This is not only an African concern. As Penner (2010) points out, the run-up to the Beijing Olympics in 2008 involved an effort to build 'throne-style' as opposed to squat installations, while images of the immodest double throne went viral in advance of the Sochi Winter Games in Russia. For much of the planet's population, toilets remain a highly charged index of relative pollution, hygiene and civilization. In this sense, it is welcome to note that the current Gates Foundation webpage describing the Reinvent the Toilet Challenge now contains a crucial fifth essential element. In addition to removing germs and recovering resources, operating off-grid, operating cheaply and promoting sustainable and financially profitable sanitation services in poor, urban settings, the ideal toilet should be 'a truly aspirational next-generation product that everyone will want to use—in developed as well as developing nations'.[6]

Concluding Thoughts

This chapter has contrasted the global plans of humanitarian designers to redesign the toilet for a more healthy and sustainable future with recent sanitation activism in South Africa, and demands for immediate inclusion within existing infrastructural norms. We suggest that for many South Africans in informal settlements, any toilet technology other than the modern, porcelain flush model is simply old buckets in new containers; they are simply associated with everything about the Apartheid past that the new democratic constitution strives to overcome. The modern flush toilet, the chapter argues, is a sign of modern citizenship in a democracy in which the disposal of human waste ought to be the problem of modern state infrastructure. This, it would seem, is the promise and expectation of democracy, and Gate's alter-native, eco-friendly 'Toilets for Africa' are unlikely to be accepted as substitutes for expectations of rights, dignity and 'proper' citizenship. Technical visions of the future must come to terms with this egalitarian political desire, as well as deeply held sentiment about the colonial past. From such a perspective human waste is hardly a neutral substance, defined by its chemical properties.

To underscore this last point, we will close with an anecdote from the latest episode of sanitation protest. On 12 March 2015, a thirty-year-old, fourth-year political science student at the University of Cape Town named Chumani Maxwele flung a plastic container filled with human waste on the statute of Cecil John Rhodes at UCT's upper campus. Standing shirtless in front of the massive statue and wearing a bright pink mineworker's hardhat, he told an assembled crowd of students and journalists that he had chosen his target because he felt suffocated by the overwhelming presence of colonial names and memorials on the campus. Elided in the days and weeks of heated discussion that followed his action was a poignant and deeply personal explanation he gave to a reporter. He said that he had thrown the faeces and urine contents of a portable flush toilet container at the statue to highlight his feelings of shame. As he put it, 'We want white people to know how we live. We live in poo. I am from a poor family; we are using portaloos. Are you happy with that?' he asked the journalists. 'I have to give Cecil John Rhodes a poo shower and whites will have to see it' (*The Times*, 13 March 2015).

Notes

1. See http://www.humanidesign.org/contesttoilets1.html [accessed 17 May 2011] sadly no longer exists. See http://humanidesign.blogspot.com [accessed 29 May 2015].
2. See http://www.coolersolutionsinc.com/ [accessed 16 May 2011].
3. See http://www.humanidesign.org/dignitytoilet.html [accessed 17 May 2011]. See http://bridgeable.com/bringing-dignity-to-the-third-world/ [accessed 29 May 2015].
4. See http://forum.susana.org/forum/categories/53-faecal-sludge-management/ 406-ladepa-is-a-faecal-sludge-pelletising-machine-in-ethekwini-durban [accessed 29 May 2015]. See also All Africa (2011).
5. See http://www.peepoople.com/peepoo/start-thinking-peepoo/ [accessed 29 May 2015].
6. See http://www.gatesfoundation.org/What-We-Do/Global-Development/ Reinvent-the-Toilet-Challenge [accessed 2 March 2015].

References

All Africa (2011) 'South Africa: Turning Human Waste into Fertilizer Pellet by Pellet'. Available online: http://allafrica.com/stories/201107130001.html [accessed 12 January 2012].

Allen, Michelle (2007) *Cleansing the City: Sanitary Geographies in Victorian London*, Athens: Ohio University Press.

Chalfin, B. (2014) 'Public Things, Excremental Politics, and the Infrastructure of Bare Life in Ghana's City of Tema', *American Ethnologist* 1 (1): 92–109.

Dutton, M., Seth, S., and Gandhi, L. (2002) 'Editorial: Plumbing the Depths: Toilets, Transparency and Modernity', *Postcolonial Studies* 5 (2): 137–42.

Fardon, R. (2013) 'Citations Out of Place. Or, Lord Palmerston Goes Viral in the Nineteenth Century but Gets Lost in the Twentieth', *Anthropology Today* 29 (1): 1–2.

High Court of South Africa (2011) 'Beja vs. Premier of the Western Cape and Others', Western Cape High Court Records. Case No: 21332/10.

Laporte, D. (2000) *History of Shit*, Cambridge, MA and London: MIT Press.

Loveless, M. (2011) 'Bringing Dignity to the Third World', Blog post, 26 September. Available online: http://bridgeable.com/bringing-dignity-to-the-third-world/ [accessed 15 January 2012].

Mail & Guardian (2010) 'ANC Youth League Calls for Trashing of Cape Town', 25 May.

Mathews Burwell, S. (2011) 'Reinventing the Toilet'. Available online: http://www.gatesfoundation.org/speeches-commentary/pages/sylvia-mathews-burwell-2011-reinventing-the-toilet.aspx [accessed 19 July 2011].

Mehta, L. and Movik, S. (2011) *Shit Matters: The Potential of Community-Led Total Sanitation,* Rugby: Practical Action Press.

Morgan, M. (2002) 'The Plumbing of Modern Life', *Postcolonial Studies* 5 (2): 171–95.

Otter, C. (2008) *The Victorian Eye: A Political History of Light and Vision in Britain, 1800–1910*, Chicago: University of Chicago Press.

Penner, B. (2010) 'Flush with Inequality: Sanitation in South Africa', *Places Journal*, November 2010. Available online: https://placesjournal.org/article/flush-with-inequality-sanitation-in-south-africa/ [accessed 29 May 2015].

Redfield, P. (2012) 'Bioexpectations: Life Technologies as Humanitarian Goods', *Public Culture* 24 (1): 157–84.

Rees, T. (2014) 'Humanity/Plan; or, On the "Stateless" Today (Also Being an Anthropology of Global Health)', *Cultural Anthropology* 29 (3): 457–78.

Robins, S. (2014) 'The 2011 Toilet Wars in South Africa: Justice and Transition between the Exceptional and the Everyday after Apartheid', *Development and Change* 45 (3): 479–501.

Rossouw, M. and Dawes, N. (2011) 'Voting Gets Down to Basics', *Mail and Guardian*, 13–19 May, 2.

Sustainable Sanitation Alliance (SuSanA) (2011) 'Large-scale peri-urban and rural sanitation with UDDTs eThekwini Municipality (Durban) South Africa'. Available online: http://www.susana.org/_resources/documents/default/2-791-en-susana-cs-south-africa-ethekwini-durban-uddts-2010.pdf [accessed 12 January 2012].

Swana, Z. (2015) 'A House Full of Faeces in Khayelitsha', *Ground Up*, March 2015. Available online: http://groundup.org.za/features/faeces/house_faeces_0005.html [accessed 15 May 2015].

Van der Geest, S. (2002) 'The Night Soil Collector: Bucket Latrines in Ghana', *Postcolonial Studies* 5 (2): 197–206.

–11–

Locating the Local: Untangling Ownership over Security Sector Processes of Peace-Building in Southern Thailand

Paul Chambers
Napisa Waitoolkiat
Srisompob Jitpiromsri

Introduction

This study examines 'conflict' and local ownership of conflict transformation. 'Conflict' and 'conflict transformation' are two concepts which imply social construction across time. 'Local Ownership' has been defined in terms of the respective capabilities of various stakeholders to establish and assume responsibility for a development agenda and to locate and achieve support for it over time (Saxby 2003: 2).

Deeply entrenched conflict has existed in what is currently called 'southern Thailand' for well over 100 years. The tension involves a clash between a Buddhist Thai nation-state and a minority of Malay Muslims.[1] In January, 2004, however, the conflict escalated and has been raging ever since. Until today, no government has succeeded in taming the insurgency, despite a litany of proposals intended to defuse it. This study argues that any progress in resolving the southern Thai conflict ultimately rests with the state's willingness to undertake serious reform of how it administers local people in the far south; the extent to which it accepts local input into adjusting these policies; and the extent to which it is willing to enter into a sincere dialogue with its southern opponents. In this paper we seek answers to the following questions. Under what set of lenses might we comprehend and diminish the tension? What is the historical background of and causes for the current conflict? Who are the stakeholders involved? What are the perceptions of each stakeholder group regarding the crisis and its solution? What might be the most viable proposals to diminish tensions in the region? Finally, we ask what might be the future trend for the conflict?

Understanding and Altering the Crisis: Conflict Transformation

'Conflict', as John Paul Lederach (1995: 9) says, is a 'socially-constructed cultural event'. Conflicts can be deeply entrenched with no clear beginning of ending. As Galtung (1995: 52) states, conflicts are '... phenomena that have no clear beginning or end ... they wax, wane and transform themselves through patterns of dependent co-arising. ...'. To understand 'conflict', Galtung posited the 'Conflict Triangle'.

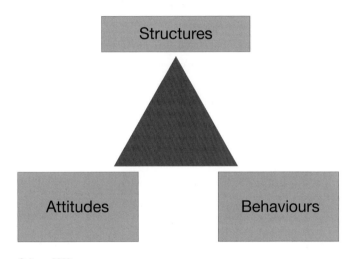

Based upon: Galtung 2000

Figure 11.1: The Conflict Triangle

In Galtung's Conflict Triangle (Figure 11.1), attitudes, behaviours and structures of people in a conflict area influence and reinforce each other. By attitudes, we mean the positive or negative perceptions/misperceptions (including stereotypes) among the actors involved of themselves and their societal enemies. Meanwhile, behaviour can be cooperative or coercive, conciliatory or hostile. By structures, we mean the political, economic and societal mechanisms, processes, institutions and history that influence the distribution and satisfaction of the needs and interests of the actors.

Galtung also derives the ABC triangle which balances attitudes, behaviours and competition: 'Attitudes' refer to feelings of hatred, fear, insecurity and distrust. For conflict transformation, the idea is to transform such attitudes into non-hatred. As for 'behaviour', this refers to violence. Violence is only a symptom of conflict. The idea in conflict transformation is to transform violence into institutionalized (and peaceful) competition. 'Contradictions' involve poverty, oppression, exclusion of an ethnic/linguistic/cultural group; stereotyping tends to stimulate greater hatred and violence (Galtung 2000: 3). When contradictions become fuelled with negative attitudes and behaviour, then conflicts commence (ibid.) (Figure 11.2).

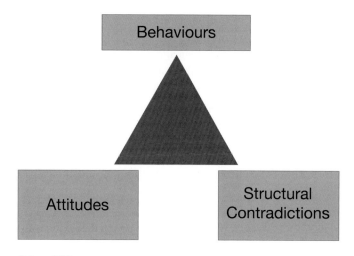

Based upon: Galtung 2000

Figure 11.2: Galtung's ABC model

Finally Galtung discusses a violence triangle (Figure 11.3). Such violence can be visible or invisible. He contends that 'it is the failure to transform conflicts that leads to violence' (ibid.: 4). His violence triangle examines the interconnectedness among structural violence, cultural violence and direct violence. Structural violence is simply where social structures or institutions prevent people from meeting basic needs. Cultural violence is much more indirect, as it means the intent to harm, injure or even kill an identity, through the use of words and images. Lastly, direct violence takes the form of physical, psychological, and vocal attacks (ibid.).

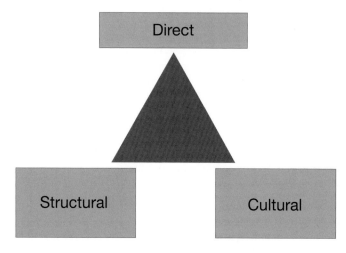

Based upon: Galtung 2000

Figure 11.3: Types of violence

Given that conflicts can be so deeply embedded, any conflict's transformation toward non-conflict is often a hard-to-achieve social construction. Moreover, 'conflict transformation is … a process of engaging with and transforming the relationships, interests, discourses and, if necessary, the very constitution of society that supports the continuation of violent conflict' (Miall 2001: 4). There are intense contradictions which might likely prevent any moves toward reconciliation and peace. Indeed, it is these contradictions which have continued to propel violence forward. Yet despite the embedded tensions in society, there are also contradictions through which it is necessary to navigate in order to achieve a lasting peace. The method of navigation through these contradictions is what Galtung terms 'creativity'. Creativity means that both sides seriously, patiently and incrementally negotiate together toward the beginnings of empathy and reconciliation. Thus, direct violence begins to subside, structural violence diminishes and cultural violence is reduced.

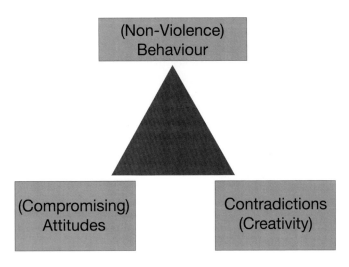

Based upon: Galtung 2000

Figure 11.4: Transforming towards peace

Figure 11.4 illustrates the potential for 'creativity' (e.g. an acceptable peace proposal), which can lead to more compromising attitudes that give rise to negotiations that lead to more accommodating behaviour or moves toward non-violence. But this changed event may take a long time: it is not meant to be a sudden, all-encompassing 'antidote'. As a result of the new contradiction of creativity and a new attitude of empathy, changed behaviours follow suit. These new behaviours include non-violence as well as new efforts toward moving toward multiculturalism,[2] mutual economic projects, and even mutual political government. Galtung views the process of achieving peace as incremental, involving sacrifices on both sides, and lengthy. He then defines peace:

By *peace* we mean the capacity to transform conflicts with empathy, without violence, and creatively never-ending process; by *transforming conflicts* we mean enabling the parties to go ahead in a self-reliant, acceptable and sustainable manner; by *without violence* we mean that this process should avoid any cultural violence that justifies direct or structural violence; by *with empathy* we mean the ability also to understand the conflict the way the parties understand the conflict themselves; by *creatively* we mean channeling conflict energy toward new realities, accommodating the parties and meeting basic human needs. (Galtung 2008)

Understanding conflicts as socially constructed events and their possible transformation toward non-conflict or lesser-conflict status appears quite applicable to the insurgency in southern Thailand. We turn next to an explication of this conflict's history.

The Conflict: A History

The current conflict in Thailand's far south originally centres on the modern Thai provinces of Pattani, Yala and Narathiwat, which, together with parts of northern Malaysia, generally covered the area of the Muslim sultanate of Patani. This kingdom, originally Hindu–Buddhist, converted to Islam around 1450. This shift in religious identity 'began to institutionalize the differences between the Malay and Thai worlds' for Patani (Rahimmula 2003: 99). Regardless, the sultanate became an uneasy vassal to the mighty northern Buddhist kingdom of Ayutthaya.

In 1786, Ayutthaya's successor, Siam, forcibly subjugated Patani, eventually dissecting it into seven provinces. Siamese forces quelled numerous insurrections and ultimately incorporated the provinces of Pattani, Yala and Narathiwat into Siam in 1902 – the four others being ceded to Britain in 1904 and 1909. Yet Siam's violent repression merely provoked local resistance (ICG 2005: 2). From 1902 until 1980, harsh laws and assimilation policies were generally applied against the southern Malay-Muslim community. Melayu (Yawi) language was banned in public offices, Malay state employees were required to assume Thai names, Muslim-Malay attire was forbidden in public, Islamic law was forbidden, Buddhist statues were placed in schools and Malay-Muslim children forced to bow before them (ibid.: 3). In 1948, a protest in Narathiwat was stifled when police killed 400 demonstrators. Two Malay-Muslim insurrectionary groups emerged in the 1960s – the Barisan Revolusi Nasional (BRN) and the Patani United Liberation Organization (PULO) – which became the principal rebel organizations (Thayer 2007: 7).

In the early 1980s, the Prem Tinsulanond government improved security in the south by allocating more money to security institutions; enhancing cooperation with moderate Muslim leaders and pursuing conciliation (ibid.: 10). This policy stressed economic development, an amnesty for rebels and the establishment of two inter-government agencies (ICG 2005: 13). The first agency, Civilian-Police-Military

Command 43 (CPM 43), coordinated security operations of civilians, police, and the military. The second agency (the Southern Border Provinces Administrative Center [SBPAC]) sought to increase cooperation among government agencies on political issues in terms of the southern insurgency. Also, the SBPAC initiated dialogue with the Malay-Muslim civilians.

By the mid-1990s, the insurgency had been temporarily staunched thanks to three factors. First, post-1988 democratization in Thailand allowed members of the Wadah Muslim parliamentary faction to gain influential positions in Thai cabinets. Thus, many Muslim moderates threw their support behind cooperating with Bangkok. Second, following the Asian financial crisis, Malaysia agreed to help Thailand arrest suspected rebels who fled across the joint border. Third, SBPAC conciliation efforts were beginning to pay off. Fourth, in the late 1990s, Thai military manoeuvres against rebels who refused government amnesties were increasingly successful (Thayer 2007: 11–12).

In 2001, Thaksin Shinawatra was elected Prime Minister in a landslide. Considering Malay-Muslim insurgents as mere bandits and wanting to reduce the leverage of his political rivals in the south, Thaksin in 2002 dismantled CPM 43 and SBPAC. He saw these agencies as mechanisms of his nemesis, ex-prime minister, now Privy Council chairperson Prem Tinsulanond (McCargo 2007: 39). Thaksin placed control over southern security matters mostly in the hands of police commanders, exacerbating tensions between the army and police, while police became accused of greater human rights abuses in the south. Meanwhile, following the 11 September 2001 terrorist attacks in New York, insurgent incidents in Thailand's far south intensified (Thayer 2007: 13).

These strikes culminated in a well-organized insurgent attack on an army camp in Narathiwat province on 4 January 2004. The militants seized approximately 350 weapons and executed four soldiers. The state immediately responded with repression: Thaksin declared martial law in Narathiwat, Yala and Pattani. Such a strategy reflected the mindset of what southern Malay-Muslim politician Surin Pitsuwan condemned as 'Bangkok knows best' – national problems in Thailand were to be dealt with by the centre, without local input (Pitsuwan 2004: 7).

Thereafter, state repression bred insurgent counterattacks and each side became increasingly implicated in human rights abuses. Soldiers and police now worked together in counter-insurgency operations. Security forces were soon accused of murdering prominent Thai human rights lawyer Somchai Neelaphaijit, who disappeared on 12 March 2004 in Bangkok. He was defending five Muslims accused of stealing some of the 350 guns (BBC News 2006). In 2004 alone, there were two massacres. On April 28, following a seven-hour stand-off with Thai soldiers, thirty-two suspected guerrillas took shelter in Krue Se mosque. Thereupon soldiers stormed the mosque, killing all thirty-one, as well as eighty other insurgents (Thayer 2007: 13–14). Then on October 25, after soldiers arrested several protestors at the border town of Tak Bai and transported them to an army base, it was discovered that seventy-eight had died en route of suffocation. The Krue Se and

Tak Bai incidents infuriated the Malay-Muslim community and insurgent attacks skyrocketed. Moreover, the incidents gave Thaksin a poor public image (ibid.: 15). In 2005, Thaksin adjourned a National Reconciliation Commission (NRC) which was tasked to suggest ways to bring peace to the troubled south. Its 2006 recommendations included: 1) making Melayu the official language for the three provinces of Pattani, Narathiwat and Yala; 2) merging administration for the provinces; and 3) re-introducing Islamic law. Yet Thaksin and Privy Council Chair Prem rejected these proposals (Nation 2006). Though the state persisted in using repression against the insurgency, it continued unabated. Criticism of Thaksin's policies grew within the military, the Privy Council and the palace. Ultimately, Thaksin's southern policy played a role in his 19 September 2006 overthrow (Askew 2008: 191). Following Thaksin's ouster, the newly appointed Surayudh Chulanondh government sought to revive Prem's policy of conciliation, even issuing a public apology to Malay Muslims and announcing a new economic stimulus programme for five southern provinces (including also Satun and Songkhla) (ibid.: 192). It re-established the SBPAC and CPM43 to coordinate security and political policies on the ground in the South. However, the insurgency refused to dissipate. Rebel attacks against Buddhist temples (where the Thai military sometimes stored its hardware) between 2004 and 2007 resulted in the deaths of five Buddhist monks and exacerbated tensions between Malay Muslims and southern Thai Buddhists (Joll 2010: 260).

In 2007, the military began to adopt a far more aggressive counter-insurgency policy, with more security officials dispatched to the region. Nevertheless, by 2009 violence had skyrocketed. This was a consequence of the fact that security forces, through their increased counter-insurgency operations, were simultaneously violating more and more human rights, which exacerbated Malay-Muslim grievances against the state, and again gave insurgents more propaganda to rationalize continuing support for their cause (Jitpiromsri and McCargo 2010: 163).

In 2009, the newly appointed coalition government of Democrat Abhisit Vechachiwa proclaimed that a new paradigm of 'Politics Leading the Military' would henceforth commence in terms of southern counter-insurgency policy. This meant that civilians would now lead the way in establishing peace and justice in that region. Yet such a 'leading role' proved to be superficial as the army was ultimately in charge of counter-insurgency policy (Askew 2010: 244, 250).

The 2011–2014 Yingluck administration initially continued the policy of favouring repression over conciliation in weakening the insurrection, as a state of emergency remained in effect. However, in 2013, her government began serious negotiations with the BRN. It even pushed the notion of creating an autonomous zone encompassing the three southernmost provinces (Nation 2013). Yet after three rounds of dialogue (with the help of Malaysia as mediator), the talks stalled. The Thai army was mostly leery of these negotiations. Since Thailand's May 2014 military coup, the Thai-BRN dialogue appears to have been at least temporarily scrapped.

The year 2015 brings southern Thailand to its eleventh year of relentless insurrection. From 2004–14, there were 6,097 deaths and 10,908 injuries relating to the violence. Such incidents are multiplying on a year-by-year basis. Meanwhile, bombings grew from 276 in 2012 to 320 in 2013 (Iaccino 2014). Ironically, in 2013, a year in which serious peace negotiations appeared to begin in earnest, violence skyrocketed to a level not seen since 2005–7.

Various explanations suggest why the insurgency has grown and continued since 2004. First, entrenched religious hostility between Muslims and Buddhists has certainly given life to the Malay-Muslim insurrection (Joll 2010: 261). Second, the globalization of militant Islam (especially after the 11 September 2001 terrorist attacks and Western invasions of Afghanistan and Iraq) lends credence to a snowballing effect of increased Muslim militancy in the world, including in Thailand in 2004 (Liow 2006: 91). Third, socio-economic factors may have helped to spark the imbroglio. Yala, Narathiwat and Pattani possess the lowest average income – especially among Muslims – of all southern provinces (Melvin 2007: 18). Illiteracy in the three provinces is much higher among Muslims than Buddhists (Jitpiromsri and Sophonvasu 2007: 96–104). Fourth, state policies toward Malay Muslims have been both biased and heavy-handed (Bajoria and Zissis 2008). Fifth, long-lasting state repression has contributed to Malay Muslims desiring political legitimization via insurgency (Jitpiromsri and McCargo 2010: 170–1). Sixth, given that the counter-insurgency budget has been immense, state agencies are hesitant to negotiate peace seriously with insurgents.

The continuing cycle of rebel attacks, followed by state repression, followed by more southern grievances which builds support for insurgency continues to persist. In the next section, we delineate the different perspectives of stakeholders involved in the crisis.

Alternative Perceptions About Security Sector Processes of Peace-Building

The inability of traditional counter-insurgency strategies to halt the rebellion has led to efforts toward a more inclusive form of peace-building – with local input. However, the interface between the national and local level in its political, social, religious and ethnic forms has been difficult. Amidst differing perceptions, needs, objectives and capabilities from all stakeholders involved in the conflict, including even different local groups, there remains little consensus on what constitutes justice and peace in the region. In this light, notions of political legitimacy in the Malay-Muslim South remain contested. This section explores these different standpoints.

1: Local Politicians[3]

Regarding problems faced by local level politicians, this study approached three elected politicians at the level of Sub-district Administrative Organization. The interviewees told us that they have been unfairly targeted by the Thai state. This is because they are Muslim. So they perceive that the Thai state does not trust them. These local politicians supported the Yingluck Shinawatra government's efforts in terms of connecting with Muslims and giving them a greater voice in far southern affairs. This reflects the willingness of local Muslim politicians to work via formal channels to resolve the conflict. Regarding the budget, they complained that the state does not provide sufficient monetary allocations to local politicians to assist in the peace process.

2: Malay-Muslim Women[4]

The second group interviewed was the Women's Civic Network for Peace in the southern Border Provinces (WCNP). It engages in leadership training for Muslim women and works to lobby the state for the rights of Malay-Muslim women. According to WCNP, southern Muslim women have been negatively affected by growing violence and worsening health care, which has led to increased maternal mortality. Moreover, with more Thai soldiers providing security, there has been an increase in sexual violence in the form of rape. Furthermore, many women whose husbands have died in the southern violence have been forced to lead families alone. WCNP has pushed the state to adopt civil-society-inclusive policies and focus on justice for female victims. It seeks more power-sharing and autonomy for local people (specifically women). Simultaneously, it has been willing to work with the state to achieve peace.

3: Journalists[5]

The third group of persons interviewed comprised Thai journalists who have worked since 2004 on the southern Thailand insurgency. This group stated that to achieve local ownership of peace processes in southern Thailand, the 'environment' must be drastically improved. Melayu language must be promoted by the state. CSOs at all levels must be committed to peace. There should be less military involvement, especially given the army's tendency to view all Malay Muslims as the enemy. Moreover, ordinary people need to be more involved. Another 'environmental' problem is education in the far south. Many local people see teachers in state schools as enemies if the teachers are not from the far south. Halal food does not often exist in schools; state schools often exhibit little recognition of Ramadan; the curriculum generally shows little recognition of history of Patani kingdom. These education 'problems' must be addressed by the state.

4: Academics[6]

We discussed the situation in the far south with two Thai academics that specialize in southern Thailand's insurgency: Dr Mark Tamthai, Payap University, Chiang Mai, and Ms Daungyewa Utarasint, University of Songkhla, Pattani, Thailand. They agreed that the problems in southern Thailand result principally from repression by the Thai state and army over southern Malay-Muslim people. There must be step-by-step change in the far south. The region needs less military but more efficient administrative oversight. Dr Tamthai supports an autonomous zone similar to the Greater Bangkok Metropolitan Area for the far south. For Ms Utarasint, it is important to educate students and other people there on the need for peace-building. The government should create a special cabinet ministry responsible for the Deep South. Autonomy might be a good idea but an autonomous zone in the far south could become quite inefficient.

Ultimately, both Dr Mark Tamthai and Ms Daungyewa Utarasint support more peace talks and 'peace constituencies' in the far south. They represent a moderate voice seeking a negotiated settlement to the conflict.

5: State Security Forces[7]

Two groups of military officials were interviewed. The first (Army [progressive], January 2013) represented soldiers who support more moderate moves toward achieving peace. These progressive officers emphasized the need for bureaucratic unity in support of the military as the method to quell the insurgency. Moreover, the military should cooperate better with civilian authorities; listen more attentively to the points of view of Malay Muslims in the south; and work to improve the perceptions of Malay Muslims about soldiers.

The second group of security officials interviewed comprised conservative, hard-core military types, including soldiers themselves and paramilitary rangers. Their Facebook page, called 'Dark South', is considered the mouthpiece of hard-line Thai military/rangers, launched on 6 May 2013 (Dark South Watch, 6 May 2013). It considers insurgents as outlaws and bandits, who manipulate academics, students, NGOs and international organizations into sympathizing with them. Dark South opposes any international actors interceding in the Deep South imbroglio, supporting a repressive solution to restore order.

6: Non-Governmental Organizations (NGOs) in the Deep South[8]

Some non-governmental organizations have been deeply involved in looking for reconciliation in the far south of Thailand. One NGO is the Wetland Research Project. The representative of this NGO is a moderate Buddhist. To diminish tensions, she supports elections for governors (which do not currently exist) or autonomy.

The second NGO representative interviewed is Muslim and works with the southern

Islamic Culture Foundation in the Deep South. His proposed solution is that the state should increase autonomy for people in the Deep South. Autonomy must occur in policies of education, economics, culture and investment. He stated that participatory decision-making is the key to peace. With regard to peace talks between the state and BRN, he wants to see more international involvement. The state should play only a supportive role in the Deep South and open up the border area so that Malaysians can more easily move to and from the three-provinces area of the Deep South, to improve economic, political, and social ties between Thailand and Malaysia.

7: Insurgents[9]

A key local group in the southern conflict is the insurgents themselves. This study was able to discuss the southern conflict with an anonymous member of the insurgency. He is a youth who has experienced the violence. He faults the repressive policies of the centralized Thai state for causing the problems in Thailand's Deep South. The 2013 development whereby the BRN (Barisan Revolusi Nasional Melayu Patani) began negotiating with the Yingluck government was a process of moving from a military process to a political process. However, in his view, a militaristic strategy remains necessary. Moreover, disseminating views through social media can be used to support militant radicalism. PULO (Patani United National Liberation Organization) is another group that is still active. PULO adheres more to violence than BRN. PULO relies on BRN as a bridge to larger goals – secession. Ultimately, Pattani's problems should be resolved via a peace process leading to incremental secession by the provinces of Narathiwat, Yala and Pattani to become their own country. The Thai state should accept that it cannot solve the Malay-Muslim problem.

8: Buddhists in Deep South[10]

Sino-Thai Buddhists have been the elite in the far South for over 100 years. Nevertheless, these Buddhists are demographically in the minority. In the three provinces of Narathiwat, Yala and Pattani, Buddhists constitute only 20 per cent of the population, and the number has dwindled as Buddhists have fled the violence (Abuza 2006). The root problem in the Deep South derives from power-seeking among local Malay-Muslim politicians. A second problem is government policy, which has been too financially accommodating toward southern Muslims. Third, southern NGOs are biased in favour of Malay Muslims. International and local NGOs never talked to local Buddhists. For her, 'Peace will come when it benefits all groups, not just particular group, in the area.' Her solution to end the problems is to maintain Thailand's centralized state. She said that Muslim people need to learn how to live with other people as well. She sees negotiations with insurgents as 'a sham" Also, she is suspicious of Malaysia's helping to mediate between the BRN and Thai government. The Yingluck government supported negotiations merely to expand its electoral base. The Thai army is the only institution which can balance off the overwhelming power of Muslim local politicians in the Deep South. She said, 'It is only the army who can make the nation survive.' She is suspicious of foreigners seeking peace in southern Thailand. Finally, the media has harmed peace efforts as it tends to negatively depict the Thai state.

9: National Politicians[11]

According to the anti-Thaksin Democrats, insurgency in Thailand's Deep South derives from first, a Malay-Muslim desire for independence from Siam; second, Thailand's traditional repression of the region; third, the particular policy of Thaksin to transform the Deep South into 'a police state'. Thaksin dismantled the dialogue-centric SBPAC. Thaksin's violent policy helped to bring the separatists and PULO back to the fore. When the Democrats assumed office in 2008 they used a 'reaching out and development policy'. The government initiated a cabinet structure for the far south and launched several welfare programmes there; promoted bi-lingual education and supported the SBPAC. The overall policy became known as 'Politics Leading the Military'. He supports an end to state authoritarianism in the Deep South. Local ownership under the Yingluck government has not succeeded because Thaksin uses a top-down approach, failing to consult with relevant agencies. Malaysia's involvement in peace talks is a big mistake.

10: National Politicians (Yingluck Government): Interview with National Security Council Adviser Paradorn Pattanathabutr[12]

Paradorn Pattanathabutr stated that it is the Yingluck government's position that the establishment of an autonomous region covering the provinces of Pattani, Narathiwat and Yala is a viable solution to the problem in Thailand's far south. Paradorn, as well as SBPAC head Tawee Sodsong, stated that the creation of the autonomous zone would be possible. Also, they support a wholesale pardon for various types of insurgents on the security authorities' wanted list. However, the army Commander, Prayuth Chan-ocha has not been supportive of these goals.

11: International Organizations Involved in Southern Reconciliation[13]

A final actor comprises international organizations. Perhaps the most prominent of these is the Berghof Foundation, a German NGO. Berghof trains 'Insider Mediators' to increase dialogue among local groups in far southern Thailand to identify locally developed approaches toward finding peace. Berghof, however, does not talk to groups intent on violence. It instead seeks to build 'peace constituencies', defined as a 'network of actors … who are pledged to non-violence and committed to community-oriented purposes, [acting] as a counterweight to the ethnopolitically or religiously segmented society'.

Such constituencies must comprise local academics and civil society organizations, are expected to work against 'war constituencies' and accept external support from international actors (Berghof Foundation 2012: 72). Through peace constituencies, Berghof seeks to promote public policy change and negotiations. So far, Berghof has succeeded in promoting various forums by local actors seeking a mediated peace (Burke et al. 2012: 49).

Berghof's point-person on southern Thailand is Norbert Ropers. For Ropers, the problem in southern Thailand points to a basic dilemma – ownership over the peace process is contested by different actors. It is a problem which most directly affects local actors. The peace process must be locally driven, and this includes insurgent participation. Solutions must derive from local people seeking sustainable peace.[14]

The above eleven interviewed groups demonstrate the diversity of standpoints in far southern Thailand. Yet disunity or clashes among these organizations has hindered peace efforts. In the next section, we apply conflict transformation theory to southern Thailand's crisis.

Conflict Transformation Theory as Applied to Thailand's Southern Conflict

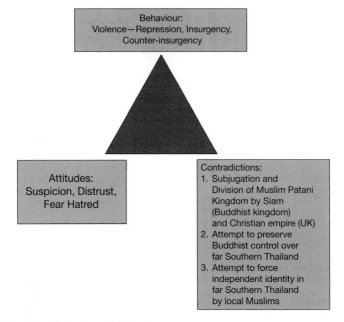

Figure 11.5: The Southern Thailand conflict triangle

Based upon Galtung's Conflict Triangle Concept (Figure 11.5), the historically evolved contradictions of subjugation of the Muslim Patani kingdom by Siam and its subsequent division by non-Muslim outsiders Siam and the UK were instrumental contradictions which were to shape attitudes of suspicion, distrust and fear by most of the Muslim population in what became the far south of Thailand. The part of the Patani kingdom over which the UK established colonial control later became Muslim Malaysia. Thus, only the Siamese-held parts of Patani continued to simmer with enormous tensions. The tensions produced by Siamese-created contradictions led to attitudes of suspicion, distrust, fear and even hatred by most of the Malay Muslim population against Siam (later renamed Thailand). Such negative attitudes were felt by the Thai Buddhists, many of who came to settle in Thailand's far south. Eventually, these attitudes gave way to violence. First there was repression by the state. Second there occurred on-again, off-again resistance and insurgency by Malay-Muslim guerrillas. This led to more state repression and counter-insurgency. The continuing cycle of a mutuality of negative attitudes and behaviour has kept the crisis in far southern Thailand alive until today.

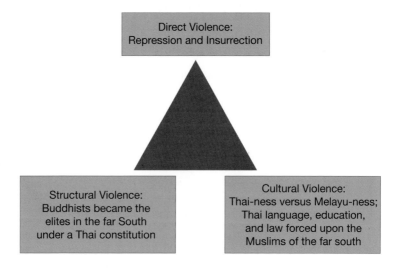

Figure 11.6: Triangle of types of violence in Far Southern Thailand

The types of violence in Thailand's far south have been of three types (Figure 11.6). There is the direct violence which is the physical confrontation between the Thai state and insurgents. Then there is structural violence, which was the creation of institutionalized, long-lasting subjugation by Buddhist Thai elites and the constitutions which legitimized their economic and political hold over the far south. Finally, there has been cultural violence. Such violence is the enacted behaviour of Thai 'we-ness' versus Melayu (southern Malay Muslim) 'we-ness'. This refers to the various, forced cultural forms of repression including use of Thai language over local Melayu language and the requirement that Malay Muslims be part of the Thai education system, while private, Muslim-led Pondok schools have, during much of the far south's history, been harshly restricted by the state. Finally, there is the refusal by the Thai state to apply Muslim Sharia law. Such a triangle of types of violence has only helped to entrench the bitter attitudes (on both sides) which have led to more violence.

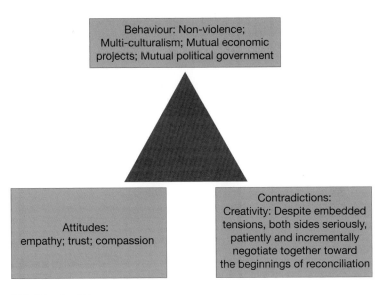

Figure 11.7: Triangle of Peace

Galtung's triangle of peace (Figure 11.7), applied to far southern Thailand above, offers a blueprint for conflict transformation in this long-tense region. The region has experienced intense contradictions that have prevented reconciliation and peace. What needs to occur is an increasing devotion by all sides toward 'creativity'. In this way, there can be a serious, patient and incremental negotiation together toward the beginnings of empathy and reconciliation. New behaviours would be needed, including a move away from violent acts and a dedication to multiculturalism, mutual economic projects and even mutual political government. By multicultur-alism, we mean that there needs to be the state-supported social construction of a bi-cultural identity, which includes both Thai Buddhists and Thai Malay Muslims. By mutual economic projects, we mean that there needs to be state-supported joint projects between Thai Buddhists and Thai Malay Muslims that mutually bolster the economic clout of the two groups together. By mutual political government, we mean allowing for an autonomy zone in the far south comprising the provinces of Narathiwat, Pattani and Yala; or, permitting direct governors elections in the far south; or, allowing for a special ministry for the far south; or permitting the existence of political parties for the far south which would exist in the national parliament; or, finally that in the far south there should be a quota of seats which must always be part of the national parliament – to ensure representation for far southerners. Such a process of 'creativity' leading to 'political transformation' will be time-consuming, will necessitate trust and will involve sacrifices by all sides.

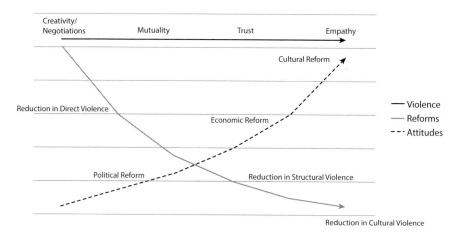

Figure 11.8: Southern Thailand's potential conflict tranformation

Figure 11.8 offers a roadmap toward peace in the far south of Thailand. The vertical side depicts the ethno-religious conflict between Thai Malay Muslims and Thai Buddhists/State in the far south. The horizontal side depicts levels of violence tapering off following negotiations. It also illustrates the changing attitudes among both sides once negotiations have commenced. Negotiations must be serious, and include the military, rebels and other armed groups, in addition to actors that are already working toward peace. Finally, for peace to be lasting there will have to be moves toward inclusive transitional justice for southern Malay Muslims and Buddhists alike.

Conclusion: Future Trends Toward Conflict Transformation

The 2014 coup has had a deleterious effect on southern Thailand peace efforts with the military regime prioritizing military security over mediation. Yet if the junta continues to rely on force alone (while ignoring the longer-term need to address issues of justice, political participation, socio-economic challenges, Malay-Muslim identity problems and perceptions of discrimination by Malay Muslims), then the insurgency will continue unabated. At least the Yingluck Shinawatra initiated a dialogue with rebels and appeared willing to implement structural reforms in the Deep South. Likewise, the junta should negotiate.

In recent years, Amnesty International has condemned both the insurgents and government for committing gross human rights violations (Amnesty International

2011). Meanwhile, Thailand's army has been reluctant to support peace talks, partly because soldiers have been principal targets of rebel groups. In 2015, insurrection-related violence appears on the rise, confounding the Thai government in terms of how to respond adequately.

Local ownership in this conflict remains diverse. Among the stakeholders involved are the following: 1) a plethora of rebel organizations; 2) Thai southern Buddhists; 3) bureaucrats associated with the more moderate policy of the Yingluck government; 4) The military, which itself tends to be suspicious of negotiations but without which no peace talks will ever be successful; 5) Thailand's Democrat Party which supports mediated settlement but disagrees with the creation of an autonomous zone; and 6) NGOs and academics that continue to work toward more rights for Muslims and a peace conducive to the needs of the Malay-Muslim majority. Not only actors dedicated to peace but rather all stakeholders (including soldiers) must agree to talk to each other before any serious negotiations can begin to take southern Thailand down the road toward mutual empathy, diminished violence and lasting peace. The role of international facilitators such as the Berghof Foundation can only be auxiliary: all real negotiations depend upon the Thai actors involved.

Neither violent repression to maintain the status quo nor violent insurrection to achieve secession is favoured by the majority of Thai citizens in southern Thailand. Regarding the Democrats' idea of a Ministry of Southern Affairs, it would probably become a peripheral actor astride continuing military domination of policy toward the Deep South. Also, what good is such a ministry without some form of autonomous zone or provincial decentralization? Ultimately, the only middle-ground solution is that of establishing a regional autonomous zone for the three southernmost provinces. But such an autonomous area must represent a sincere attempt to govern the people of the three provinces even handedly and justly: Thailand's military and police must not be allowed to act with impunity. Any future peace in the southern border region depends upon the level of commitment by both insurgents as well as civilian and military policy-makers in Bangkok. Each will have to find it in their interest to agree to an autonomous area as the final plan. Economic incentives such as more employment opportunities and increased development projects for the south will have to be implemented. At the same time, Malay Muslims need to be encouraged to be more involved politically at the national level of Thai politics in order to increase political linkages between Muslims and Buddhists. Meanwhile, national-level political parties must develop quotas so that some Malay-Muslim candidates can be included in the upper rungs of political party lists during elections.

Ultimately, the mindset of Thai policy-makers needs to change from looking for a military solution which vanquishes resistance to prioritizing serious negotiations along with a willingness to compromise. The judicial system in the southern borderlands must be revamped to consider the realities of Malay Muslims living under a Thai Buddhist state. Education in the region must permit the free expression of education in Pondok schools. Implementation of these reforms must not be haphazard but rather applied over a long period of time. But such a solution does not mean that rebel attacks should be allowed to continue interminably. Moderates in the three provinces need to work with the Thai state to guarantee security from Muslim and Buddhist militants alike. Only with such reforms can the beginning of a secure peace be achieved in southern Thailand.

The key to attaining this goal, however, is for both sides to become willing to understand that their long, hostile conflict must be transformed so that attitudes of empathy and trust can begin to prevail over suspicion and hate. This is the key to any solution involving notions of conflict transformation. Yet before a step toward realizing moves toward attitude shifts and behaviour shifts, each side needs to become unified. Thus, for the insurgents, there must be unity to negotiate with the state rather than one faction negotiating while another group fights. Moreover, Thailand's civil government, police and military need to all speak with one voice. Finally the Thai state and militants must realize that they will have to find ways to incorporate less moderate southern actors into the peace process. Ultimately, any conflict transformation is not going to happen overnight but rather will take a long time to implement.

Notes

1. Muslims account for fewer than 5 per cent of Thailand's religious population while Malays comprise approximately 3.5 per cent of the ethnic population.
2. Galtung refers to multi-culturalism as a social phenomemon deriving from globalization. For him, multi-culturalism possesses four approaches: intolerance, where one culture kills or destroys another; tolerance, where one culture permits the mere existence of another; inter-cultural dialogue, based upon mutual respect and curiosity; and finally active coexistence with mutual cultural enrichment. It is multi-culturalism as inter-cultural dialogue which is alluded to later on in this chapter (See Galtung 2002: 12, 36–8).
3. Interview with Local level politicians, Pattani, Thailand, 14 January 2013.
4. Interview with Jamjuree, Soriya; Kamnung Chamnankij, Network of Civic Women for Peace, Pattani, Thailand, 22 January 2013.
5. Interview with Thai journalists (Mohamed Ayubpathan and Dan Pathan) who focus on problems in Thailand's deep south, Pattani, Thailand, 15 January 2013.
6. Interview with Mark Tamthai, Chiang Mai, Thailand, 11 May 2013; Skype interview with Daungyewa Utarasint, 11 July 2013.
7. Army Officers (progressive) stationed in Region 4, Yala Province, Pattani, Thailand, 25 January 2012; *Dark South Watch*, Facebook, 6 May 2013.
8. Representative, Southern Islamic Culture Foundation, Pattani, Thailand, 12 May 2013; Representative, Wetland Research Project, Pattani, Thailand, 12 May 2013.
9. Anonymous insurgent, Pattani, Thailand, 11 May 2013.

10. Interview with anonymous Buddhist Sino-Thai Businessperson who has lived her entire life in Pattani Province, Southern Thailand, 28 July 2013.
11. Interview with Thavorn Senniam, Deputy Secretary General, Democrat Party, Deputy Interior Minister, 2009–11, 13 August 2013.
12. Interview published in *Nation* (2013).
13. Skype Interview with Norbert Ropers, 5 May 2013.
14. Skype Interview with Norbert Ropers, 5 May 2013.

References

Abuza, Z. (2006) 'The Islamist Insurgency in Thailand', *Current Trends in Islamist Ideology* 4 (1 November 2006). Available online: http://www.currenttrends.org/research/detail/the-islamist-insurgency-in-thailand [accessed 10 May 2013].

Amnesty International (2011) 'Thailand: Insurgents Must Stop War Crimes against Civilians', Press Release, 27 September 2011. Available online: http://www.amnesty.org/en/news-and-updates/report/thailand-insurgents-must-stop-war-crimes-against-civilians-2011-09-26 [accessed 20 May 2013].

Askew, M. (2008) 'Thailand's Intractable Southern War: Policy, Insurgency and Discourse', *Contemporary Southeast Asia* 30 (2): 186–214.

Askew, M. (2010) 'The Spectre of the South: Regional Instability as National Crisis', in M. Askew (ed.) *Legitimacy Crisis in Thailand*, Chiang Mai: Silkworm Books.

Bajoria, J. and Zissis, C. (2008) 'The Muslim Insurgency in Southern Thailand' (10 September 2008), *Council on Foreign Relations*. Available online: http://www.cfr.org/thailand/muslim-insurgency-southern-thailand/p12531?breadcrumb=%2Fregion%2F290%2Fsoutheast_asia [accessed 1 August 2013].

BBC News (2006) 'Search for Justice in Thai South,' 8 August 2006. Available online: http://news.bbc.co.uk/2/hi/asia-pacific/5255054.stm [accessed 12 May 2013].

Berghof Foundation (2012) 'Berghof Glossary on Conflict Transformation', March 2012, Berlin. Available online: file:///C:/Users/Acer/Downloads/Documents/glossary_2012_complete_2.pdf [accessed 12 July 2013].

Burke, A., Tweedie, P. and Poocharoen, O. (2012) *The Contested Corners of Asia: Subnational Conflict and International Development Assistance – the Case of Southern Thailand*, San Francisco, CA: Asia Foundation.

Deep South Watch (2014) 'An Inconvenient Truth about the Deep South Conflict: a Decade of Chaotic, Constrained Realities and Uncertain Resolution', 2 July 2014. Available online: http://www.deepsouthwatch.org/node/5904 [accessed 5 August 2013].

Galtung, J. (1966) *Peace by Peaceful Means: Peace and Conflict, Development and Civilization*, London: Sage.

Galtung, J. (1995) 'Conflict Resolution as Conflict Transformation: The First Law of Thermodynamics Revisited', in K. Rupesinghe (ed.) *Conflict Transformation*, London: Macmillan.

Galtung, J. (2000) *Conflict Transformation by Peaceful Means (the Transcend Method)*, Tokyo: United Nations.

Galtung, J. (2002) 'Rethinking Conflict: the Cultural Approach', a Speech presented at the Intercultural Dialogue and Conflict Prevention Project, Directorate General IV: Education, Culture and Cultural Heritage, Youth and Sports Directorate of Culture and Cultural and Natural Heritage Cultural Policy and Action Department, Council of Europe, Strasbourg. Available online: https://www.coe.int/t/dg4/ cultureheritage/culture/Completed/Dialogue/DGIV_CULT_PREV(2002)1_ Galtung_E.PDF [accessed 25 May 2015].

Galtung, J. (2008) '50 Years – 100 Peace & Conflict Perspectives', Transcend University Press, Transcend Peace University. Available online: https://www. transcend.org/tpu/ [accessed 2 July 2014].

Iaccino, L. (2014) 'Thailand: Policeman's Wife Shot Dead and Set on Fire in Revenge Attack', *International Business Times*, 10 February 2014. Available online: http://www.ibtimes.co.uk/thailand-policemans-wife-shot-dead-set-fire-revenge-attack-1435809 [accessed 2 July 2014].

ICG (International Crisis Group) (2005) 'Southern Thailand: Insurgency, not Jihad', *Asia Report* 98 (18 May 2005). Available online: file:///C:/Users/ Acer/Downloads/Documents/098_southern_thailand_insurgency_not_jihad.pdf [accessed 15 June 2013].

Jitpiromsri, S. and McCargo D. (2010) 'The Southern Thai Conflict Six Years On: Insurgency, Not Just Crime', *Contemporary Southeast Asia* 32 (2): 156–83.

Jitpiromsri, S. and Sophonvasu, P. (2007) 'Unpacking Thailand's Southern Conflict: the Poverty of Structural Explanations', in Duncan McCargo (ed.) *Rethinking Thailand's Southern Violence*, Singapore: National University of Singapore Press.

Joll, C. (2010) 'Religion and Conflict in Southern Thailand: Beyond Rounding Up the Usual Suspects', *Contemporary Southeast Asia* 32 (2): 258–79.

Lederach, J. P. (1995) *Preparing for Peace: Conflict Transformation across Cultures*, Syracuse: Syracuse University Press.

Liow, J. C. (2006) 'International Jihad and Muslim: Radicalism in Thailand? Toward an Alternative Interpretation', *Asia Policy* 2: 89–108.

McCargo, D. (2007) 'Thaksin and the Resurgence of Violence in the Deep South', in D. McCargo (ed.) *Rethinking Thailand's Southern Violence*, Singapore: National University of Singapore Press.

Melvin, N. J. (2007) 'Conflict in Southern Thailand: Islamism, Violence and the State in the Patani Insurgency', *Stockholm International Peace Research Institute*, Policy Paper 20, September. Available online: file:///C:/Users/Acer/ Downloads/Documents/SIPRIPP20.pdf [accessed 29 July 2013].

Miall, H. (2001) *Conflict Management: A Multi-Dimensional Task*, Berlin: Berghof Research Center for Constructive Conflict Management.

Nation (2006) 'Prem Disagrees with Proposed Use of Malay as Official Language', 25 June 2006. Available online: http://nationmultimedia.com/2006/06/25/headlines/headlines_30007268.php [accessed 11 May 2013].

Nation (2013) 'NSC Chief Exceeds his Brief?' 13 March 2013. Available online: http://www.nationmultimedia.com/national/NSC-Chief-exceeds-his-brief--30201835.html [accessed 1 June 2013].

Pitsuwan, S. (2004) 'Seven Pointers to Claiming the South', *Nation*, 17 February 2004: 7.

Rahimmula, C. (2003) 'Peace Resolution : A Case Study of Separatist and Terrorist Movement in Southern Border Provinces of Thailand', *Songklanakarin Journal of Social Sciences and Humanities* 10 (1) (January–April 2004): 98–112.

Saxby, J. (2003) *Local Ownership and Development Co-operation – the role of Northern Civil Society*, Ontario, Canadian Council for International Co-operation.

Thayer, C. (2007) 'Insurgency in Southern Thailand: Literature review'. Available online: http://www.scribd.com/doc/17965033/Thayer-Insurgency-in-Southern-Thailand [accessed 12 July 2014].

Lessons from Anthropological Projects Related to the Great East Japan Earthquake and Tsunami: Intangible Cultural Heritage Survey and Disaster Salvage Anthropology

Hiroki Takakura

Introduction

The exceptionally destructive Great East Japan Earthquake and Tsunami had one of the strongest impacts of any recent disaster, not only in Japan but also around the world. The author is an anthropologist and a survivor of the disaster who lives and works in Sendai, Miyagi, one of the cities closest to the epicentre. Many scientific projects and social programmes were implemented after the earthquake. The responses of anthropologists in Japan reflected various individual forms of behaviour, from participating as volunteers, through organizing public lectures or workshops, to carrying out applied surveys. This paper explores the contribution of these anthropologists' activism to the afflicted region and its communities. It asks what kind of social engagement the anthropologists' responses represented, and examines the related effects that the anthropologists' activities produced among the public.

This paper examines these questions from the perspective of my personal experience, because the author was also personally embedded in the post-disaster contexts. Before the earthquake, I carried out field trips in Miyagi prefecture and surrounding areas for the purposes of training students in anthropology, while my main research concerns were in Siberian indigenous issues in the Russian Arctic. But given the difficulties that the region where I lived now faced, I decided to find a way of participating in applied research projects at home. As a researcher, I started out in anthropological projects with some hesitation because of the immediately apparent catastrophic condition of the disaster sites. Soon I learned that anthropologists had a unique way of contributing to the disaster recovery process. In particular, while I worked as a leader of the contracted project surveying damage to intangible cultural heritage caused by the tsunami in Miyagi prefecture, I identified a sense of overlap between the requirements of recovery policy managers and anthropological expertise. Here is a retrospective review of the project and some reflections on it from the anthropological point of view. I try to provide a case study rather than a general discussion of either disaster anthropology or social engagement. Any giant disaster should be idiographic rather than nomothetic subject matter, although I do believe that particular findings can be made applicable to a much broader context through inductive reasoning.

Firstly, I describe my project on intangible cultural heritage and the tsunami with reference to the Japanese context. Then I turn to discussing its meaning from the viewpoint of the discipline, proposing possible modes of anthropological social engagement against disasters.

Anthropologists in Japan After the Disaster

Following the powerful earthquake off the Pacific coast of northeastern Japan and massive tsunami, which caused deep damage and devastation unprecedented in the history of Japan, as well as a series of accidents at an affected nuclear power plant, anthropologists all over the country asked themselves how they could take part in relief efforts as citizens, and how they could also contribute as scholars and researchers generating specialized knowledge. For instance, the Tohoku Regional Colloquium of the Japanese Society of Cultural Anthropology met on 15 May 2011, in Tohoku Gakuin University for 'A Gathering about the March 11 Great Earthquake: Sharing of Experiences as Victims and Experiences as Researchers'. I myself planned the meeting. More than fifty anthropologists participated and I still clearly remember the discussion among participants both from inside and outside the affected region and the sharp contrast of opinions about the pros and cons of conducting a post-disaster survey.[1]

In my view, however, the tone of the discussion at that gathering was predominantly negative, suggesting that Japanese anthropological expertise could not be of direct use in dealing with the 11 March 2011 disaster. The same sentiment also appeared in the following publications. While saying, 'I don't intend to criticize all of the actions of the researchers and experts ... who rushed into the quake-stricken areas as being either self-righteous or self-serving,' one researcher warned that their surveys and research really did little to help the victims of the disaster (Suga 2013: 2). Another scholar, seeing the disaster unfolding before his very eyes, writes, 'There is no field of science or methodology that can help to physically improve the situation,' concluding that 'all we can probably do is remain engaged on a long-term basis' (Kimura 2013: 14). A characteristic of anthropology is that it can make any social or cultural phenomenon an object of research, engaging in participant observation while closely relating to the people of the specific area under study. Anthropological participant observation here meant conducting surveys while staying in the evacuation centres and temporary housing along with victims whose homes as physical spaces had been destroyed by the tsunami. It seemed potentially very bad timing in terms of not only survey ethics but also survey methodology for building up trust relationships with participants to launch fieldwork immediately after a disaster. In the light of those issues, the negative tone of the discussion mentioned above was only to be expected.

Under such difficult conditions, however, anthropological surveys were in fact conducted. As revealed in the books on the March 11 disaster published in succession in 2013, some anthropologists did launch substantive fieldwork projects immediately following the disaster. One is Shōichirō Takezawa (Takezawa 2013a, 2013b), who stayed at evacuation centres in Ōtsuchi-chō in Iwate prefecture for nearly eight months, and whose book describe the reconstruction process – including local residents' management of the evacuation centre – from a local point of view. In a collection of essays edited by himself and others, Tom Gill, professor of social anthropology at Meiji Gakuin University, discusses the choices made by disaster-affected individuals and communities, and how they grasped the situation that they were in. He examines the functions of cultural continuity in the emergency situation of a disaster and the emergence of innovative changes (Gill et al. 2013: 9).

We should probably keep in mind, however, that those anthropologists who did research adopting this approach were rather exceptional. I do not in the least question the scholarly ethics of these exceptional researchers. On the other hand, considering the many anthropologists who wanted to make use of their expertise in the face of the unprecedented disaster, I thought it useful to consider the somewhat easier-to-begin survey approach and its effectiveness as a response.

The survey of the disaster-affected intangible cultural heritage was conducted in the stricken areas in a way that differed from conventional anthropological fieldwork. As a government-commissioned project, moreover, the survey also differed in nature from a pure research project. In that sense, readers may think it inappropriate to juxtapose the results of this survey with those of the above-mentioned studies. This paper considers how, precisely because of that difference, the intangible cultural heritage survey project can be placed in an anthropological context. I contend that this approach in disaster-stricken areas can become part of the stock of research methodologies in the field of anthropology.

As a researcher who works in the quake-hit area, I believe that the anthropologists should contribute to the recovery policies and, in fact, the local administration expected that contribution from anthropologists. Based on this experience, I propose disaster risk reduction anthropology as an option for public anthropology.[2]

Earthquake Disaster Reconstruction Plan and Commissioned Project

Prior to the 2011 earthquake disaster, the Agency for Cultural Affairs (Bunkacho) in Japan launched the Program for Promoting Tourism and Regional Invigoration by Making the Most of Cultural Heritage (*Bunka Isan o Ikashita Kankō Shinkō / Chiiki Kasseika Jigyō*). This programme was a response by the Agency to the Japanese government's guiding principle of economic policy that the cultural heritage of each part of Japan should be utilized for promoting local tourism, industry and other areas of regional revitalization. Not long after the 2011 disaster, Iwate, Miyagi and Fukushima were invited to apply for the programme for a second time because it was judged that the disaster had made it difficult for these prefectures to submit an application in response to the first invitation.

It was the executive committee of the Miyagi Prefecture Regional Cultural Heritage Reconstruction Project that submitted the application from Miyagi prefecture. The committee consists of several NGOs for promoting folk-culture and the Prefectural Government Cultural Properties Division – which serves as the secretariat of the committee. One of the projects planned by the committee was the 'Survey of Intangible Cultural Heritage affected by the Great East Japan Earthquake in Miyagi Prefecture'. The project aimed to obtain data promptly concerning the potential for the recovery of local communities with intangible cultural heritage in the tsunami-affected coastal areas of Miyagi prefecture, as well as information about the damage to tangible cultural heritage. The project was to provide such data and information to help the local government make appropriate judgements concerning its culture administration activities. From this, the local government regarded their local intangible cultural heritage as playing a certain role in regional community revitalization in the reconstruction plans following the disaster. This project was commissioned to the Tohoku University Center for Northeast Asian Studies where the author works.

One organizational feature must be kept in mind regarding this commissioned project. The prefecture's Cultural Properties Division, along with the Education Planning Office, the Lifelong Learning Division, and so forth, is an office under the Miyagi Prefectural Board of Education. This meant that the survey project was affiliated with the hierarchic structure of the prefecture's board of education, and that therefore the prefectural board of education was able to request the boards of education on the city, town and village levels to extend cooperation to the project.

The staff members of the commissioned project first visited the city, town or village board of education in the district to which they were assigned when they conducted their first round of survey. These municipal boards of education supervise information related to intangible cultural heritage in their local areas, especially information about the societies for preserving *kagura* (a type of Shinto theatrical dance) and other folk performing arts. At the request of the prefecture the local boards provided us with such information. In most cases it was representatives of these preservation societies who were our first informants. After acquiring information from them, we easily found people to interview one by one, as is done in an ordinary anthropological survey. The presence of such an organizational system was a great boon in that we were able to assure contact with specific informants prior to entering each target area for the survey. It was an advantage for the city, town and village boards of education as well, because even in the initial stages of the field survey they were able to know what kind of people would enter and conduct the surveys, and in what way. We built a network of connections with the cultural preservation societies, the municipal boards of education and the prefecture, partly as a way of resolving difficulties such as the possibility that a person who had accepted to be interviewed might later make a complaint. We had also decided beforehand that as a rule more than one survey staff member would visit a target area so that they would visit the homes and temporary housing where victims were residing together. In cases where trust with the interviewers was established after several visits, one staff member was later allowed to visit alone.

The survey was conducted from November 2011 to March 2013, a period of approximately a year and a half. The survey organization consisted of twenty-two researchers (as surveyors) and approximately ten graduate and undergraduate students in the city of Sendai (as assistant surveyors). The surveyors were assigned to districts of which they were in charge, and when conducting the survey as a rule they were each paired with an assistant surveyor. The municipal boards of education would introduce us to the preservation societies for intangible cultural heritage, and we would go into the field to conduct the survey. Each surveyor was assigned to a district to assure continuity in the successive stages of the survey. Each survey lasted one to two days, and over the period of one and a half years the surveyor generally visited the assigned district six to eight times, although the actual number of days varied according to the individual surveyor. The primary method for collecting information was the interview, but when an event was held the surveyor might collect information as a participant.

This method resulted in the uniform documentation of verbal interview responses taken down and recorded, collected, and sorted by district. The surveyors conducted the surveys over a total of 152 days. From interviews with approximately 120 persons (257 persons in cumulative total), 1,000 250-word pages, if translated into English ethnographic documentation, and 250 photographs were collected. The unique features of this survey project were the establishment of a methodical survey system and the obtaining of a huge volume of formal records (Takakura and Takizawa 2013).

Salvage in Disaster and in Anthropology

In my understanding, this was a disaster salvage anthropology project. The essence of the project was the documentation of the disappearing cultural heritage. In the Oxford Advanced Learner's Dictionary definition, salvage is 'the act of saving things that have been, or are likely to be, damaged or lost, especially in a disaster or an accident'. Here, then, is the perfect example of cultural salvage. There is, however, a further assumption: the documentation of its intangible cultural heritage should make a contribution to the future development of the local community.

The salvage project became popular in Japan after the disaster. Many institutes, organizations and even individuals tried to excavate the memories and to organize recordings of the disaster. Due to the development of information technology such as social media, vast volumes of the fragmented information, images and sounds were accumulated and circulated both in organizational and personal terminals on the Internet. National and local newspapers, individual journalists and many local Non-Profit Organizations (NPOs) and Non-Governmental Organizations (NGOs) published the narratives of the survivors and local photographs from before and after the disaster. Some institutions such as libraries and universities started to video interview participatory projects in which they rented video cameras to citizens to record the narratives of family and friends.[3] All those concerned found it necessary to record the effects of the disaster in some way. Oblivion was a sin and salvage was good for remembrance.

I believe that the contracted project fits into this pattern. The local government entrusted the duty to us as part of a social trend. However, anthropologists need to discuss why salvage is required, and ask what kind of contributions could be possible for the academics in these social contexts. The reason lies in the history of discipline. The word 'salvage' carries a special meaning in the anthropological context. The postmodern critique has made it impossible to reproduce a notion of the anthropological subject as an 'other' that exists in a time not contemporary with our own (Fabian 1983). Does 'salvage' denote the construction of the 'eternal primitive culture'? (Shimizu 1992). Therefore at first we need to consider the grounds for 'salvage' in the context of anthropological knowledge.

Here I would like to reflect on the stimulating ideas on this issue offered by three anthropologists. The first opinion is that of American anthropologist Jacob W. Gruber (1970), who claimed that ethnographic salvage lies at the very foundations of anthropology:

> Salvage provided the opportunity for human contact and human contrast .... we feel that in the disappearance of the savage, in the irrevocable erosion of the human condition, we inevitably lose something of our own identity. (Gruber 1970: 1298)

The phrase 'the disappearance of the savage' must be a target for contemporary anthropological criticism. However, what happens if we replace it by 'the aftermath of the disaster'? Certainly the survivor of the disaster somehow reconstructs something in some way, but it is also true that some things, and some people, are lost forever. Recognizing and recording what was lost is a typical act of salvage, which opens an encounter between peoples on the basis of difference. This is my inter-pretation of the phrase of Gruber. In a setting of disaster, a sense of loss should be treated in a proper way, which facilitates people's finding something that is related to their recovery. This is the essence of the cultural salvage. Remember that many anthropologists in Japan hesitated to embark on fieldwork in the heavily stricken area of the disaster. Those who did not act may have lost the chance of human contact and the sense of human contrast as a way of making an anthropological contribution.

Gruber also states that any science should have a unique 'organization of the particular kind of information' as a methodology and 'system of explanation' as a theory. The accumulation and use of data on human differences from the eighteenth century onwards shaped the forms of systematic explanation that would come to constitute anthropological theory (Gruber 1970: 1289–90). This implies the possibility of data-gathering other than according to our canon. Certainly the intensive participant observation method properly and accurately focuses on human differences and universals, but other methods also can offer the data in different ways. The sense of disappearance or sense of loss justifies salvage, which affords its own perspectives on human differences and cultural diversities. This is a persuasive logic in the context of disaster.

The idea of salvage or 'the disappearing' may remind us of colonial anthropology. I do not deny the negative history of the discipline's treatment of the researched peoples. On the other hand, salvage and 'disappearing' may be invoked in alternative fields such as visual research. Margaret Mead stated her thoughts on the issue as follows:

> The recognition that forms of human behavior still extant will inevitably disappear has been part of our whole scientific and humanistic heritage .... because these are disappearing types of behavior, we need to preserve them in forms that not only will permit the descendants to repossess their cultural heritage, but that will also give our understanding of human history and human potentialities a reliable, reproducible, reanalyzable corpus .... (which) can never be replicable in laboratory settings. (Mead 1995: 3, 8, 10)

This is an argument in her article on 'visual anthropology in a discipline of words' for defending the importance of photography and film as a research method. The 'salvage' is justified without any hesitation precisely because there is a presumption that any cultural behaviour and concept is not 'eternal' but always changing. Among such things we need to find something that deserves to be a record against oblivion, which contributes to our search for 'human potentialities'. In the aftermath of disaster, the 'potentialities' might be community development or resilience. As far as visual anthropology is concerned, at this moment in history both in the site of fieldwork and at home we are now sitting in front of our digital technology terminal, which is what now provides the encounter that is our 'decisive moment', to use the famous phrase of photographer Henri Cartier-Bresson. We always come to a crossroads for the salvage of the disappearing something.

David Koester and Liivo Niglas recently discussed the role and value of visual salvage ethnography in the context of Siberian studies. For the Itelmen or the Kamchatka indigenous people filmmaking as a part of ethnographic practice contributes not only the recording of culture but also sensitive and powerful measures against the trends of cultural loss. Koester and Niglas claim that: 'Salvage anthropology in the 21st century is enriched by adding this sensorial, individualizing, and inherently temporizing dimension to the documentation processes' (Koester and Niglas 2011: 58).

We can therefore conclude that salvage does not always contribute to the construction of an 'eternal primitive culture' but rather opens up new encounters with human potentialities, which in turn can contribute to socio-cultural revitalization, in particular in disaster settings. I can now elaborate on my claim that salvage anthropology deserves to be organized as an option of applied anthropology in disaster situations.

The Context of Policy Tasks

Anthropological fieldwork is often more about identifying tasks than about testing hypotheses. This feature makes it possible to apply methods of analysis to various societal and cultural spheres, which is normally an advantage, but in times of disaster has come to be perceived as a problem. To elucidate this point further, specialist fields such as urban engineering, civil engineering or clinical psychology are explicitly demarcated areas of study, making it easy to conduct surveys in those fields as part of disaster-area research support. In comparison, anthropology has surprisingly few areas where it can demonstrate uniquely specialized expertise. Anthropology excels at relativizing the views of existing specialized fields, or providing alternative frames of reference. Yet it can be said that such features of anthropological expertise have worked against researchers in this case. To utilize specialized expertise in disaster recovery support effectively requires that the research areas prescribed within the specialized field itself match the needs in the field for support, to a greater or lesser degree.

In this regard, we carried out the project commissioned from us on condition that it tied directly into regional rehabilitation in an institutional way, affirming the importance of passing down folk- and traditional culture. It is important to consider the fact that anthropological expertise was sought in the disaster recovery support field to assist in the government-designated area of intangible cultural heritage. This facilitated our access to survey locations. The ethical issues related to conducting surveys in disaster-stricken areas were resolved in a relative sense by this system of government outsourcing. In practice, when we began to conduct the survey, the participants generally understood why we were there and we encountered no open opposition to the objectives of the survey.

A sceptical anthropologist might doubt that intangible cultural heritage such as folk performing arts could really contribute to rebuilding a local community. The reality that needs to be emphasized here is that the three prefectures of Iwate, Miyagi and Fukushima all recognized such a contribution in their earthquake recovery plans (Takakura and Takizawa 2014: 296). So, I would like to examine our project anew in the light of this key premise.

From the point of view of Miyagi prefectural government policy,[4] engaging in the survey project meant carrying out a 'project to support the restoration of intangible cultural heritage' as a specific recovery effort within the administrative category of 'rebuilding the local community'. Policy categories at the same level in the disaster reconstruction plan were 'lifestyle support for victims', 'securing housing for victims' and 'ensuring a safe living environment'. Their specific recovery efforts were 'disaster support financial loans', 'construction of disaster recovery public housing', and 'promotion of earthquake-resistant structures'. Basically, this arrangement positions the revival of intangible cultural heritage at the same level as moving people to higher ground within the policy structure.

However, it goes without saying that including intangible cultural heritage at this level does not mean that it has the same priority from a policy point of view. That is self-evident, given the fact, for example, that the promotion of earthquake-resistant structures has a much greater priority in terms of things like budget size and the social impact of how soon construction is carried out. Yet the important point to bear in mind here is not the size of the budget, but that policy issues exist in the government's recovery plan in which fields like anthropology have a positive contribution to make.

The local governments themselves do not conduct surveys and research. For this reason, disciplines such as anthropology, folklore and qualitative sociology are assumed to be specialized fields related to intangible cultural heritage administration and a system is in place to outsource studies to researchers in these fields. Another key point is that in the three prefectures affected by the disaster, these projects are supposed to be carried out in the short- to medium-range phases immediately following the earthquake and tsunami (2011 to 2017). As I mentioned earlier, a feature of anthropological fieldwork is the establishment of relationships with local communities over the long term. However, the government has requested short-term involvement limited to the immediate post-disaster period.

Within this administrative reconstruction context, another point must be noted, which is that when the specialist expertise of anthropology is called on to play a role in the response to the Great East Japan Earthquake, the subject of research is limited. As a former leading Japan anthropologist Tamotsu Aoki once argued, it might be true that 'studying anything from any angle' is a strength of this discipline (Asahishinbun 1995: 10). But the above statement appears undeniably naïve when one considers what this discipline can do in the face of an earthquake disaster as compared with what can be accomplished by the more 'practical sciences'. This is what makes it important that the government sought out the specialized knowledge of anthropology to assist with intangible cultural heritage as part of its recon-struction policy in Japan. It did so because the expertise of anthropology in the area of intangible cultural heritage has been considered necessary for the reconstruction effort by society and the government on the basis of anthropological research results to date. In Japan the applicability of anthropological expertise, and its ability to meet social needs, has largely been associated with development issues, ethno-regional conflict and refugee issues in developing nations. It is important to remember that intangible cultural heritage is just one area similar to the above in the context of the Japanese earthquake and tsunami disaster.

In a disaster-stricken area, various disciplines work in collaboration. In such a context, the areas that can be handled by anthropology are defined by its achievements in the past and their social ramifications. It needs to be understood that anthropology is not championing the ability to research absolutely anything, but that the discipline has special spheres in which it can meet societal needs. As a profession, we need to construct augments about where anthropology's strengths lie.

Breaking Away From the Long-Term Participant Observation Method?

The meaning of the negative stance toward surveys and assistance projects related to the revival of intangible folk cultural heritages is understandable when it comes to researchers' academic pursuits in ordinary times. In the wake of the Great East Japan Earthquake, however, such attitudes seem extremely anti-social and nihilistic. As I have repeatedly stressed up to this point, the prevailing premise in the administration of reconstruction after the Great East Japan Earthquake is that, not in urban areas but in small-scale rural areas, intangible cultural heritage can contribute in some way to the rebuilding of local communities. Based on this premise, I believe that anthropologists should use their specialized expertise to become more involved in society. They need to ask what types of conditions make intangible cultural heritages useful in helping to rehabilitate local communities. Or conversely, under what types of conditions is revival of intangible cultural heritages not useful? Trying to answer these questions is what is required of anthropologists in the area of disaster recovery policies.

The reason that nihilism is to some degree convincing may have something to do with long-term participant observation methods in anthropology. As I mentioned at the beginning, it is not easy for researchers to enter a disaster-affected area from either the ethical or the logistical point of view. We need to remember, however, that the long-term participant observation method is no more than one 'ideal' method. In the ordinary process of getting a Ph.D. in social anthropology we conduct long-term participant observation. But do we continue with such studies on the same scale after we enter academia? It may well be possible, were one to continue with the same study village, that this could be achieved. But in many cases, later studies are conducted by the comparative method or over extended areas – in ways that do not rely solely on long-term participant observation. The survey that we conducted in the area hit by the disaster naturally included some participant observation, but it was based more on written records of oral recollections drawn from interviews done over a relatively short term of time. It was an organization-extensive survey. I think that the appropriateness of survey activities based on this kind of method warrants further scrutiny. To begin with, a disaster recovery assistance project requires that a relatively short-term survey be carried out as soon as possible. And after personally having carried out this survey, I came to believe that at the very least an emergency survey to assess affected intangible cultural heritages in the aftermath of a disaster is in some measure effective and socially meaningful.

Conclusion

The concluding statement I wish to make is that, in the aftermath of a major disaster in which a regional community has suffered immeasurable damage, a viable option for professional anthropologists is to cooperate with the government administration of local cultural heritage, rather than standing aloof from it, so as to engage in a collaborative endeavour to improve local cultural heritages administration in desirable ways. Such an approach may well be a framework embedded in Japanese society that defines government expectations of anthropologists, and anthropologists' relations with government, based on the historical development of anthropology in Japan. In different regions and with different types of government, there must be different organizational structures. However, it is our knowledge of culture and our fieldwork methods that define the expectations of non-anthropologists about the contributions of anthropology, and these are universal in all countries and regions. Inventing a way to use our expertise in an emergent situation is a critical lesson for anthropologists after the Great East Japan Earthquake. I am not saying this is the only path for anthropologists to follow. But I would like to emphasize that in the post-11 March 2011 disaster world, in response to the question put to anthropologists regarding how we are to be involved with disasters, reviving intangible cultural heritages as a means of social recovery requires us to think deeply about method, theory, and organization.

It is important to reiterate that this survey project was set to take place in the initial phase of the prefecture's disaster recovery plan – the recovery phase. In any disaster there is an initial stage in the recovery measures. Such were the conditions for the project, which needed to adopt a specialized type of survey method and, in the case of Japan, implementation of a cooperative effort between the anthropologists and the government. In a different context the collaboration might have involved a different kind of organization and different kinds of agencies. To put it another way, the possibility still exists for different assistance projects or pure research projects to be carried out in the regeneration and development phases. A famous Japanese human geographer and anthropologist who conducted research on the post-1933 Sanriku tsunami disaster, Yaichirō Yamaguchi (2011 [1943]), began his research approximately three years after the devastating tsunami. His theme was 'why people return to areas prone to tsunamis'. This topic and his survey methods still provide us with certain pointers today. When to begin a survey is of great significance in disaster research, and each period following the disaster poses its own questions and demands survey methods appropriate for dealing with them.

This is not only the case in Japan. UNESCO regards intangible cultural heritage an important factor in maintaining cultural diversity in the face of globalization. Its understanding is that intangible cultural heritage helps promote intercultural dialogue, and encourages mutual respect for other ways of life. From my project it became clear that intangible cultural heritage also contributes to the construction of community resilience. The project was embedded in the Japanese social context. One could organize this kind of work in collaboration with NGOs and NPOs in some other contexts. In the case of Hurricane Katrina 2005 in the USA, for example, American folklorist Carl Lindahl organized a project in which survivors conducted interviews among themselves (Lindahl 2007). Les Field and Richard Fox (2009) discussed the practical social value of anthropological knowledge: they argued for the importance of collaboration and co-theorizing in the ethnographic research. Collaboration should be the foundation of the ethnographic process, from project conceptualization, to fieldwork and the writing. Disaster salvage anthropology should be conducted among many stakeholders: anthropologists, government, NGOs and the people affected.

Regardless of differences in local context, disaster salvage anthropology for local intangible culture using methods of extensive and short-term survey offers an effective and socially valued applied research response to disaster. So I would like to end by emphasizing that anthropologists need to be prepared to organize, at any time, teams of researchers capable of conducting a systematic emergency survey of disaster-affected intangible cultural heritage both in a fieldwork region and a home region where the anthropologist lives and works. It should be articulated to the disaster risk reduction policy context.

Notes

1. In 2011 alone, significant meetings other than those mentioned here included an open lecture meeting on "The Great East Japan Earthquake As Witnessed by a Folklorist" (Tohoku University), held on 25 June under the auspices of the Folklore Society of Tohoku, the 206th regular meeting of the Chubu Anthropology Colloquium held on 23 July to discuss 'Anthropology in Crisis Part I, Anthropology's Role in Disaster: Lessons from the Great East Japan Earthquake' (held at Sugiyama Jogakuen University), and the 860th meeting of the Folklore Society of Japan on 3 December 2011, 'Memories and Accounts of the Earthquake Disaster: Toward Rebirth of Folklore' (Tohoku University).

2. One such attempt was the publication of United Nation Office for Disaster Risk Reduction (UNISDR 2008). This book clearly insisted that the indigenous and local knowledge in terms of anthropologist view could be an effective tool for disaster risk reduction, in particular in the context of participation of local people and integration of science and technology in the community processes.

3. In order to grasp the development of the related salvage projects, I recommend the Japan 2011 Disasters Archive managed by Harvard University Reischauer Institute of Japanese Studies for non-Japanese readers (http://jdarchive.org/en/about) and, for those who understand Japanese, Michinoku Shinrokuden, Tohoku University Archiving Project (http://shinrokuden.irides.tohoku.ac.jp) is one of most integrating databases of the projects.
4. See http://www.pref.miyagi.jp/site/ej-earthquake/fukkou-keikaku.html [accessed 6 December 2014). English version is available online: http://www.pref.miyagi.jp/uploaded/attachment/36634.pdf [accessed 1 December 2014].

References

Asahishinbun (1995) *Jinruigaku ga wakaru [Understanding Anthropology]*, Tokyo: Asashi shinbun.

Fabian, J. (1983) *Time and the Other: How Anthropology Makes its Object*, New York: Columbia University Press.

Field, L. W. and Fox R. G. (2009) 'Introduction: How Does Anthropology Work Today?' in L. W. Field and R. G. Fox (eds) *Anthropology Put to Work*, Oxford and New York: Berg.

Gill, T., Steger, B. and Slater, D. (eds) (2013) *Higashi Nihon Daishinsai no jinruigaku [The Great East Japan Earthquake and Anthropology]*, Kyoto: Jinbun Shoin, 2013. (Published in English as *Japan Copes with Calamity: Ethnographies of the Earthquake, Tsunami and Nuclear Disasters of March 2011*, Pieterlen: Peter Lang AG.)

Gruber, J. W. (1970) 'Ethnographic Salvage and the Shaping of Anthropology', *American Anthropologist* n.s. 72 (6): 1289–99.

Kimura, S. (2013) *Shinsai no kōkyō jinruigaku: Yure to tomo ni ikiru Toruko no hitobito [Earthquake Disasters and Public Anthropology: Earthquake Tremors in the Lives of the People of Turkey]*, Kyoto: Sekai Shisōsha.

Koester, D. and Niglas L. (2011) 'Hunting in Itelmen: Filming a Past Practice in a Disappearing Language', *Sibirica* 10–3: 55–81.

Lindahl, K. (2007) 'Storms of Memory: New Orleanians Surviving Katrina in Houston', *Callaloo* 29 (4): 1526–38.

Mead, M. (1995) 'Visual Anthropology in a Discipline of Words', in P. Hockings (ed.) *Principles of Visual Anthropology*, Berlin: Mouton de Gruyter.

Shimizu, A. (1992) 'The Eternal Primitive Culture and Peripheral Peoples: A Historical Overview of Modern Western Anthropology' [in Japanese], *Bulletin of National Museum of Ethnology* 17 (3): 417–88, Osaka.

Suga, Y. (2013) *'Atarashii no no gakumon no jidai e' ['Toward a "New Field Science" Era']*, Tokyo: Iwanami Shoten.

Takakura, H. and Takizawa, K. (eds) (2013) 'Higashi Nihon Daishinsai de hisai shita Miyagi-ken Enganbu ni okeru minzoku bunkazai chōsa (2012 nendo hōkokushū)' [Survey on Miyagi Prefecture Coastal Area Folk Cultural Assets Damaged by the Great East Japan Earthquake (Collected Reports 2012)], Sendai: Tohoku University Center for Northeast Asian Studies.

Takakura, H. and Takiwazawa, K. (eds) (2014) *Mukei minzoku bunkazai ga hisai suru to iukoto* [*What Does the Damage to the Intangible Cultural Heritage Mean?*], Tokyo: Shinsensya.

Takakura, H., Takizawa, K. and Masaoka, N. (eds) (2012) *Higashi Nihon Daishinsai de hisai shita Miyagi-ken Enganbu ni okeru minzoku bunkazai chōsa (2011 nendo hōkokushū)* [*Survey on Miyagi Prefecture Coastal Area Folk Cultural Assets Damaged by the Great East Japan Earthquake (Collected Reports 2011)*], Sendai: Tohoku University Center for Northeast Asian Studies.

Takezawa, S. (2013a) 'Tsunami no hakai ni taikō suru hisai komyunitī: Ōtsuchi-chō no hinanjo ni miru chiiki genri to tasha to no kankeisei' [*An Affected Community Facing the Devastation of the Tsunami: The Relationship between the Principle of the Community and the Other*], *Bulletin of National Museum of Ethnology* 37 (2): 127–98, Osaka.

Takezawa, S. (2013b) *Hisai-go o ikiru: Kirikiri, Ōtsuchi, and Kamaishi funtōki* [*Living in Post-disaster Areas: A Record of All-out Efforts in Kirikiri, Ōtsuchi, and Kamaishi*], Tokyo: Chūō Kōron Shinsha.

UNISDR 2008 *Indigenous Knowledge for Disaster: Good Practices and Lessons from Experiences in the Asia-Pacific Region.* Bangkok: United Nations Office for Disaster Risk Reduction, Regional Office for Asia and Pacific. Available online: http://www.unisdr.org/files/3646_IndigenousKnowledgeDRR.pdf [accessed 1 December 2014].

Yamaguchi, Y. (2011) [1943] *Tsunami to mura* [*Tsunami and Villages*], Masami Ishii Masami and Shūichi Kawashima (eds), Tokyo: Miyai Shoten.

Index